Business, Integrity, and Peace

Ethical business behavior has an unexpected payoff: it may reduce the likelihood of violence. This insight forms the basis of *Business, Integrity, and Peace*. Academic and popular interest in the topics of corporate responsibility and Peace Through Commerce has surged in recent years. This book demonstrates that the adoption of generally accepted ethical business practices does not require wholesale changes in corporate governance. It does require, however, the development of more reflexive and self-regulating models of corporate decision-making, drawing upon three strands of existing corporate responsibility approaches: the legal, the managerial, and the aesthetic. Fort introduces the concept of Total Integrity Management, providing an integrative framework that transcends disciplinary boundaries to create ethical corporate cultures, which in turn offer the best opportunity for corporations to become instruments of peace.

Business, Integrity, and Peace is an important and provocative work that will appeal to academic scholars, business leaders, and policy-makers alike.

TIMOTHY L. FORT is the Lindner-Gambal Professor of Business Ethics at George Washington University Business School and an academic advisor for the Business Roundtable Institute for Corporate Ethics. He is Director of the Program on Peace Through Commerce at George Washington University's Business School and is also an adjunct Faculty Member of the George Washington University School of Law.

Business, Value Creation, and Society

Series editors
R. Edward Freeman, *University of Virginia*
Stuart L. Hart, *Cornell University* and *University of North Carolina*
David Wheeler, *York University*

The purpose of this innovative series is to examine, from an international standpoint, the interaction of business and capitalism with society. In the 21st century it is more important than ever that business and capitalism come to be seen as social institutions that have a great impact on the welfare of human society around the world. Issues such as globalization, environmentalism, information technology, the triumph of liberalism, corporate governance, and business ethics all have the potential to have major effects on our current models of the corporation and the methods by which value is created, distributed, and sustained among all stakeholders – customers, suppliers, employees, communities, and financiers.

Forthcoming in this series:

Korine & Gomez *Entrepreneurs and Democracy*
Moon, Crane & Matten *Corporations and Citizenship*
Painter-Morland *Ethics as the Everyday Business of Business*
Yajizi & Doh *Corporate Governance, NGOs and Corporations*

Business, Integrity, and Peace

Beyond Geopolitical and Disciplinary Boundaries

TIMOTHY L. FORT
George Washington University Business School

CAMBRIDGE UNIVERSITY PRESS
Cambridge, New York, Melbourne, Madrid, Cape Town,
Singapore, São Paulo, Delhi, Tokyo, Mexico City

Cambridge University Press
The Edinburgh Building, Cambridge CB2 8RU, UK

Published in the United States of America by Cambridge University Press, New York

www.cambridge.org
Information on this title: www.cambridge.org/9781107402898

First published 2007
First paperback edition 2011

A catalogue record for this publication is available from the British Library

ISBN 978-0-521-86298-1 Hardback
ISBN 978-1-107-40289-8 Paperback

To Nancy, Kurina, Steven, Theo, Scooby, and Rose

Contents

Tables

Foreword

Tim Fort has written an important book for our times. At a point when the world seems more fragmented and torn apart by differences among fundamental beliefs, Fort has the audacity to suggest that we rethink our institutions, especially business. If we do so, he argues, we will find multiple opportunities for the creation of peace and the subsequent human flourishing that results. Fort has long suggested that we see business as a "mediating institution" in society, especially relevant to the way that we solve our conflicts with each other. Now, he goes further and shows how taking "ethical business" seriously can lead to dramatically different consequences for societies.

The first step in Fort's argument is to delineate what business can really be: an instrument of value creation and trade that affects many parts of society. We need to look beyond economics and profits to see the real impact of business on civil society. In fact all businesses create value for stakeholders, i.e., customers, suppliers, employees, financiers, community, and others in civil society. Business executives must take this broad role seriously to create "ethical businesses". And, policy makers need to begin to see business as an instrument of peace and civility, rather than mere means to advance whatever policy agenda happens to be in power. Citizens have a role to play as well, and Fort's argument suggests that they need to see the possibility inherent in business as creating peace and prosperity rather than being based on individual self-interest and greed. All must demand the highest standards of ethics and responsibility from business. By focusing on what he calls "total integrity management" we can come to expect business and its executives to be "honest brokers" who build trust in civil society, and act from a position of trust.

By integrating the work done in management, corporate responsibility, stakeholder theory, law, anthropology, and other related disciplines, Fort has given us a complex and multi-layered argument that continues to set the direction for a new conversation about business and its role in society. Indeed it is a perfect introductory volume for the series on *Business, Value Creation, and Society*. The purpose of this series is to stimulate new thinking about value creation and trade, and its role in the world of the 21st century. Our old models and ideas simply are not appropriate in the "24/7 Flat World" of today. We need new scholarship that builds on these past understandings, yet offers the alternative of a world of hope, freedom, and human flourishing.

R. Edward Freeman
Olsson Professor of Business Administration
The Darden School
University of Virginia
Charlottesville, Virginia, USA

Special acknowledgment

I met Dr. Walter Neiswanger for the first time in 1990. Walter is a retired pathologist and a lifelong resident of Davenport, Iowa, not far from where I grew up. Walter was a skilled pathologist in the Davenport area. A few minutes with him demonstrates why. He pays meticulous attention to detail and is just flat-out smart. He brings to the people he encounters a profound interest in their well-being and an infectious, joyful approach to life.

In addition to being a successful professional and wonderful neighbor, colleague, and friend, Walter is one of the most philanthropically active human beings I have ever encountered. His generosity is legendary in the community. Reflecting his own interests, Walter's philanthropy covers a wide range of areas ranging from medicine to art to education to homeless services and much beyond, many of which I undoubtedly do not know about because Walter quietly supports individuals and organizations. He is one of those people who gives because he wants to help, not because he will be recognized for his generosity.

Sometimes Walter's gifts are so significant, though, the charities themselves insist on honoring him. Among Walter's most prized philanthropies is the Neiswanger Institute at Loyola University Chicago, which engages the ethical issues surrounding medicine, bioethics, and physician care. He also has been an enthusiastic supporter of the Figge Museum of Art, particularly with respect to his passion for the art and people of Haiti.

Walter has been my friend for many years. When I was transitioning from the University of Michigan to George Washington University, Walter saw the potential for this book and offered to underwrite my 2005 summer research so I could get the major work of the manuscript completed. I am grateful to Walter for his support, without which this book might still have been completed, but certainly not as quickly nor as well. Walter is a person who, if we replicated his actions, would probably cause there to be no need for this book. He is a person who inspires peace and justice and whose life and work I honor.

Acknowledgments

Any list of acknowledgments is bound to be incomplete, but I'd like to do my best to recognize those individuals and institutions who have helped to make this book possible.

First, I'd like to thank Cambridge University Press and its representatives with whom I have had the pleasure of now writing two books. Chris Harrison, Katy Plowright, and Paula Parish have been great to work with. My thanks too to Ed Freeman for his leadership in creating this series for Cambridge and the continuous great support he gives to colleagues, including his review of the manuscript of this book.

Second, this book was written in transition between two universities. I began the work at the University of Michigan and finished at George Washington University. Both institutions, their deans, and colleagues have been very supportive of my research. Many scholars at each – and at other academic, non-government, and government bodies – have read drafts of the manuscript and have provided helpful comments. I need to give particular recognition to Cindy Schipani, George Siedel, Gretchen Spreitzer, Mark Starik, Jennifer Griffin, Jorge Rivera, Stephen Ladek, Frances Milliken, and Tara Radin for their engagement on these issues at conferences. The Association to Advance Collegiate Schools of Business thrilled me by making this concept of Peace Through Commerce one that deserved a special task force. As a result of the leadership of Carolyn Woo, Dean of the Mendoza School of Business at the University of Notre Dame and her task force, of which I was honored to be a member, I am enthused that the concepts of this book will become mainstream business school topics. I am also grateful to Igor Ambramov, the Director of the US Department of Commerce's Good Governance Program for reading the entire manuscript and offering numerous helpful suggestions.

Third, I have benefited from truly remarkable work from a series of research assistants. At George Washington, Michelle Westermann-Behaylo did terrific work and is someone the field will quickly be paying attention to for the work she does in her own right. At Michigan, Aaron

O'Donnell, James Noone, Matt Morris, and James Devaney got this project going when I didn't have much of a clue as to what I was doing. Kevin Eckerle (both at Michigan and at George Washington), Bethanie Archbold, and Michael Herbst didn't directly contribute to the book, but their work on corporate responsibility issues gave me quite a few ideas. At George Washington, doctoral students Andie Young, Chuck Koeber, and Tim Clark took my classes and, in the process, critiqued many of the ideas of the book.

Finally, a wonderful secretarial staff not only helped in the preparation of the manuscript, but over the years have transcribed my research notes so that they were both legible and also electronically available for me to use in building the manuscript. At Michigan, Cheryl Strickland, Tami Gibson, Connie Allen, and Shelly Whitmer carried the burden of this effort. At George Washington, Rochelle Rediang patiently responded to each and every request with her trademark cheerfulness.

Last but certainly not least, my thanks to my wife Nancy, my children Kurina and Steven, and even Rose and Scooby. Given this book was written while moving halfway across the country – and at the same time I wrote another book, *Prophets, Profits, and Passions* – the time I had to take to sneak in writing took time away from them too. My thanks to them for their love and patience.

Thanks to all of you, and thanks to all of those who also helped, but which my addled brain has failed in providing the memory to give you adequate recognition.

Publication acknowledgments

Previous versions of Chapters 1 and 2 appeared in the *American Business Law Journal* as "The Times and Seasons of Corporate Responsibility".

The excerpt on natural law in Chapter 3 has had several versions, the most recent of which was in my 2001 Oxford University Press book, *Ethics and Governance: Business as Mediating Institution*.

A portion of Chapter 5 appeared in the *Fordham Journal of Corporate and Financial Law* and was co-authored with David Hess and Robert McWhorter under the title "The 2004 Amendments to the Federal Sentencing Guidelines and Their Implicit Call for a Symbiotic Integration of Business Ethics".

All excerpts appear in this book pursuant to agreements with the previous publishers and with permission from my co-authors.

Notes on citation style

The citation style for this book is The Uniform System of Citation, also known as "The Bluebook". This is a system used by lawyers in the United States and is applied here with three major exceptions. First, while The Bluebook calls for citations to appear at the bottom of the page of the item referenced, I have placed them at the end of each chapter in order to be available to the reader, but not interrupt the flow of the text. Second, The Bluebook requires any proposition or statement that is supported by another source to identify that source immediately. In other words, just about each sentence will require a footnote. In fact, many times, there can be multiple footnotes within a single sentence. Particularly to the extent that such footnotes refer to the same source (i.e. in one paragraph, I may cite the same page of Steven Salbu's article multiple times), The Bluebook can wear on the reader. Based on conversations with the editors of Cambridge University Press, I have adopted an approach I have used previously, which is to limit citations as much as possible to the same source one time per paragraph. In doing so, I believe there is a good balance between appropriate recognition of authorities without cluttering the text. Third, The Bluebook specifies particular abbreviations for the names of journals. These work well in pure legal scholarship where most readers are Bluebook-trained. The abbreviations can be a bit mysterious for a broader readership. Thus, I have tried to set out full journal names as much as possible unless the abbreviation easily identifies the full name of the journal.

PART ONE

Peace Through Commerce

1 | *The times and seasons of corporate responsibility*

> There is a time for everything, and a season
>   for every activity under heaven:
> A time to be born and a time to die,
> A time to plant and a time to uproot,
> A time to kill and a time to heal,
> A time to tear down and a time to build,
> A time to weep and a time to laugh,
> A time to mourn and a time to dance,
> A time to scatter stones and a time to
>   gather them,
> A time to embrace and a time to refrain,
> A time to search and a time to give up,
> A time to keep and a time to throw away,
> A time to tear and a time to mend,
> A time to be silent and a time to speak,
> A time to love and a time to hate,
> A time for war and a time for peace.[1]

In 2001, less than two months after the September 11 attacks, I co-hosted the first conference on Corporate Governance and Sustainable Peace at the University of Michigan's William Davidson Institute. In the two years preceding that conference, I had been developing ideas about how businesses might contribute to reduced violence and my ruminations were met, generally, with polite bemusement. The idea of business contributing to peace seemed to be a stretch for most people. It sounded like something more likely to come from the mouth of a leftover sixties peace activist or a contender for Miss Universe (neither of which I am) than from a business ethics scholar. A few fellow adventurous academics were willing to try thinking about the idea, perhaps because they didn't want me to fail completely, but for the most part, peace through commerce had a tilting with windmills aura.

Yet in the days and weeks following 9–11, people from just about everywhere wanted to do *something* to try to contribute to peace. Those who lived far away from New York and from my current home in Washington, DC felt shock at the attacks and wanted to contribute something to prevent a similar catastrophe. Yes, they could console those who had been directly affected and support government leaders, but there was a yearning to do more. A conference on how one's daily work might make such a contribution caught people's attention. And so, we had quite a good conference. The focus wasn't the connection between business and terrorism *per se*; governance and sustainable peace were a set of broader topics pre-dating 9–11. But the events of 9–11 certainly impacted the conference significantly.

Many interesting themes came out of that conference, some of which will appear in this book. One of the more noteworthy themes was the conviction that no one had the power to do anything about issues of global violence. Government leaders felt constrained by the limits of sovereign power, particularly in an age of globalization where the Internet, transportation, and other communications made borders harder to control. Today, countries have trouble protecting borders from external content, including not only Internet information but also the trafficking of illicit goods, and in controlling national currencies. Non-governmental organizations (NGOs) felt constrained because they simply had the power of ideas, and some limited power through courts of law and through public opinion. Businesses felt constrained because issues of violence were of government concern, not of business. Thus, while all the parties agreed that the goal of peace through commerce was worthy, none of them believed that it was within their reach to actually do anything to achieve it.

They have a point. After all, what can one person or one company, even a large multinational enterprise, do to thwart violence? What can a single NGO do? Or even, perhaps, one country? Yet, given what we have seen in the world, given terrorism, changing borders, a proliferation of weapons of all kinds of different levels of destruction, given ethnic warfare and given the ecological damage wrought by war, how can we not try to think through how we might create conditions of peace – politically, religiously, and economically?

The good news is that this effort has already started. The United Nations, the World Bank, and many NGOs, such as the Prince of Wales Business Leadership Forum, have already thought through and set out ways for businesses to contribute to a lessening of violence in "zones of conflict". Conceptual frameworks demonstrating how business can contribute to peace have been articulated by the William Davidson Institute (WDI) Conferences at the University of Michigan from 2001 to 2003. The WDI conferences were published by the *Vanderbilt Journal of Transnational Law*, and follow-up conferences at George Washington University's Institute for Corporate Responsibility Program on Peace Through Commerce were published by the *American Business Law Journal*. Cindy Schipani and I synthesized a good deal of this work with our own in our book, *The Role of Business in Fostering Peaceful Societies*. The University of Notre Dame, in partnership with the UN, held a 2006 conference, and published the work of those participants in a book by Notre Dame Press. The *Journal of Corporate Citizenship* has published a special issue on the topic. So too has the United States Institute of Peace and International Alert.

We are not, then, starting from scratch. Moreover, the field of corporate responsibility has reached a stage of maturity so that some comprehensive integration can be undertaken. In this book, I want to show how an integration of contemporary approaches to business ethics contributes to sustainable peace. This approach, which I call *Total Integrity Management*, pulls together legal, managerial, and aesthetic/spiritual approaches to business ethics. These approaches are well-developed but rarely interact with each other. Total Integrity Management integrates them, showing how they can be more effective by building on each other. As I will argue in this book, they also arise directly out of what has been separately identified as contributions businesses can make to sustainable peace as well as our biologically rooted impulses that arise, when integrated, in a way that help to resolve conflict. In other words, we may have a chance for a more peaceful world by aligning our biological propensities with extant, disparate contemporary thinking. Thus, the central aim of this book is to show the historical and theoretical realities of the opportunities businesses have to create Peace Through Commerce and then to demonstrate how existing practices can make that happen.

Achieving that focus *does not* require a wholesale transformation of corporate governance. It does require a stronger focus on commonly accepted understandings of ethical business practices. Many businesses already endorse these practices and implement them to some degree. But if they realized that in doing so they might reduce violence, my sense is that the corporations and the individuals who comprise them, might find additional incentives for taking these ethical practices seriously. Put a different way, ethical business behavior is an achievable goal with an unexpected payoff. It may be too much to think that one's daily work could achieve peace, but one's daily work can be ethical. But by being aware that ethical business behavior could make peace more likely, ethical business behavior itself becomes a more valuable goal and a more meaningful one.

Adopting this goal and this mindset may also require a recognition that a shareholder-only model of corporate governance may not be the optimal approach to achieving sustainable peace. In fact, companies have set out to contribute to peace already. When they do so in Afghanistan, Bosnia, Burundi, Columbia, El Salvador, Guatemala, Israel, Kosovo, Nepal, Nigeria, Northern Ireland, Palestine, Philippines, Sierra Leone, Somalia, South Africa, and Sri Lanka, they *do not* embrace the short-term pursuit of profitability. They may believe that a concern for peace will have long-term beneficial impacts on shareholder profitability, but to get to that goal, they need to engage non-economic values. At the same time, the shareholder paradigm is not a bad place to start.

Corporate governance, shareholder priority, and shareholders' priorities

In the twenty-first century, economic globalization will continue to increase the power of corporations vis-à-vis the nation-state. If this results in a breakdown of archaic bureaucracies and oppressive authoritarian regimes, globalization may yield great benefits. Yet, if the state is the primary check on business, the continued weakening of the state may also lead to the increased vulnerability of individuals and societies, undermining a social fabric that previously held a society together. People in marginalized circumstances (or those who wish to exploit the marginalized's plight for their own political objectives) may well react, perhaps violently, to the loss of protections and the transformations of their cultures. That poses a quandary for businesses: how do they pursue their quest for profitability if their practices sow the seeds of instability? Businesses generally thrive on stability. Businesses best pursue profitability single-mindedly when there is a state that can enforce legal norms and protect (or rectify) the excesses of greed.

As Colin Powell once said, "money is a coward".[2] Most businesses prefer stability, reliable rules of law, and non-corrupt governments. They do not thrive in corrupt, unstable markets. The interesting test will be how businesses will secure stability, rule of law, and transparency as they simultaneously augment their ability to make geopolitical boundaries irrelevant.

The answer, I believe, lies in the understanding that, in the twenty-first century, businesses will best ensure their profitability if they also mindfully contribute to the public good. History shows how this is possible, although learning from history is difficult to do because of the current polarization of the debate over the "shareholder vs. stakeholder" models of corporate governance.

The free market model is well-established in many countries and its results have been spectacular. Under any metric, the level of economic expansion and wealth creation in the last one hundred years eclipses anything previously known in human history.[3] There are more material goods, more jobs, more infrastructures, more technology, better hygiene, better medicines, and more conveniences than have ever been known. This phenomenal growth does not simply create opulence – although there is that – but also provides personal freedom. A person who can use their earnings to feed, clothe, and educate a family enables family members to develop talents and interests that would otherwise be submerged in a daily quest for sustenance.[4] Parents are able to educate their children, and the educational value-added in a society tends to create the kind of economic differentiation that leads away from violent, destructive civil wars. Economically vibrant countries are less violent than moribund ones.[5] With such a record, and in the wake of communism's downfall in 1989, optimistic assessments of free market capitalism and liberal democracy claimed the "end of history";[6] that is, it won the argument as to the best way to organize society. The liberal, capitalist model has performed spectacularly, albeit selfishly, over the past one hundred years with visible benefits.

One version of the free market model is the "value-maximization model". It takes capitalism in a particular direction, one that measures effectiveness in quantifiably ascertainable metrics obtained when managers focus on shareholder profitability. This approach is not solely justified by profitability, however. The ability to conduct such measurements provides definable accountability of managerial actions. It hems in managers who want to use shareholder assets for their own benefit. This model has been seized upon and impressively developed by scholars residing in schools of management and in many law schools. In fact, it is not an exaggeration to argue that the value-maximization approach has become the entrenched paradigm in business schools.

Today, however, that governance "paradigm" is being challenged in a most unexpected way. The challenge comes from another group of scholars residing in, of all things, schools of management, who favor notions of "corporate social responsibility" (CSR) as opposed to an economic system based on a single-minded focus on profit. Although it is dangerous to simplify what any one "school" of thought says, CSR advocates believe that corporations have obligations to the greater society as well as to shareholders, whereas the shareholder advocates believe that managers should focus solely on the interests of the shareholders and to enhance their profits. While the so-called shareholder school is diverse, perhaps the seminal statement of the position was in the *New York Times Magazine*, where Milton Friedman argued that businesses do the most social good by focusing on attention to shareholder value rather than trying to engage in social concerns. In his article, which is not quite as polemic as its title, "The Social Responsibility of Business Is to Increase Its Profits", Friedman does acknowledge that corporations can engage in a variety of social contributions and initiatives as long as it is related to a business strategy, an argument that might well be made by many "stakeholder activists". Further, Friedman also argues that businesses should be attentive to rules of law. Nevertheless, Friedman's article does emphatically argue that managers using corporate funds to contribute to their own conception of good works (a) commit theft (because the money belongs to the shareholders, not the manager) and (b) attempt to realize social goods that they are unable to attain through legitimate political processes.[7]

The peculiar thing is that CSR advocates typically present themselves as challenging the entrenched shareholder paradigm whereas, in reality, it is very difficult to find a time and place where the shareholder paradigm actually represents the legal duties of managers. In the United States, arguably one of the most shareholder-focused countries, the legal duty of managers in a public corporation is not to maximize profitability *per se*, but to carry out the lawful directives of the shareholders. The famous 1919 case, *Dodge vs. Ford*, did hold that even an executive as powerful as Henry Ford could not simply decree that extraordinary dividends could be diverted from shareholders (including the Dodge Brothers) to his favored stakeholder groups (employees and customers).[8] But the more prevailing rule is that managers *do* have a great deal of latitude to sacrifice immediate profit in favor of a reasonable good. This was true in *Shlensky vs. Wrigley*, where the court held that the Chicago Cubs could refuse to undertake the profitable strategy of playing night baseball as long as there was some sensible strategy for not doing so.[9] A later case, *Paramount Communications vs. Time Warner*, said that boards of directors could decline a higher bid price for a company takeover and consider the bid's impact on the corporate culture of the company as a reason to decline the bid.[10]

In a similar vein, profitability may always be a shareholder interest, but so too, for example, may the *New York Times'* interest in adhering to standards of journalistic excellence,[11] or Johnson & Johnson's commitment to its *Credo* (where obligations to shareholders come last after those of other stakeholders), or Timberland's commitment to giving its employees forty hours a year to do volunteer work. More than half the states in the United States have corporate constituency statutes where managers may take into account non-shareholder constituents; the most influential state for incorporation, Delaware, allows much of the same through judicial opinions. In Europe and Asia, companies more typically have a greater focus on social and national goods.[12]

Thus, we are in the bizarre position of shareholder advocates holding onto an "entrenched" paradigm that does not legally exist, while CSR advocates struggle to articulate a position against the paradigm when, in fact, the neoclassical model has never really had full sway. Why this strange juxtaposition?

First, value-maximizing theorists have good reason to want to protect shareholders. Shareholders aren't necessarily big, bad, rich people. In many ways, they are vulnerable themselves. A distressed shareholder has little ability to challenge management. A small number of large shareholders or institutional shareholders (such as pension or mutual funds) may be able to force changes in the executive suite. So too can the market as a whole. But managers abuse shareholders too, especially minority shareholders. And so, one way to look at those advocating shareholder protection is to see them as speaking out for another stakeholder group that needs protection from managers. Such theorists do have concerns, however, that managers given the discretion to consider non-shareholder constituents will always be able to find a stakeholder group that would be happy with a particular course of action. Thus, a shrewd manager, seeking only self-interest, could play one stakeholder group off against the other, guided only by who supports the manager's position of the moment. For that reason, value-maximizing theorists view "stakeholder theory" as a framework that has the potential to marginalize a shareholder, who has then even less ability to hold management accountable for its actions.

Second, the argument between the shareholder-only conception of corporate governance and the stakeholder-too model is largely an academic and civil society struggle. This does not mean that the argument is not important. Academic and civil society issues influence political and legal ones, but the battle for primacy more frequently occurs in the press and in academia than it does in the courts. More importantly, it is hard to deny the increasing influence of the value-maximization variation of capitalism. In their seminal article on today's corporate governance, Michael Bradley, Cindy Schipani, Anand Sudnanram, and James Walsh argue that more traditionally communitarian governance systems, such as Germany and Japan, are moving toward the contractarian (i.e. value-maximization) model.[13] While I think Bradley *et al* overstate the case for this shift, it is hard to dispute the basic truth of their claim. Value-maximization's success in business and law schools has influenced the way courts and legislatures analyze corporate responsibility.

Third, there is a psychological argument that remains unsettled. That argument goes to the heart of capitalism, the genius (or bane) of which is that by being selfish, the world gets better. Morally, this is a deeply unsettling position and it is one that has been at the heart of debates about capitalism for centuries. No matter how successful capitalism and value-maximization might be quantitatively, the notion that good is done via selfishness runs hard against the grain of most philosophies and religions, and also against human instincts. That argument will *never* be settled and so whenever there is a claim to have settled it, which value-maximization attempts to do, a contrary reaction will be triggered.

Fourth, although the *law* is more than willing to have corporations act philanthropically, responsibly, and ethically, the *market* may have a different set of standards. That is, the capability of being able to move in and out of a stock position of a company a dozen times *a day* means that executives banking on a strategy that good citizenship will pay off in the long run (because goodwill and reputation matter) have no long-run strategy to ensure their plan. If the market doesn't like next month's financials, shareholders can and will sell the company's stock and perhaps fire the CEO. This pressure virtually mandates that corporations manage for the short term and further mandates that corporations attend to concrete financial performance to the detriment of soft, less-measurable aims of citizenship. It is this governance mechanism, not that of the law, that is making the debate over what a manager should do so contentious. The law permits more socially engaged corporate strategies as well as a more shareholder-focused one; it does not mandate either. Moreover, when managers do prioritize interests of non-shareholders over those of shareholders, as many bad things can happen as good. The scandals of, for example, Enron and Worldcom were, after all, not those of employing sweatshop labor to increase profits, but of managers prioritizing *themselves* over *both* shareholders and employee interests.

Because the market governance mechanism is financial, when issues of corporate responsibility are raised, attention is understandably paid to finding ways to link good ethics with good business. Thus, as described in Part Two of this book, a good deal of scholarship is directed toward the establishment of links between corporate social performance and corporate financial performance. Yet, as long as the metric is financial, the justifications will be financial, and that then begs the question as to whether the financial justification of behavior, economic or otherwise, is sufficient to fully account for moral virtue. In other words, can moral virtue, journalistic excellence, volunteerism, meaningful work, or sustainable peace, really be captured by stock valuations on the New York Stock Exchange or NASDAQ? Or, even more importantly, given the times and seasons of our lives in the opening years of this millennium, does the exclusive focus on profitability serve us well in creating sustainable peace and security?

Today's time and season

The message of this book is that an exclusive focus on profitability does not serve us well. Rather than repeating the traditional moral claims about the deficiencies of value-maximization – concerns that I do share – I want to suggest that regardless of the moral propriety of focusing only on profitability, the risk for the twenty-first century is that such an approach imperils us all, including businesses and the free market.

When Khalid Sheikh Mohammed, the mastermind of the 9–11 attacks, selected the targets for hijacked planes to crash into, he focused equally on government targets in Washington and on economically prominent centers in Manhattan and California.[14] Some of the emphasis on economic sites was undoubtedly psychological and symbolic. At the same time, disrupting economic, commercial vibrancy was seen by terrorists as a way to bring America to its knees. Economics has, of course, always been a central underpinning of political power. In a global economy, economics provides the wherewithal to build "hard power" in terms of military capability as well as "soft power" through the projection of capitalist – frequently American – values across the globe.[15]

The difficulty is that these expansions of values, even if well-intended, can raise antagonisms in countries as traditional ways of life are challenged. Indeed, researchers have suggested that one of the causes of terrorism is that in recoiling from the intrusion of external ways of life, including ways of doing business, parts of a society can attempt to reclaim their identity by focusing on a select strand of a religious tradition, investing it with a prominence new to the religion itself.[16] In that recoiling, charismatic leaders can rally a portion of the society against western ways of life, sometimes non-violently but sometimes quiet violently, because the very survival of traditions are deemed to be at stake. In such dire, extreme times, terrorism becomes a mechanism to preserve the perception of the tradition to be maintained. The militant fundamentalists who follow this path may not do justice to their own tradition, but the phenomenon does become a reality. This in turn affects business, because businesses are part of the globalization phenomena against which the tradition is being protected.

Business interests may believe that the protection of society from violence is the responsibility of government. They would be right. But businesses, like it or not, are in the midst of today's wars of terrorism both in terms of responsibilities to keep employees and material resources safe and also to reduce the disaffection that can breed or give refuge to and support for those trying to attack the free market

itself. At other times and places in world history, businesses may have
been able to rely on a neat distinction between government and corporate responsibility, but in today's globalized economy, terrorist groups
are empowered by the technologies (provided by globalization) that
can disrupt business itself. And so, businesses get caught in the midst of
twenty-first century battles whether they want to or not. In some
respects, this is not new; in other respects, it is quite different.

Of course, destroying the capability of an enemy to sustain itself is
nothing new; it is what siege warfare and blockades were all about.
Consistent with a long line of military strategy, painstakingly detailed
by Phillip Bobbitt[17] and described more fully below, contemporary
warfare from at least the time of Napoleon has sought to win battles
by symbolically, psychologically, and sometimes literally attacking the
population at large.

Napoleon, Bobbitt argues, traded constitutional protections of basic
rights and protections via the Napoleonic Code in order to justify the
conscription of large numbers of the population. Once the entire population is in some sense mobilized, it also becomes part of the army the
enemy seeks to attack. This is a strategy that terrorism follows today.
Terrorism is, of course, not a new tactic either. Political assassinations
have marked human history going back to biblical times. Yet, twenty-
first century terrorism is markedly different and that difference has
implications for the organization of economic enterprise for at least
two reasons. First, as Chapter 3 notes, globalization diminishes borders
and, in doing so, national sovereignty. It is much harder for countries to
control what goes in and out of their borders because of advances in
telecommunications, transportation, and the Internet. Governments
must pay close attention to international global markets in making
their investment decisions or else there can be a run on a country's
currency. And the technology that empowers individuals also makes
the traditional, albeit the most minimal function of the state – its
capacity to control violence – far more difficult.

Second, there is a market for weapons technology, telecommunications, the Internet, and financial products. Unfortunately, under a
value-maximizing approach, businesses have a built-in incentive to
shoot themselves in the foot or worse. The shareholder model of the
corporation has great difficulty saying "no" to a profit opportunity.
Indeed, with capital markets mandating short-term financial returns,
that difficulty may be more akin to impossibility. A bit more cynically

put, a manager could simply rationalize that the business is selling a component. What an end-user does with that component is beyond a corporation's control. To put it even more cynically, why not make money selling products, even components of weapons of mass destruction (WMD), to terrorists as long as one doesn't get caught? How does a manager say no to such a profit opportunity if by saying no the market punishes him by demanding his job? One might answer that a company should obey the laws on the topic. But what if the laws are unclear (which is the case in controlling sales of WMD components)? We have all heard (and perhaps even have said when doing our tax returns or driving above the posted speed limit) that a given law is just too inconvenient and too expensive to follow. If "everyone else is doing it" and if the risk of getting caught for violating a law is low, why not try to make some money to boost the bottom line?

Further, market-based solutions typically (a) rely on government to provide the base infrastructure and laws that are the only constraint to exploiting market opportunities, (b) take advantage of legal expertise to circumvent whatever laws are in place, and (c) lobby in order to arrange the playing field for additional market opportunities rather than in creating level playing fields and just legal systems. The result is that in a time and season when one of the most dangerous physical threats to existence is terrorism, the purposes we mandate for corporations do not protect either the general population or the corporations themselves. *A model of corporate responsibility that mandates that managers justify decisions only on the basis of a financial metric will never include enough other threats to the business to prevent a literal physical disaster.*

Interestingly, one response to the question of how to reduce the threat of the sales of materials to be used to create weapons of mass destruction (or the sale of WMD themselves) has been to call for corporations to develop the right kind of corporate culture. This approach is popular on many fronts in the area of corporate responsibility today. With respect to sexual harassment issues, the US Supreme Court constructed a process whereby corporations could mitigate their liability by creating internal training programs and dispute resolution forums.[18] With respect to more general notions of corporate misbehavior, the 1991 Amendments to the Federal Sentencing Guidelines constructed a legal system whereby if corporations took good faith steps to implement effective compliance programs, their potential liability for misconduct would be reduced.[19] In 2002, Congress followed the same approach in the Sarbanes-Oxley Act, requiring high-level officials to become more personally responsible for truthful reporting of company financial statements and to adopt and abide by ethics programs with checks and balances to make them effective.[20] In 2004, Amendments to the Federal Sentencing Guidelines went beyond having corporations adopt compliance programs and instead mandated that companies develop legal *and ethical* corporate *cultures*.[21]

These reflexive models of corporate decision-making attempt to make businesses into institutions that have some degree of moral maturity. That is, rather than insisting that corporations act like a toddler – grasp for anything you can unless you are going to get caught – these mechanisms are trying to get corporations to, in a sense, grow up. The value-maxmization model, on the other hand, encourages – in fact essentially mandates – that corporations act like toddlers. They are to grasp and push and try to get around rules until they get caught. There is little encouragement for corporations to develop a sense of moral maturity so that they build in a wisdom that allows them to renounce market opportunities in light of other, important goods. The reflexive legal models ask corporations to be more attentive to legal and ethical norms by making them into self-regulating institutions with legal oversight examining the sufficiency of their moral maturity. Without such balancing of complex and potentially contradictory goals, there is little guarantee that any mature corporate culture will ever be created.

Let me be careful though. Corporations have no conscience. They are not human beings. They have no soul. They are things. And so when I say that shareholder theory encourages corporations to act like toddlers, it is a bit unfair. Corporations are never going to possess moral maturity in the sense that an adult transcends the maturity of a toddler (at least we hope). Yet, organizations do have cultures and traditions. And those cultures and traditions can be grasping and narrow or they can be complex and balancing. That does require some level of cultural maturity and sophistication.

In a similar fashion, non-governmental organizations, typically through media or Internet sources, try to impose social expectations on the corporation. Just as the law imposes negative consequences (typically in the form of fines) on a company for misbehavior, so NGOs attempt to blacken the eyes of corporations so that corporate image and reputation lead to negative financial consequences. Such consequences could be in lost sales or through the threat of more regulation as a result of legislative attention to popular outcry against the misbehaving corporation. While regulation remains at the core of a strategy constraining corporate behavior, these reflexive models (both legal and social), seem to be moving corporations to attend more to their legal, ethical, and social obligations.[22]

The rationale for why corporations *should* be attentive to such groups is because of a loose consensus that corporations have responsibility to their stakeholders. Thus the stakeholder view, in innumerable guises, has become a preponderant analytical model. Yet there is great variation in stakeholder models. People draw very different circles as to which stakeholder should count, in what ways, and how much. Some scholars attempt to prioritize specific stakeholder groups; others attempt to prioritize specific principles.

After exploring the stakeholder model in the 1930s and again in the 1970s-80s, normative and legal scholars have developed and refined alternative models of corporate responsibility. They range from a virtue-based approach that emphasizes attending first to corporate culture and community as a way to instill the predisposition and habit to regularly think about corporate responsibility, to multiple forms of contract theories that presuppose varying implicit and explicit social contracts. Another school attempts to find ways in which corporate responsibility can lead to profitable business. It is fair to say that while the stakeholder framework provides a jumping-off metaphor to contrast with value-maximization, most contemporary legal and normative theories of corporate responsibility focus on particular dimensions, such as human rights of workers or indigenous populations, the development of corporate culture, or the efficacy of social initiatives.

Yet, at the end of the day, because of market pressures, corporations must make a profit and will be judged primarily according to whether they are successful in doing so. As long as this is true, additional goals and aims will be idiosyncratic or tangential to business behavior.

The question is whether corporate responsibility as an idiosyncratic or occasional aim of business behavior is adequate for today's time and season. In this book, I argue that it is not because the incentives and structure for business behavior do not adequately protect against the real threats to human existence. In the short run, that threat is terrorism and violence. In the long run it is ecological and environmental (differentiated from ecological in the sense of "environment" attending to social implications of poverty) sustainability. The free market's energy should rely on free market incentives, but the free market must be free from terrorism that could vaporize Manhattan with a nuclear device and that could undermine a basic material and social infrastructure. The argument of this book is that while government certainly has the primary responsibility for preventing such horrors, the stakes of preventing them are so great and the current structure so porous so as to require a re-thinking of corporate responsibility for this time and season of human history.

Peace Through Commerce

It is not unreasonable for harried business executives to complain that they have enough to do without having to worry about creating world peace. At the same time, business needs relatively stable conditions in order to survive. There are, of course, significant industries that profit from supplying military material and from rebuilding war-torn societies, but the vast majority of commercial firms benefit from stability and are significantly harmed by violence and unrest. Moreover, there has long been a school of thought, stretching from philosophers such as Kant and Montesquieu to late twentieth-century economists such as Hayek, arguing that trade promotes peace. This reciprocal relationship – that business needs peace to thrive and thriving businesses promote peace – suggests a particular role for business in fostering peaceful societies.[23]

Since the turn of the century, considerable attention has been devoted to businesses working in zones of conflict. Three are of particular note. Jane Nelson, in her 2001 book, *The Business of Peace*, developed five principles of corporate engagement: strategic commitment to developing and embedding policies that address human rights, corruption, and security issues; risk and impact analysis with respect to the nature of the conflict in which the company does its business; dialogue and consultation with the relevant stakeholders; developing mutually beneficial and transparent partnerships with governments, other companies, and NGOs; and developing accountability metrics in order to evaluate corporate actions. Nelson argued that with only 4 percent of the world's GNP related to military expenditures, the vast majority of business thrives on peace and stability. Stability brings with it better investment opportunities, reduced operations costs, and more efficient acquisition of funding.[24] Nelson illustrates her points with specific examples of companies' actions that mostly relate to the work of business in zones of conflict, but which could be extended more generally as well.

The United Nations' Global Compact built on Nelson's work and initiated a series of dialogues with (mostly European) companies, academics, governments, and NGO leaders to develop several models of corporate engagement. These included developing conflict impact assessment and survey tools, fostering and profiling multi-stakeholder dialogue, assisting in community development projects, providing for revenue transparency, certifying commodity extraction in a way that does not benefit warring parties, and developing human rights-protecting security arrangements.[25] The UN also developed case studies of multi-stakeholder partnerships and of revenue sharing strategies. In the UN's work, business has a significant role to play in developing practices that mitigate the possibility of violence in conflict-sensitive regions.

In 2006, International Alert released a book-length report advocating the concept of "peace entrepreneurship". It grouped the actions corporations could take in response to conflict into three categories on a continuum of conflict sustaining to conflict reducing/peacebuilding, with a coping strategy in the middle. Businesses *have already* contributed to peacebuilding, according to International Alert, by engaging in formal peace negotiations (usually in a supporting role), addressing economic contributions, building relationships that reach across conflict lines, helping to protect their own security, and encouraging women entrepreneurs.[26]

These three sources are deep wells for businesses working in conflict-threatened economies to draw from. The lessons learned from this scholarship may extend beyond businesses working in such challenging circumstances. Yet seeing how businesses can contribute to peace does become harder when the corporation is not in the direct threat of war. One of the themes of this book, however, is that there are still actions businesses can take. The goal of ethical business behavior is one that captures what businesses can do and which acts as an intermediary goal. In other words, ethical business behavior contributes to peace. Even if one does not perceive one's business in a conflict-threatened situation (and today, most of us may be in such situations whether we recognize it or not), achieving ethical business behavior is a goal that is graspable by managers even if Peace Through Commerce is not. The unexpected payoff of ethical business behavior, however, is that it may reduce violence.

For example, in previous work, Cindy Schipani and I argued that businesses have the opportunity to contribute to less violent conditions in countries in which they work and that they can do so by creating ethical organizational cultures that replicate anthropologically substantiated characteristics of peaceful societies. Conceptually, businesses do possess the capability to reach across borders and to get people who may not otherwise work together to do so, even if the only common goal they have is profitability. Some businesses even intentionally hire employees from otherwise conflicting ethnic or religious groups in order to get them to have the experience of cooperating. The World Bank and the United Nations have each produced studies demonstrating that poverty-stricken countries tend to be more violent than prosperous ones. One reason for this relationship seems to be that the productive engagement of individuals in work prevents leaving them idly occupied and therefore ripe for charismatic leadership pointing them into violent acts. An additional reason may be that the competition for resources is so severe in poverty-stricken societies that violence may be the preferred means to secure them.

Business may be in a position to damper fires leading to violence simply by providing economic opportunity. On the other hand, businesses that are perceived to be exploitative or culturally undermining could sow the seeds for resentment and violence. It is, therefore, a particular kind of company that provides necessary economic development, but does so in a way that is constructively engaged in communities where they work: in short, an ethical business company.

More specifically, there are three contributions business can make to sustainable peace. The first is the aforementioned contribution to economic development. Profitable companies provide economic development through employment which, as has already been noted, is likely to contribute to less violence, particularly if jobs provide "value-added" work. The World Bank's studies show that when the primary export of a country is an undifferentiated commodity – such as oil, diamonds, or timber – the likelihood of civil war is dramatically magnified. When businesses add value to the product, violence decreases. Moreover, the benefits of economic development are not simply those of employment. With employment by a multinational company frequently comes managerial training and technology transfer. That is, multinational companies train local citizens on how to effectively run organizations. Not only is this good for the local subsidiary of the company, but given job changes, individuals who have been trained in state of the art management techniques may use them in other businesses as well. Moreover, many multinational companies train their supplier companies in good management techniques in order to assure the quality of the product being supplied to them.

Not only are managers trained, but technology is transferred. In the case of Motorola in Malaysia, it is estimated that almost $1 billion of technology transfer occurred.[27] Given that the value-added component of business is a particularly important dimension of getting a country beyond violence-prone, commodity exports, this kind of transfer has significant potential for harmony-producing benefits.

Beyond economic development, companies also contribute to the non-violent aspects of a country if they avoid corruption. In our book, Cindy Schipani and I showed that there is a direct, linear correlation between how countries fare on Transparency International's Corruption Perception Index and whether disputes are handled violently or not. To summarize the study, those countries that fared the Transparency International's index settled disputes by violence 60 percent of the time; those in the third quartile (next most corrupt), settled disputes by violence 44 percent of the time; those in the second quartile settled disputes by violence 26 percent of the time; and those that were the least corrupt settled disputes by violence 14 percent of the time.[28] The study is correlative not causative; there could be a third factor explaining both. Yet, it is hard to think that more corruption is likely to dampen feelings of frustration and injustice in a given society.

Thus, to the extent that corporations are open to the external evaluation of their conduct, such as avoiding corruption, they can make a contribution to less violence. Similarly, to the extent that corporations support other external kinds of regulation and dispute resolution, such as supporting the development of the rule of law, dispute resolution systems, and property rights, corporations may enhance the peacefulness of the community.

A third contribution is that of building a sense of community. By this, we mean engaging with communities in a constructive way, something typically called corporate citizenship. This is a common-sense notion that if corporations treat their host communities poorly, they do little to enhance good relations. At a minimum, corporate citizenship would include protection of ecological resources of a host community, respect of the human rights of individuals affected by corporate actions, and an overarching sense of sensitivity to local customs, religions, and traditions. Although global protestors frequently complain about large multinational corporations, there are not only good stories about corporate behavior, but a recent study shows a surprisingly favorable impression of corporations among developing countries.[29]

A 2003 Pew Research Study showed that citizens in a wide variety of countries have a positive view of "large corporations from other countries". With the exception of Argentina, every Latin American country had strong majorities holding a favorable view of large companies from other countries; the same was true in Eastern Europe with the exception of Poland and Russia. The favorable impression was even more pronounced in Africa where only one country (Tanzania at 53 percent) showed a favorable rating less than 65 percent. Asian countries were less enthusiastic, but still showed plurality favorability ratings. Among developing countries, only the Middle East showed significant ambivalence. This general attitude toward corporations is further supported by evidence indicating a skeptical view among emerging countries toward anti-globalization protestors and a favorable disposition toward trade. Yet, at the same time, people also raise concerns about the gap between rich and poor and the worsening treatment of workers.[30]

This seems to suggest that corporations have a platform from which to have a positive impact on a society, but that the way in which they go about doing it and the ultimate results of the activities can make people uneasy. Hence, the engagement of corporate citizenship provides a way for a large company to contribute more positively while reducing the negative impacts.

Perhaps more interesting is the building of community within the corporation. Many contemporary management techniques stress the importance of having employees contribute to problem-solving and to point out defects in current systems in order to assure quality production. This kind of contribution can only occur when there is a baseline of essential respect for and protection of the human rights of employees. The experience of speaking out to contribute to problem-solving is a democratic skill and if it is true, as it seems to be, that democratic countries tend to avoid warring with each other, there could be a positive political spillover effect to the development of this skill in the corporation.

This enhancement of the participatory aspect of work in organizations suggests the importance of daily interaction occurring within the corporation. It also suggests that the daily ethical behavior occurring in business may have an impact beyond what occurs within the daily life of a manager or worker. Indeed, in a 2001 book, I argued that a way to distill the central dominant theories of contemporary business ethics is within a conception of a business as a mediating institution.[31] Mediating institutions are the relatively small communities in which human values are developed because there is a direct, recognizable consequence to actions.[32] In such communities, such as family, neighborhood, and religious and voluntary organizations, individuals obtain a sense of meaning of who they are as human beings, in part as members of an organization that interfaces with the rest of the world, but also in part in terms of the values that must be internalized and regularly practiced in order to be a good citizen of the family or neighborhood. One cannot hide unethical behavior in such organizations, they are small enough so that it is found out.

Interestingly, the connection between the relationships to be nourished in such a community and the rules necessary to sustain those relationships is one that seems to be connected to the size of the organization itself. For instance, in his work on the development of language, Robin Dunbar noted that human beings and our primate cousins have a very large neocortex in relation to our body mass. If, as many believe, the neocortex is significantly responsible for human cognition, it would seem that we are evolutionarily developed to rely heavily on our brain wattage rather than our speed or size. This rather common-sense notion is connected, however, to a second dimension; the sizes of communities in which we develop our language are relatively small. Dunbar notes that primates live in only certain sizes of groups; beyond a certain size, the group fissions and will not exceed its ceiling. Plotting known group sizes of primates against the neocortex ratio (size of neocortex compared to total body mass) yielded his prediction that the maximum (meaning where there was still a tangible understanding that one was in an important relationship with other members of the community) optimal size of a human grouping was

150. As Dunbar colloquially put it, there are about 150 people that you know well enough so that if you saw them at a bar, you'd be comfortable pulling up a chair and having a beer. Dunbar further substantiated this number by finding surveys showing that 150 was the average number of names in an address book, the size of the company unit in the military, and the optimum size of a religious body.[33]

These rather small numbers suggest that human beings cognitively understand the importance of their actions to a relatively small number of individuals and that within those groups, some kind of moral character is developed. The kind of character, of course, can vary. Small group sizes may be associated with peaceful societies, as noted below, or they may also characterize a militia or youth gang. What is important is that these small groups, for better or worse, seem to be a hardwired feature of our human nature and do form some moral dispositions.[34]

Businesses could be constructive mediating institutions, particularly if they aligned participatory features of the workplace with the goal of sustainable peace. People do adapt their behavior to fit in at work. A small mediating institution could foster the kinds of communal, empathic kinds of moral behavior that are beneficial and, if aimed toward non-violence, can do so with constructive contributions to the larger society. This conception of business behavior is one that infuses ethical considerations in business so that there is concern for the well-being of corporate stakeholders. It may be too much to ask corporations to take into account the impact of their actions on *all* stakeholders, but companies could efficaciously regularly consult and empower employees and shareholders. Doing so may possibly provide a sense of voice to other stakeholders since employees are also community members affected by the environment. If corporations were to manage for the benefit of employees and shareholders, they would create a kind of business community that is not as far-flung as what a full-blown stakeholder model might suggest, but may be able to create a corporate community in which there is mutual decision-making about the way the business works. It would then be a corporate community that could help to instill virtues appropriate for ethical business behavior and create a different kind of social contract for business leading to good business actions. In short, it could combine the best features of the three leading business ethics frameworks – stakeholder, virtue, and contract – in a way to optimally promote good ethics in business.

Total Integrity Management

Anthropologists have conducted studies as to what features define peaceful societies and they look and feel a good deal like mediating institutions. David Fabbro's research demonstrated that peaceful societies tend to be relatively small, with consensus and egalitarian decision-making, little hierarchy, an ethical commitment to non-violence, and absence of a standing military force.[35] Further, such communities tend to have some distance between them and other communities; with the nature of globalization pushing communities together, that characteristic may be rare today, but it also may enhance the importance of these other characteristics, which I have described as central features of mediating institutions.

Raymond Kelly has analyzed "non-violent" societies and argues that the key feature that differentiates violent from non-violent societies is a notion of "social substitutability".[36] When the members of a society are so interchangeable that there are few, if any, defining individual characteristics, it becomes much easier to resort to killing a de-humanized body. That is, the more a person is a thing or a number, the easier it is to eliminate them. The more a person is a father, daughter, or neighbor, the harder it is to kill.

To summarize, there has been significant, theoretical, and empirical work demonstrating that (1) businesses may be able to contribute to the reduction of violence, (2) a central way to actualize the leading theories of business ethics is through the notion of businesses being mediating institutions, an approach that emphasizes that the size of the organization must be small enough to allow its members to connect moral principles to actual consequences, and (3) such organizations are also a feature of non-violent societies, as least as long as other egalitarian, participatory, and non-violent goals and practices are explicit. While these connections provide a plausible framework for businesses to be contributors to peace, however, they are only a plausible starting point. Taking into account the biological and moral importance of mediating institutions, together with the idea of Peace Through Commerce, suggests that there may be a way to achieve Peace Through Commerce through a management approach that emphasizes the various dimensions of ethics; something I call Total Integrity Management. The goal of this book is to more fully articulate that framework and to demonstrate its depth so that it becomes more than plausible – so that it instead becomes a testable hypothesis and potentially practical proposal for reforming corporate governance in order to address the challenges of today's time and season.

That effort is the focus of Part Two of the book. "Business as mediating institution" shows how organizational design can nourish the empathic moral sentiments. It is a design that taps into caring about ethics. Peace Through Commerce suggests that a reason to be ethical is because of the unexpected, positive impact that may result. It becomes an aspirational aim. Together, these two features create what I call the Good Trust dimension of Total Integrity Management. Good Trust is about engaging the innate desire human beings possess to be good. That desire, if actuated, leads to both ethical business behavior and Peace Through Commerce. The desire is not actuated by legal rules nor economic payoffs. At the same time, caring is not enough. Emotional sentiments must join with compliance to societal expectations of proper behavior largely reflected by law. I call this dimension Hard Trust. It too must also be joined with managerial strategies that make good ethics good business. That links and reinforces the reasons for being ethical. I call this Real Trust. The three kinds of trust: Hard Trust, Real Trust, and Good Trust *integrated together*, can create the corporations that contribute to sustainable peace. In turn, these three dimensions of trust also link to three other important dimensions of ethics. First, they are very similar to the three contributions to peace: rule of law aspects (Hard Trust), economic development (Real Trust), and building empathic communities (Good Trust). Second, these three kinds of moral approaches come from well-developed yet distinctive approaches to ethics: legal regulation (such as the Federal Sentencing Guidelines), managerial scholarship (descriptive social science and normative), and spiritual/aesthetic questions for moral excellence. Unfortunately, these three disciplinary approaches rarely interact with each other. In this book, I want to integrate them because I believe the integration is necessary for Total Integrity Management and more importantly to achieve Peace Through Commerce. No one approach can achieve ethical business behavior nor can one dimension achieve sustainable peace. Finally, these three dimensions are rooted in nature itself. As will be described in Chapter 2, William Frederick has shown that there are three value clusters through all nature: economizing (linking in my terms Real Trust, economic development, and managerial ethics scholarship), power-aggrandizing (linking in my terms Hard

Trust, rule of law, and legal ethics scholarship), and ecologizing (linking in my terms Good Trust, community building, and a spiritual/ aesthetic ethics scholarship). Thus, my argument is that our human nature, history, and contemporary scholarship about corporate responsibility and about Peace Through Commerce are extant resources that can be integrated to create a logical argument for how business can practice ethical business behavior and thereby contribute to sustainable peace.

The framework of this book

For those readers who are already convinced that business could have a role in fostering sustainable peace, you may wish to skip Chapters 2 and 3 and proceed directly to Chapter 4 where I begin to discuss *how* they could do so. While I think the arguments are important to situate businesses' role in a larger context which allows them to contribute to sustainable peace, there is some tough sledding in these chapters. Depending on what the reader wants to gain from this book, these two chapters may or may not be essential.

Chapter 2 provides a brief historical account of business, history, and warfare. Its central point is that businesses may be far from instruments of peace. They can be exactly the opposite. Frequently, businesses have been the instruments of obtaining and increasing national power. This is particularly true of transnational corporations. As an example, the British nationalism of Cecil Rhodes in southern Africa, or that of the East India Company, linked corporate and nationalistic ambitions. In Germany, a central legal, corporate responsibility, established since the Third Reich, has been one to the welfare of the *volk*. France's Credit Mobilier had nationalistic charges. Amy Chua has documented how Chinese immigrants throughout Southeast Asia serve to spread China's power and influence and are frequently resented (in Cambodia, Vietnam, and Thailand) as a result. A common complaint against globalization is that it serves as extension of American "soft power", by spreading values of individualism, profit, and consumerism.

Chapter 2 also looks anthropologically at how peace-making is part of our hardwired nature, and in doing so shows that we human beings can also adapt and change our social structures. Yes, nature may be "red in tooth and claw", but harmony is also part of our nature. It is worth recalling that aspect of our nature and drawing upon it in resolving conflicts today. Thus, this chapter looks at our primate heritage for clues as to the ways in which reconciliation is part of our genetic heritage. It also looks at human development to examine the characteristics that have been identified as attributes of peaceful societies and how those attributes are increasingly difficult to maintain in today's globalized economy. Difficult, but not impossible, and within the phenomena of globalization itself lies the potential for peace as well.

These examples suggest that transnational businesses have historically been linked to nationalistic ambition and continue to be so in many respects today. That malleability includes corporate governance. Moses did not bring down any specific rules on the topic when he returned from Mt. Sinai's peak. Corporate governance has been malleable throughout history and today may be the time and season for its focus to incorporate a commitment to sustainable peace. Thus, following the work of legal historian Reuven Avi-Yonah, Chapter 3 will show that in the United States, corporations generally evolved from nonprofits to family businesses to national concerns to transnational firms. At each step, the theory of the firm began with an aggregate model (partnership-like activities) to a concession model (the state specifying the rights and duties of the organization) to an entity approach (where the institution takes on its own character). This evolution works reasonably well until firms reach the transnational stage, at which point they become much more difficult to control by national sovereigns. To the extent that businesses are the extension of national self-interest, some issues are best addressed by the political nation-state system. However, to the extent that corporate self-interest transcends that of the nation-state, which seems to be happening increasingly today, additional sets of questions arise as to what we are to make of this power and opportunity. Indeed, this is a time and place in history where the power of transnational corporations vis-à-vis nation-states is different than at any other time in history because of the capability of corporations to move their facilities from country to country. As a result of this mobility, questions about corporate consideration of labor standards, human rights, and environmental standards increasingly arise. So too the connection between corporations and private military organizations raise questions about corporate-sanctioned violence. Thus, this chapter shows how the response to corporations becoming their own reflexive, adult institutions runs into problems. Although Part Two will argue that this approach is on the right track, the issue of WMD (as well as other illicit commercial activity) reveals many of the problems with the corporate culture approach. In particular, the approach tends to be overly focused on law to the neglect of other aspects of culture-building.

Part One, then, is about how corporations fit into today's geopolitical framework. They do not fit in easily. Corporations cross geopolitical boundaries and therefore approaches to corporate governance, business ethics, and corporate social responsibility must also be boundary spanning. Corporations are geopolitical actors in their own rights and need to be accounted for as such. If they do, they can foster Peace Through Commerce. But how do we get there? This question is approached in Chapter 4, which is about how, in order to conceive of a model for corporate governance, business ethics, and corporate social responsibility today, no one disciplinary approach is sufficient. In fact, any attempt to create corporate cultures that attend to public goods needs to blend multiple strands of analysis, the integration of which has been sorely lacking. While Chapters 2 and 3 deal with some rarefied concepts, Chapter 4 and the following chapters tend to become much more pragmatic and conversational.

Chapter 4's aim is to provide a set of metaphors that create a different model for corporate behavior. The chapter sketches an overarching sense of how contemporary scholars attempt to provide structures, arguments, and rationales for business to obtain the trust of the public and thereby legitimize its existence and special privileges, such as limited liability, continuity of life, free transferability of shares, and centralized management. Rather than relying on a metaphor of maximizing profit, one can instead conceive of businesses as Honest Brokers. That is they are honest within the meaning of how a professional, such as a broker, can be honest. They are Honest Brokers in the sense that there is a sense of trustworthiness about them. And they can be the kinds of individuals and organizations that others turn to in order to resolve their own conflicts. The attributes that make individuals Honest Brokers can be identified and extended organizationally so that corporations could become Honest Brokers too through attention to rule-based notions of propriety, through the pragmatic activities of reliability, and through a vision of harmony that transcends day-to-day life. This chapter introduces Part Two, which will attempt to synthesize these concepts through the idea of Total Integrity Management.

Together, Hard Trust, Real Trust, and Good Trust provide ways for corporations to act so that the public has confidence in their legitimacy. No one of the three can address the complexity of corporate issues. All three, in an integrated way, need to be blended to be mutually reinforcing. In doing so, they may meet the requirements of so-called "reflexive" corporate governance strategies, where the institutions become organizations of, if not justice, at least compliance with legal standards. More than legal standards, however, are necessary even to create just institutions that result in compliance.

Chapter 5 looks at contemporary efforts to rein in corporate misbehavior, such as the OECD Anti-Corruption Convention, the EU Privacy Directive, the Sarbanes-Oxley Act, and the US Federal Sentencing Guidelines (particularly the 2004 Amendments). Legislatures have not been reticent to require that corporations adhere to public demands. There is a need for the public to be able to repose a certain degree of trust in business institutions, and so law-making establishes a sense of Hard Trust. The hardness of trust is that there is direct punishment for violation of legal duties. The law is not capable of creating other dimensions of trust, but it is an essential part of an integrated approach that can make businesses into Honest Brokers.

Building on the notion of reflexive regimes, Chapter 6 shows how corporate cultures might be developed to address critical problems such as proliferation of WMD. Further, to create a global sense of justice, corporations acting as citizens become important to "drain the swamp" of perceived injustices that could otherwise provide support for terrorists. Further, speaking ecologically, an integrated model suggests ways to approach critical environmental issues. This management section will summarize the two strands of dominant research, one normative and the other social scientific. The normative aspect emphasizes considerations of justice, human rights, social contracting, virtue and community, and stakeholders. The social scientific dimension stresses the construction of social capital, organizational justice, trust, and corporate citizenship.

A good deal of contemporary scholarship has been devoted to Hard Trust and Real Trust, albeit not by those names. However, there is a final aspect of trust that enervates them both. This is Good Trust, the topic of Chapter 7, or an affective quest for moral excellence. Like the quest for peace, this is also an aspect of human nature. It is worth identifying and building upon. It cannot ensure trust and peace on its own any more than Hard Trust and Real Trust can ensure good behavior on their own. This psychological, even spiritual aspect, however, is an overlooked aspect of corporate responsibility. Unleashing affective notions does not come without its own set of dangers. This chapter presents the positive potential for Good Trust while also pointing out some of the dangers associated with zealous quests for the good.

The final chapter suggests, as final chapters tend to do, a set of next steps. These steps come directly from the three kinds of trust. They also suggest how much work there is to do in refining how businesses can foster peace.

Conclusion

The view of the corporation as one in which the primary duty of managers is to ensure the profitability of shareholders is not so much wrong as in need of maturity. Demanding that managers only pursue profitability, as long as they do not violate the law (more particularly, as long as they do not get caught violating the law) or staying out of the cross-hairs of negative media and NGO attention, is akin to what Lawrence Kohlberg described as a pre-conventional stage of moral development.[37] This stage, something of a toddler level of moral maturity, has success in a toddler, or corporation, getting what they want, but it is not a stage that is well-suited for sorting out the moral complexities that regularly occur in the world. There may have been a time and place in which compartmentalizing corporate thinking served a useful purpose. Today, however, with corporations enmeshed in a world of many competing needs, governments less able to control their own borders because of the power and reach of corporations and the technologies developed that encourage the crossing of borders, and the urgency of particular threats to the existence of all humanity, including corporations and their constituents, a toddler's moral maturity is not sufficient. Faced with threats such as the accessibility of weapons of mass destruction, it would help to have a growth of corporate conscience. Corporations still have a vital role to produce goods, services, and wealth, but they must do so with a mind to how that can be sustained, and such sustainability includes draining the swamp of resentments that can occur in contemporary society, and also turning an eye away from profit when there is reason to believe that misuse might be made of corporate products.

The foundational resources have already been built for the development of moral maturity. Laws, philosophy, and management theories already provide a strong foundation upon which to build. What needs to be done is to integrate some of the more controversial dimensions of human motivation, including attending to our hardwired characteristics and to our religious impulses, and to connect their better parts with an overarching goal and commitment to sustainable peace. This particular goal is especially suited for our current time and season both because of the threat of violence itself and, perhaps more importantly, because research that demonstrates how peace is achieved tends to funnel moral passions constructively and away from destructive tendencies. Undertaking that goal with a specific mind toward the differentiation among the kinds of firms and organizations is a task necessary for corporate responsibility.

My colleague at the University of Michigan, Bob Quinn, shows his human resources and leadership students an example of different leadership styles by contrasting General George Patton and Mahatma Gandhi. Both men are tough and demanding, but in nearly every other respect, they are quite different. Patton is domineering, impatient, and demeaning. Gandhi is self-effacing, gentle, serving, and patient. Both men and both styles can lead. There may be times and seasons for each. The question is the appropriateness of each style for their time and place. This book does not reject the impressive organizational capability of value-maximization. I simply wish to argue that it needs at least to be paired with a harmony-building version of capitalism in the twenty-first century, one that generates Peace Through Commerce.

Notes

1. Ecclesiastes 3:1–8, 22.
2. Colin Powell, quoted in Ted C. Fishman, *The Myth of Capital's Good Intentions*, HARPER'S MAGAZINE 34 (August 2002). Fishman rejects Powell's statement, arguing that business makes a great deal of money from war and instability.
3. See e.g. F. A. HAYEK, THE FATAL CONCEIT (1988), arguing that *all* members of society tend to be better off with the free market.
4. AMARTYA SEN, DEVELOPMENT AS FREEDOM (1999).

5. Paul Collier, *Economic Consequences of Civil Conflict and Their Implications for Policy* 6 (June 15, 2000), at http://econ.worldbank. org/files.13198_EcCausesPolicy.pdf.

6. FRANCIS FUKUYAMA, THE END OF HISTORY AND THE LAST MAN (1998).

7. Milton Friedman, *The Social Responsibility of Business Is to Increase Its Profits*, N.Y. TIMES MAGAZINE (September 13, 1970).

8. 170 N.W. 668, 684 (Mich. 1919).

9. 237 N.E.2d 776 (Ill. App 1968).

10. 571 A.2d 1140 (Del. 1989).

11. See FRANK H. EASTERBOOK AND DANIEL FISCHEL, THE ECONOMIC STRUCTURE OF CORPORATE LAW (1991) noting that, under current law the shareholders are free to choose to pursue non-economic as well as economic goals.

12. R. J. Welford, *Corporate Social Responsibility in Europe and Asia: Critical Elements and Best Practice*, 13 JOURNAL OF CORPORATE CITIZENSHIP 31–47 (2004).

13. Michael Bradley, Cindy Schipani, Anand Sudnanram, and James Walsh, *The Purposes and Accountability of the Corporation in Contemporary Society: Corporate Governance at a Crossroads*, 62 LAW AND CONTEMPORARY PROBLEMS 3, 9–86 (Summer 1999).

14. 9–11 COMMISSION REPORT 153 (2004).

15. See e.g. JOSEPH NYE, SOFT POWER: THE MEANS TO SUCCESS IN WORLD POLITICS (2004).

16. See MARTIN MARTY AND SCOTT APPLEBY, FUNDAMENTALISM AND THE STATE (1993).

17. PHILLIP BOBBITT, THE SHIELD OF ACHILLES: WAR, PEACE AND THE COURSE OF HISTORY (2002).

18. Burlington Industries Inc. vs. Ellerth 118 S. Ct. 2257 (1998). The Court clarified that employers were indeed liable for the harassing actions of an employee while working within the scope of his employment. This extension of traditional principal-agent law, however, was softened by the opportunity the Court gave for companies to require an alleged victim to use company-based resolution mechanisms prior to filing suit, provided that the company-based mechanisms met certain good faith standards.

19. U.S.S.C. Section 8A1.2.

20. Sarbanes-Oxley Act of 2002, Pub. L. No. 107–204, 116 Stat. 745. Sarbanes-Oxley largely is an extension of the philosophy underpinning *Burlington Industries* and the Federal Sentencing Guidelines in that it attempts to specify certain institutional practices and structures meant to assure that companies themselves are undertaking the efforts necessary to comply with law.

21. U.S.S.C. Section 8B2.1af (2). The Amendments went into effect on November 1, 2004, and could have a tremendous impact on corporations by requiring them not simply to comply with the law, but to design "ethical cultures" that lead to compliance.

22. PETER SCHWARTZ AND BLAIR GIBB, WHEN GOOD COMPANIES DO BAD THINGS: RESPONSIBILITY AND RISK IN AN AGE OF GLOBALIZATION (1999).

23. TIMOTHY L. FORT AND CINDY A. SCHIPANI, THE ROLE OF BUSINESS IN FOSTERING PEACEFUL SOCIETIES (2004).

24. JANE NELSON, THE BUSINESS OF PEACE: BUSINESS AS A PARTNER IN CONFLICT RESOLUTION 5 (2001).

25. *Enabling Economies of Peace: Public Policy for Conflict Sensitive Business*, 23 UN GLOBAL COMPACT. Consultants: Karen Ballentine and Virginia Haufler (2005).

26. *INTERNATIONAL ALERT*, LOCAL BUSINESS, LOCAL PEACE: THE PEACEBUILDING POTENTIAL OF THE DOMESTIC PRIVATE SECTOR 29 (2006).

27. U.S. Department of State Award for Corporate Excellence, http://www.state.gov/e/eb/cba/bs/ace/, accessed July 4, 2006.

28. FORT AND SCHIPANI, *supra* note 23, at 18–19. The study looked at Transparency International's rankings of countries ranging from least corrupt to most corrupt. Approximately ninety countries had data sufficient for TI to be able to conduct its ratings. We then bifurcated the four summary positions of the Kosimo Index (see above note) into two: whether the dispute was handled violently or non-violently (grouping violent and mostly violent together and grouping non-violent and mostly non-violent together). We then tabulated the disputes according to this bifurcation and summarized, in quartiles, the percentage of times that disputes were handled violently.

29. THE PEW GLOBAL ATTITUDES PROJECT, VIEWS OF A CHANGING WORLD (2003).

30. See *id.*, especially T-47.

31. TIMOTHY L. FORT, ETHICS AND GOVERNANCE, BUSINESS AS MEDIATING INSTITUTION 10 (2001). The notion that mediating institutions are central to moral development is not a new one. The idea that businesses might be mediating institutions has also been mentioned. See Michael Novak and John W. Cooper, *The Corporation, A Theological Inquiry*, in AEI SYMPOSIUM S. (1991). However, the nature of the moral-forming dimensions of mediating institutions emphasizes that small sizes allow for an individual to experience consequences of actions whereas the times when businesses have been mentioned as possible mediating institutions have only occurred in the sense that businesses, being neither

government nor individual, in some sense "mediate". The moral-forming dimension of this positioning had never been made clear. On the other hand, in my formulation of businesses as mediating institutions, in order to make virtues into regularized ways of action depends on an organizational arrangement within companies so that there are neighborhood-kinds of groupings that approximate the moral-forming dimension of mediating institutions.

32. *Id.* at 8.
33. *Id.* at 71–3.
34. *Id.*
35. David Fabbro, *Peaceful Societies: An Introduction*, 15 JOURNAL OF PEACE RESEARCH 67 (1978).
36. RAYMOND KELLY, WARLESS SOCIETIES AND THE ORIGIN OF WAR (2000).
37. LAWRENCE KOHLBERG, THE MEANING AND MEASURE OF MORAL DEVELOPMENT (1981). Kohlberg demonstrated that people progress in their moral reasoning and ability to behave ethically through a series of six stages, classified into three levels: the pre-conventional level, where threat of punishment controls behavior; the conventional level, where gaining approval motivates behavior; and the post-conventional level, where a genuine interest in the welfare of others motivates behavior.

2 | Red (and not so red) in tooth and claw

I N a 2006 article in *Foreign Affairs*, Robert Sapolsky related the story of "The Forest Troop", a group of baboons in a national park in Kenya. A tourist lodge expanded into their territory and with that expansion came a great deal of leftover food in the garbage dump. The baboons feasted on this. The males, who grabbed the spoils each morning, were very combative and not interested in socializing. Then tuberculosis broke out, killing most of the troop's members and all of the scavenging males. The remaining population was comprised of less aggressive males and a higher ratio of females to males. Socially, there was less harassment of subordinates and greater incidents of socialization. These attributes continued even after the remaining males left the troop, as baboons apparently do, and new males arrived. Even though the new males did not necessarily share the less aggressive nature of the surviving males, they continued the less violent culture and practices. As Sapolsky puts it, "Forest Troop's low aggression/high affiliation society constitutes nothing less than a multigenerational benign culture."[1] In short, cultures can change. That is true of our primate cousins, the baboons, and it is true of nations such as Germany, Japan, and Sweden.[2] And so, the question is, if baboons can do it, why can't companies?

This is not to say that human nature is fully malleable. It is not. It has biological constraints. Nor is it to equate baboons with nation-states or corporations. But cultures and organizations, communities and institutions can and do change. They can move from violent to peaceful. This is important to bear in mind because frankly, business often does *not* promote peace through commerce. Historically, commerce has also been the instrument of exploitation, domination, and even direct violence. Pointing out such examples, however, does not doom business to repeat violence-producing events.

The stakes here are high. As Paul Seabright writes:

If violence in the human species were an isolated and individual affair, we could perhaps be optimistic that the more different people were, the more the gains of exchange would provide reason to trade rather than fight. But human violence, like that among chimpanzees, is not only or even mainly the result of quarrels between individuals. It is also systematically and spectacularly about violence between groups, whose individuals cooperate among themselves to inflict violence more lethally and cruelly than they could ever do on their own ... The reason for the emphasis on difference with outsiders is also obvious: evolution has favored ways of targeting our violence toward those who are unlikely to be related to us and therefore our genetic rivals rather than our allies. These emotions may have served genetic survival during our evolutionary history, but today, they threaten the physical survival of everyone.[3]

Raymond Kelly notes that the key logic of war is "social substitutability". Social substitutability promotes group violence because "any member of the killer's collectivity is a legitimate target for retaliatory blood vengeance rather than the specific killer alone".[4] Thus, the logic of war is different from that of murder, duel, or capital punishment. It is not about retributive justice only. It is about building group cohesion, rage, sacrifice, power, and immortality.

This chapter and Chapter 3 together address the theme of how businesses can be part of a shift so that corporations can become instruments of peace. This chapter looks at historical and anthropological reasons for why the times and seasons suggest that this is a change that could happen, and identifies the resources for making it happen. There are historical reasons to be optimistic and there are reasons to be wary. Chapter 3 looks at theories of the firm. There too, building blocks exist for making corporations into instruments of peace and there are obstacles as well.

In the mid-nineteenth century, for instance, Cornelius Vanderbilt built a vast economic empire in the United States. He built a political and even a military one too. In the Civil War, he offered to use some of his ships to combat Confederate submarines. He organized a company militia to deal with his competitors and in a famous rejection of the authority of the law, said about it, "'tain't I got the power?". Vanderbilt believed that an important way to secure his business success was to physically ensure it himself. A war-making capability was, in fact, an aspect of his business strategy. He operated at a time when the nation-state was just being born and his corporate actions were more of an extension of his entrepreneurial personality than an institutional sense of corporate foreign policy. In some ways, however, his aggressive militarism may foreshadow the power of today's independent corporation vis-à-vis a nation-state today.

A militaristic business strategy was also implemented by Cecil Rhodes in South Africa as well as via the British South Africa Company, chartered by Great Britain. Rhodes' taking of diamond mines, for instance, was one in which business and military interests went hand-in-hand. Unlike Vanderbilt, Rhodes and the British South Africa Company advanced the defined interests of a well-organized state power: England. They operated as agents of the state.[5]

A less dramatic, but similar example occurred in Canada as Samuel Champlain secured the fur trade for France through strategic (i.e. military) alliances with select Native American tribes. His charter, too, was that of doing the hard colonial work of France. He was a business agent of state power. Although William Penn eschewed violence as a practicing Quaker, his business strategy was one of securing from Britain the right to distribute (Native American) land to settlers who paid him for it. Penn sought to parcel out the land after gaining the assent of tribes, but the basic notion was government sanctioning of land appropriation with at least a latent threat of military enforcement of the appropriation if Penn's diplomacy fell short.[6] Colonial entrepreneurship is no recipe for a just and sustainable peace.

One way to look at the interaction of business and violence is to do so on a micro level. That is, one can observe the times and places where businesses are part of violence or when their actions cause a violent reaction. For instance, in 2001, McDonald's restaurants were attacked around the world by Hindus and vegetarians.[7] Both groups were angered because McDonald's changed the way it cooked its French Fries. McDonald's had publicly announced that it would cook its fries in vegetable oil, but without announcing a change, it switched to cooking them in beef tallow. Unsuspecting Hindus and vegetarians thus unwittingly consumed beef. When this became known, several McDonald's were attacked and, fittingly enough, some of them were smeared with cow dung. French Fries may not spark a war, but how one fries them may add to senses of cultural insensitivity and domination that can fuel the resentments leading to war.

Given the historical examples of Vanderbilt, Rhodes, Champlain, and others, it may seem dubious to see a connection between business and peace. Business and war seems to be an easier fit. Dwight Eisenhower, for instance, warned of the dangers of the "military-industrial" complex. Eisenhower's point was that some businesses profit from supplying the military, and the military, in order to test its equipment and for individuals to rise in status (through successful war-making), had an interest to encourage defense spending and war-making.[8] Even deeper into history, business, government, and war-making have frequently gone hand-in-hand.

For instance, many anthropologists argue that once human economies shifted from nomadic, hunter-gatherer foraging to agriculture, both the rationale and the capability of organized warfare became more possible. Agriculture allows for the creation of surplus, which a ruler can redistribute in order to create standing armies. Part of the function of armies is to protect the natural resource – land – that serves as the basis for agriculture. Armies also provide the capability for conquering other lands that can increase the surplus accruing to the kings. Thus, the economic model that creates surplus both requires defense of the surplus-creating asset as well as creating the possibility for feeding the ambitions of rulers.

Colonialism in ancient city-state forms of Sumeria, Phoenicia, Greece, or Rome, added the economic capabilities of trade, navigation, and slave-trafficking. European colonialism, of course, continued these integrations of business and conquest through trading for precious metals and spices through an expanded notion of mercantilism, and also vastly increased the trade in and for land in the Americas.[9] European powers exploited the New World and its natural resources ranging from trees, fur, and cotton in order to fatten royal coffers, but underneath the governmental level, individual entrepreneurs had to be the agents for the acquisition of these desired products. Kings and noblemen were not going to be trapping beavers or chopping down trees. Individuals were contracted to do this for their own profit and interest as well as for the benefits of royalty.

An interesting feature of this individual business interaction with economic development and warfare is that individual businesspersons may have been dragged into conflicts they would have rather not been involved with in the first place. For instance, in their book *The Dominion of War*, Fred Anderson and Andrew Clayton write that Samuel Champlain, as briefly noted earlier, acted on behalf of France to develop relations with Native Americans in order to boost claims for land and to develop the fur trade. In the process, Champlain hoped to bring Christianity to Native Americans, but in order to secure the requisite trade with Huron, Algonquin, and Montagnais tribes, he had to join in wars against those tribes' enemies: the Iroquois.[10] Champlain's uneasy participation in such battles prefaced conflictual interaction among a variety of peoples as business and political interests were jointly being established in America:

> The peoples of the Atlantic rim shared the same fundamental human needs for goods, sex, security, and transcendence, but they participated in cultures that expressed those needs, and societies and economies that organized the pursuit of them, in strikingly different ways. Systems of war and trade, for an example, were as old as human societies in Europe, the Americas, and Africa, but were conducted according to different rules and served different ends on the continents where they had arisen.[11]

This is not to suggest that trade inevitably led to war; among the Native Americans, trade was far more complexly related. Battles may have been more feud-like or for ritual torturing in an attempt to gain the spiritual power of an enemy. Acquiring proficiency and demonstrating bravery were more important than the destruction of an enemy, which was not the goal of warfare. Trade among native peoples, however,

> differed from war in every way. Trade emphasized sociability: Based on ideals of reciprocity and traditionally conceived of as mutual gift-giving, exchanges built connections both within and between groups. Trade was therefore fundamentally *anti*competitive, since its ultimate goal was to not gain wealth but to create mutual obligations and alliances of advantage to all. The most significant items – for example, tobacco, shell beads, and crystals – were sacred in character and could not be traded without endowing the exchanges themselves with spiritual power.[12]

Colonialism in North America destabilized these practices as warfare became a tool for domination of one people over another rather than the limited notion of warfare that had previously been practiced on the continent. Not only European ambitions, but native access to arms unleashed unprecedented quests for power among the aboriginal peoples as well.[13] With respect to the fur trade, Indians allied with France and with the Dutch.

England, of course, had the most successful colonial empire. Part of the reason for that was its navy. Another part, as will be seen shortly, was its revenue system, which allowed it to finance its ambitions more efficiently than its competitors. England mastered the use of the power of its navy to open up economic opportunities from Africa to China to America. Trade tended to steer England away from war with a potential (or real) colonial outpost, not because it fostered good relations.

In short, under colonialism and mercantilism, businesses served government interests. Governments allowed businesses to exploit new resources in exchange for the national claim to sovereignty over the lands and in return for the establishment of favorable trade relations. Whether the idea for this was that of the rulers or the traders is not the point, at least for now. From the time of Adam Smith, the idea of mercantilism was that it was an economic philosophy developed by merchants and imposed by them onto rulers. Thus,

> The merchants of the great trading companies had to explain to the uncomprehending courtiers of Queen Elizabeth or Louis XIV how trading activities could be justified in terms of the military calculus that appealed more naturally to the nobility. The answer put forward by merchant pamphleteers was that trade brought gold and silver – *treasure*, it was called – into a nation, thereby enhancing its military power.[14]

But as Rondo Cameron explains, in some countries such as The Netherlands and England, the interests and power of merchants were significant enough to have a great influence on governmental decision-making, whereas in countries where the monarchy had a more paramount establishment of power, such as France and Spain, economic interests may have been more subordinate to political ones.[15] The difference is not incidental, as we shall see in looking at the resulting governance consequences, but the more specific point is that business and governmental interests were linked in a joint appreciation of the advantages of war-making as a mechanism of securing access to new natural resources and to protecting and fostering beneficial trade relationships.

This account provides a superficial understanding that business and military ambitions were two sides of a mercantilist and colonial coin. Business thrived through military domination and conquest of new lands. Rather than being instruments of peace, businesses were often agents of conflict and did much of the dirty work for ambitious monarchs wanting to add colonies to their empires.

These examples ought to make one worried about businesses partnering with government. Bloodshed, or at least the threat of it, can be a value-maximizing proposition. It can be value-maximizing in two different ways. One way is that of a business seeing violence as a mechanism for obtaining its own money and power. This was Vanderbilt's strategy and he was quite willing to break the law to achieve his interests. The other was as an agent of power within the framework of state agency as exemplified by Rhodes, Champlain, and Penn.

On the other hand, the late twentieth-century actions of Motorola demonstrate the positive side. Motorola has won two US Secretary of State's Awards for Corporate Excellence because Motorola's business expansions, first in Malaysia and then in China, brought enough positive benefits to those countries so that Motorola promoted better, more harmonious relationships between the US and Malaysia or China. Motorola's efforts are not the only ones. Several other companies have been recognized for such corporate diplomacy.

Motorola's actions are those that are better suited for the realities of the twenty-first century than are those of Cornelius Vanderbilt. They also provide better opportunities for sustainable peace than those of Cecil Rhodes. They provide a model for Peace Through Commerce much better than the alliances of Samuel Champlain. And they are more sustainable, and will lead to more sustainable peace, than the admirably diplomatic, yet still expropriative models of William Penn.

The question is on what basis do corporations get to the point of replicating Motorola rather than Cecil Rhodes? It is tempting to address that question in terms of theories of the firm. But I think we need to step further back into our anthropological history to see the forces and values we have to build upon that give rise to theories of the firm. To do this, I first want to offer some political touchstones in the next section. The following section attempts to connect such notions of culture to more hardwired features of our lives in the form of William Frederick's three value clusters. These clusters tie the tripartite political formulation to the tripartite anthropological material of the next section which pushes us back further to some anthropological considerations of war and peace. The final section then extends these considerations to issues of today's market-state to demonstrate why we have the resources to create corporations into effective instruments of peace.

Political touchstones

Political theorist Walter Mead has differentiated between sharp power, sticky power, and soft power.[16] Sharp power is attentive to military capabilities in getting others to do what one wants to do. Thus, man-power, technological capability, and natural resources welded into a trained military expertise provide a sharp instrument to shape events to one's preferences. Political realists and neo-realists emphasize this aspect of power so that representative theorists begin with Thucydides, who famously argued that Athens, for instance, domi-nated the Melians not for any demonstrated moral superiority, but because they could.[17]

Sticky power, Mead argues, comes from economic institutions. That is, in extending economic globalization, countries become caught in the West's market institutions, which are conducive to western politi-cal institutions and norms as well. No market can exist, for instance, without the reliable enforcement of rights to contract and property, yet the enforcement depends on certain kinds of laws and judiciaries, which today presupposes certain kinds of political institutions. Exceptions may exist, for instance China at the present time, but on the whole, economic rights have a tendency to lead to political rights or at least to certain kinds of legal institutions that coercively enforce necessary economic rights.

Economic development is the main focus of sticky power and, as has been argued elsewhere, there has been a good deal of "the economiza-tion of foreign policy" from many countries as they seek to obtain and project influence through economic power.[18] Because of the West's particularly adhesive sticky power, Mead argues, its institutions are boosted through globalization. Throughout history, philosophers have more generally believed that economic markets would lead to more peace and less violence. Kant[19] and Montesquieu[20] both asserted that commercial republics would be more peaceful and usher in eras of peace. Free market economists, such as F. A. Hayek, made similar, albeit less rosy predictions in arguing that trade thrives on trustworthy moral virtues, and because relationships benefiting from trust are so much in our self-interest, international trade would demonstrate the wisdom of and lead to world peace.[21] Samuel Huntington is less optimistic about sticky power, arguing that the important issue of the use of power will be driven by cultural and religious identity rather than by economics.[22] Economics, Huntington argues, is obviously a crucial aspect of power, but people will sacrifice money for identity. (Actually, this is an important point and potential resource for encouraging ethical business behavior, but for present purposes, it is worth countering Huntington's identity-centric emphasis with that of Amartya Sen, who objects that we have too narrow a sense of what identity is. People connect identity with many religious, cultural, educational, neighborhood, class and other sources.)[23] Even if it is true that identity may trump economics, that identity is complex and does not negate the fact that sticky power is important.

Soft power is about the influence of ideas and values, particularly as they can be shared in cross-cultural settings.[24] Joseph Nye is the preeminent representative of this school of thought that stresses that values like international law, human rights, the rule of law, and democracy have a moral appeal to them so that those countries advocating for them gain a sense of normative influence. Realist Henry Kissinger, for instance, recognizes the importance of moral power, both in terms of American institutions and also, prior to World War I, among central and eastern European powers. There, a moral solidarity based on historical identification with the Holy Roman Empire prevented, for some time, the deadly spiral of self-interest that eventually brought Russia, Austria-Hungary, and Germany to war.[25] Soft power can be real power. Although Stalin ridiculed the strength of the pope, his successors were unable to check the resistances fueled by John Paul II. This importance of ideas is why Bobbitt paints the entire twentieth century, in large part, as a moral struggle for ideas:

The Long War was in a deep sense a moral struggle. Each of the three contending state systems was the outcome of a particular nineteenth and twentieth century attitude about mankind, attitudes that I will roughly call the biological, the sociological, and the legal. The fascists believed in a sort of social Darwinism for states, by which the competition for survival among species was mirrored in the struggle among, and the domination of, genetically determined national groups among human beings ... The communists took a sociological view of man, by which man could not only be wholly described according to his behavior in groups, but could be changed by manipulating the incentives of groups transcending states. The partisans of the liberal democracies also agreed on a basic element of the parliamentary attitude: that the impartial rule of law, and not simply the political power of the individual or group, should govern the outcome of the state decisions. Each of these attitudes is not so much a reaction to the others, as it is to the nineteenth century self-consciousness that delegitimated the dynastic territorial states of the eighteenth century. Each tries to escape the problem of this loss of legitimacy by bringing an external, validating resource to bear. Each promises that it can best deploy the State to enhance the welfare of the nation.[26]

Soft power trades on notions of values. In using the term "values", I have in mind the multiplicity of definitions identified by William Frederick that acknowledges that values have a specific normative meaning. That is, a person "with values" is a person possessing characteristics of honesty and compassion rather than those of lust and greed. We typically don't think of the latter as being a values-driven person. Yet, at a more fundamental level, values are simply those things that people place value on. They are our preferences that we prioritize. The important question comes in the attention we pay to selected values. Certainly human beings value courage, competition, success, loyalty, and security. The combination of these values can easily lead to war insofar as people must exhibit them in order to provide security and honor. And so much of our history, indeed much of our science fiction, is about glorifying these values.

At the same time, however, humans also value compassion, serenity, love, and peace. These too are part of our nature and part of our history. Indeed, the following two sections argue that our very biological nature is more than red in tooth and claw. It is also attuned to peace and harmony. Our history oscillates between times for war and times for peace.

A values-driven approach

Phillip Bobbitt notes that five developments tend to undermine the authority of the nation-state. Those are the transnational emphasis on human rights and efforts to protect those rights even if it requires intruding across borders; the potential for the use of weapons of mass destruction by terrorist groups; trans-border threats such as ecological damage (e.g. global warming), migration, and disease; economic globalization that minimizes the ability of governments to control economic transactions within their own country; and global communications networks.[27] Bobbitt attributes these developments to the replacement of the nation-state with a new form of organization he calls "the market-state" where governments shift the justification for their legitimacy from looking out for the welfare of citizens to that of providing citizens with the opportunity to compete in the global marketplace. This shift emphasizes the activity of economic institutions, particularly corporations, so that analysis of what impact issues of justice have on violence must shift as well, at least to some degree, to the actions and opportunities of corporations. And just as each new organizational structure has carried within it the tensions for later conflict, so a market-state, with corporations as key actors, also carries with it such seeds.[28]

While it would be foolish to ignore nation-states in the dialectic of justice, ethical business behavior, corporations, violence, and government, it also is worth attempting to look behind contemporary balances of power to understand abiding dimensions of conflict. This section, therefore, looks at the anthropological rootedness of conflict and peace, in terms of biology and our closest evolutionary relatives as well as within our anthropological past. Out of a tripartite dialectic, it then demonstrates the continuity of this past with contemporary notions of distribution of power, and also as distributed among various sectors in a political economy. The point, not surprisingly, is that there must be an integration of the forces at play to produce some kind of social stability. Understanding the hardwired roots of the forces may shed light on how emerging forces might be aligned to mitigate violence. As one might suspect, the role of the corporation becomes prominent in this emerging kind of political environment not to enhance the war-making capability of the nation-state, but to stabilize an emerging economic form that triumphs because its form of justice outstrips the efficacy of violence.

Balances of power and of values

Is there something deeper to Mead's division of power? That is, beyond the sensible differentiation he articulates, does such a tripartite division manifest something deeper in our nature? I believe that it reflects basic values operating in all of life that requires some degree of expression. The dimensions of power Mead captures arise from deeper values inherent in us that do require expression in some significant way. Seeing that then suggests how we may be able to draw on that nature in the twenty-first century.

Maintenance of social harmony is based on balance of power. The configuration of those balances may differ, but multiple pieces of data indicate that violence is practically inevitable without some sort of checks and balances. The term "balance of power" need not be restricted to a form of geopolitical positioning among various nation-states in the manner of the Concert of Europe.[29] There are other kinds of balances of power, even when it appears there are few. Geopolitically, the interesting question is not whether a balance of power system might exist – it will – the question is whether it is *better*, a term that requires definition, to have one kind of balance of power as opposed to another.

The examples of balances that can be strictly hierarchical (and corrosive) go beyond geopolitical ones. The famous Milgram experiments, for instance, demonstrated how individuals are prone to obey orders, even those that require torture.[30] Studies of prisons show how easy it is for them to become places of brutality because of the practical nonexistence of meaningful checks to power.[31] Anthropologists have shown that there is a relationship between hierarchically designed societies and violent oppression.[32]

The distinguishing characteristic of those balances that are abusive as opposed to those that, if not constructive, at least limit abuse is that those that are *better* are those that blend a variety of values that are important in life. What makes them *better*, at least for present purposes, is simply their capability to ensure the survival of the species.[33] Extending the analysis beyond the human world is helpful in obtaining a sense of the values and forces in play. To do this, I want to rely on a schema developed by William Frederick that typologizes the value sectors at work in the natural world, and then examine the issue of conflict specifically within the primatology literature and the anthropological literature.

Value sectors

William Frederick provides an overview of the values at work in all human life and relates these values specifically to the existence of the corporation. Frederick argues that there are three recurring value clusters, as well as, for humans, a fourth one, the work of which is to put the three recurring clusters together.[34] These values are "natural values" not because they accord with a philosophical notion of justice or goodness, but simply because they comprise dimensions of living creation. Thus, Frederick makes no moral claim in differentiating among economizing values, power-aggrandizing values, and ecologizing values. Moreover, he does not claim that the fourth value cluster, techno-symbolic values, that are part of human nature, contains a moral superiority to it; instead, the ability to put the various value clusters into different combinations is what human beings do. One can pass moral judgment – Frederick's preferred standard is that of utility – but moral judgments differ from the value clusters that characterize the drives that define living creatures, particularly human beings.[35]

For Frederick, economizing is the extraction of energy of raw materials and the conversion of them into a useful form. At a basic level, this process is photosynthesis for plants and metabolism for animals. Each process extracts energy from raw materials that enables an organism to survive. Extending the analogy, the conversion of materials into useful forms is, socially, what corporations do. Corporations convert raw materials and labor into forms that are socially desired. More generally, economizing is a principle of exchange where parties in a given society or community trade, allocate, and distribute various kinds of economic goods.

Power-aggrandizing values are those based on drives for dominance, including positions of power, status, control, and hierarchy. Just as lions seek to dominate a relevant pride, so human beings also contend for domination and control. This can take the example of quests for political power, of course, but it also applies in terms of obtaining the desired corner office or acquiring another company in order to acquire bragging rights on Wall Street or in the media, as opposed to a takeover based on economic productivity.[36]

Ecologizing values refer to the supporting relationships that occur among individuals and even among species. At a basic level, the inter-relationship among species in a rain forest creates a mutually sustaining symbiosis over long periods of time. Individual plants and animals and particular species thrive in mutualistic interaction with one another. In many species, self-sacrificing behavior is frequently observed, certainly in terms of parents giving up their life for their young, but even among group members as well. In primates, this mutual support is raised to a conscious level where individuals understand their individual welfare to be linked to the welfare of their group. This value is communal; what is interesting is the interaction of mutualistic supportive relationships as a feature of a good deal of life, an observation that counters a simplistic characterization of nature as being "red in tooth and claw".[37]

Finally, in Frederick's typology, techno-symbolic values are the capability to manipulate these three value clusters in different ways. This value cluster is our ability to think, to philosophize, to symbolize, to create religion, to play, and to constitute our societies. Put otherwise, techno-symbolic values are our biologically rooted culture-making capacity from which the variety of human cultures arise. With this as background, one can use this typology to characterize how primates, hunter-gatherers, citizens of agricultural, industrial, and post-industrial societies interact on the dimension of peace and violence. Table 2.1 summarizes these interactions.

Anthropologists have a long history in examining the behavior of human beings and of our primate cousins. This examination includes, of course, the political distributions of power. It also includes efforts to categorize the attributes of non-violent or peaceful societies. These materials range from Konrad Lorenz's classic, *On Aggression*, to Robert Ardley's *The Territorial Imperative and the Social Contract*, to Helen Fisher's *The Sex Contract*, to Eibl-Eibesfelt's *The Biology of Peace and War*. More recently, four sources are of particular note. Frans de Waal has written several books dealing with the nature of primate politics and peacemaking in his *Chimpanzee Politics*, *Natural Conflict Resolution* (with Filippo Aureli), *Peacemaking Among Primates*, and *Good Natured*. The next section of this chapter is directed toward the primate record as distilled primarily by de Waal, particularly because of de Waal's attempt to integrate many of the insights of these scholars himself. This section looks at anthropologists who have examined the human record. These include Raymond Kelly, David Fabbro, Lawrence Keeley, Jared Diamond, and Jonathan Haas. As a non-anthropologist, it is not my aim to provide a definitive rendering of their assessments of the nature of war and peace. I do, however, want to highlight general principles that emerge from that literature in part because they can be connected to the tripartite delineation of values I have just described. Those intermediary sources thus provide a bridge for understanding a continuum of connectedness stretching from our biological heritage to modern-day globalization. In doing so, the lessons from anthropology can be brought to bear in how to construct the kinds of business organizations that may foster peace through commerce in a globalized economy and in terms of the market-state.

Anthropological rootedness of war and peace

It is sobering to read that intelligence makes human beings and our primate cousins more likely to be murderous. That is, however, a central point of Paul Seabright's book, *The Company of Strangers*.

Table 2.1. *Anthropological rootedness of peace and violence*

Natural Value	Primates	Hunter-Gatherers	Agricultural and Industrial	Post-Industrial/Mead Corollary
Power-aggrandizing	Contested; Hierarchy and Submission; Alliances	Non-violent Culture, Small, Non-Hierarchical; Egalitarian Decision-making Raiding, but Lethalness Minimal	Surplus for Armies and Bureaucrats; Hierarchical; Instability on Basis of Size	Individual Empowerment/Disempowerment; Asynchronous Volatility; Mead: Sharp Power/Military Capability
Economizing	Distributive; Justice Principles; Network Relationships	Generosity; Communal Reciprocity; Redistribution	Surplus Assets; Power Differentiations; Property Rights	Economic Opulence; Income disparity; Absolute Increases in Wealth; Mead: Sticky Power
Ecologizing	Gender Dimensions; Presence of Children; Grooming; Intervention of Outside Parties	Religion; Communal Identity	Human Rights; Coercive Stability; Ideology and Sacrifice; Social Substitution	Bobbitt's Evolution; Representation; Rights; Procedural Justice; Mead: Soft Power

Killing an unrelated member of the same sex and species eliminates a sexual rival ... In a species where contests are decided mainly by brute force, a male can eliminate a sexual rival simply by forcing him to physically submit. But the more intelligent the rival, the more likely it is that, having submitted now, he will find a way to return to his sexual pursuit later on. So eliminating permanently the rival who has been temporarily defeated is a strategy that confers much more selective benefit in an intelligent species.[38]

Comments such as these reinforce the idea not only that nature is red in tooth and claw, but also the view of human nature that one of my college professors captured in saying that we human beings are "all a bunch of little shits". Well, we're not always so bad. Our anthropological record is neither pretty nor hopeless. We have both good and bad stitched in our bones. We can neither rely exclusively on instinct nor intelligence. Human beings need to integrate both attributes if we are to create sustainable peace. Our anthropological heritage provides us with some clues as to how we might go about this.

The primate record

One of the leading primatologists, Frans de Waal, makes an important contribution to understanding issues of conflict when he situates conflict within a longer notion of relationships.[39] It is an oversimplification, he argues, to characterize aggression as antisocial behavior or as inherently evil. Instead, aggression and conflict are part of relationships that have the possibility of reconciliation, forgiveness, and producing positive outcomes. The capacity for reconciliation, he argues, is as natural as making war. Looking at the primate record, De Waal provides three characteristics as to how conflict is managed among primates: (1) contested hierarchical relationships (including hierarchy and submission), (2) exchange considerations, and (3) "softening" attributes, including gender dimensions, the presence of children, and reconciliation (including grooming).

Not surprisingly, these examples coincide with the value clusters already described. Hierarchy and submission grow out of adjustments and applications of power relationships. Exchange considerations are rooted in economizing values and softening attributes connect to a larger, long-term conception of community sustainability. In describing each of these, I am not advocating that they are equally morally preferable. The point is simply to show ways in which our primate heritage offers clues to establishing peace and security.

Contested hierarchies

According to de Waal, among most primates, quests for hierarchy and status drive a significant portion of time. Consistent with Frederick's power-aggrandizing sector, bonobos and vervet monkeys, for instance, engage in fierce competitions for status with regard to enhanced sexual availability and priority rights to food. Fights can be bloody, even deadly. In fact, contrary to romantic notions of how non-human mammals limit the severity of their battles, De Waal cautions otherwise and indicates that biologists now view human beings as "relatively pacific".[40]

Yet, in spite of fierce competition, aggression does not erode the fabric of the community, in large part because such aggression is connected to reconciliation. With males, for instance, fights erupt when the communication about acknowledged status relationships break down.[41] After fights, however, relationships quickly resume. Acting like "families", De Waal states, "primates ... have to face the fact that sometimes they cannot win a fight without losing a friend".[42] As compared with human beings, who make take years or generations to reconcile, De Waal says, "monkeys generally make up within minutes".[43] This frequently occurs through grooming that "exploits the insatiable need for contact that is characteristic of the primate order", or kissing.[44] Although perhaps intuitively unsettling, De Waal's conclusion is that aggression and subsequent appeasing can have an intensifying impact on social bonds. This is not to pass moral approval of those bonds – from psychiatry, De Waal notes, reprehensible sexual or child abuse can result in powerful attachments[45] – but instead it is simply to note that our desire for some sort of solidarity or bonding is an urge so strong that it can (although it may not necessarily) survive conflict *per se*.

Reconciliation often does have a natural feel of the softer, ecologizing sentiments that bond combatants to each other. That dimension could have egalitarian aspects of friendship, but even without that positive result, there is also a less sentimental manifestation of reconciliation based on the recognition of one's place in a power relationship. One way this bonding plays out, for instance, is through submission. De Waal reports that even within large enclosures, where the opportunity for recent combatants to avoid each other is large, there will be contact with the opponent 40 percent of the time within just thirty minutes. The nature of the contact is different, De Waal says, from normal interactions, with outstretched arms and open hands, more eye contact, helping, kissing, and soft screaming.[46] In short, primates may find stability within ordered relationships and can resume stable relationships once conflicts about one's place in the hierarchy are determined.

Exchange considerations

A second way that harmony is maintained is through exchange relationships. This occurs through two means: networking and redistribution. Primates are social creatures; they always live in groups. While dominance is a characteristic of those groups, it is not a complete description of the social relations in the group. Dominance ensures getting food first, but leadership is also maintained by sharing food with others. Without regular enactment of distributive justice principles, a dominant male's leadership is likely to be challenged by others and the leader is also bound to receive rebukes from others, particularly females. In short, power is not absolute. An alpha chimp must have concern for the material welfare of others in the group, if for no other reason than because it has a lot to do with his ability to stay in power.

Similarly, throughout the group, network relationships are important. This is particularly true among females who develop long-term relationships among relatives and members of their social class.[47] Networking allows for cooperation to occur within the groups. Without cooperation, the advantages of food sharing, protection, and grooming disappear.

Exchange relationships thus serve as a second means of stable ordering of primate societies. They establish cooperative environments, which mitigate conflict. This is not to say that conflict disappears. Conflict itself can intensify the relationships that further reinforce exchange relationships. That is, once a conflict has occurred, making up typically results in exchange considerations and that can fortify the relationship itself.

Similarly, the primate contest for power is sophisticated and strategic. De Waal relates the saga of three male chimpanzees, Yeruit, Nikki, and Luit. The eldest, a waning Yeruit, fends off Luit, his principal challenger, through an alliance with young Nikki, but the alliance is upended through jealousies and presumably, feelings of insufficient return on the commitment to the alliance. The chimps struggle to obtain and return power through their changing alliances. And they fight. In the aftermath of the climatic battle, Luit dies from his injuries. Maintaining alliances, of course, does suggest soft notions of loyalty and trust and as was the case with reconciliation, there is a blending of the value sectors. Yet the presence of reconciliation and alliances suggests that more than power-aggrandizing is at work. The more that exists can be explained by economizing and ecologizing values.

Softening attributes

Because primates are social creatures, there are a number of "soft" features that complement the "harder" characteristics related to power and exchange. These typically refer to the impact of children, intervention of outside parties to sustain relationships, and the natural desire for reconciliation itself. Researchers note cases where when two males have recently fought and reconciliation has not yet taken place, the presence of an infant serves to warm them up. Indeed, violent conflict almost never takes place when children are in the immediate vicinity. Along the same lines, outside parties frequently intervene, or mediate, conflict. In addition to infants, other members of the group will literally nudge two adversaries next to each other in order to promote their reconciliation.[48]

Why should an angry fighter succumb to the charms of a cuddly infant? What do outside mediation efforts draw upon? One answer seems to be that the desire to be in harmony with others is rooted in the very nature of primates. Forgiveness, for instance, seems to be a very ancient idea, perhaps thirty million years old. To claim that the idea arose recently in humans is, as De Waal puts it, an "uneconomical" theory requiring multiple explanations for similar behavior among different species. Humans and apes share "conciliatory gestures and contact patterns such as the outstretched hand, smiling, kissing, and embracing".[49] In short, there is a naturalistic tendency for primates to desire harmony and peace.[50]

There is, in other words, a naturalistic, soft, hardwired component to primate nature. Non-human primates certainly have a hardwired propensity for power-aggrandizing, expressed through dominance. They also possess naturalistic, hardwired attributes toward exchange relationships. Those cooperative attributes themselves soften quests for power and constitute a kind of Peace Through Commerce. Yet, even among dominance-laden social structures, there are also soft aspects of social structure that connect to an innate understanding of the need to also value harmony and reconciliation. What is important to see is that there is not any one or even two attributes. There are three and we ignore the third to our detriment.

Techno-symbolic

Beyond these three harmony-producing primate attributes – each consistent with one of Frederick's value clusters – there is the question of how these three dimensions are combined. This is, of course, Frederick's fourth value cluster: the techno-symbolic dimension. What seems to differentiate the actions of non-human primates from human beings is the sophistication of language and culture in the service of reconciliation.[51] De Waal notes that monkeys do not understand the entirety of the hierarchical structure of the society in which they live.[52] It is not easy for human beings to be able to understand the whole of their social structures either, but language and culture provide us with a better opportunity to do so. It is important to recognize that human beings still do share these naturalistic desires for peace and harmony as well as for power and money. Indeed, DNA evidence demonstrates a 99 percent resemblance between the genes of human beings and chimpanzees and bonobos. The giant apes, gorillas, and orangutans are more distantly related in terms of DNA, but the closeness of the relationships among humans, chimps, and bonobos suggests that the reconciliatory characteristics of chimps and bonobos may also exist in human beings as well.[53] Our human techno-symbolic capability allows us to structure groups and cultures in a variety of different ways and to attend on some value clusters (power-aggrandizing and economizing, for instance) at the detriment of others (ecologizing), and one reason that we tend to do so is because contemporary models of human behavior often proceed from the notion of a rational person, opportunistic and self-interested, who maximizes a very narrow version of self-interest. Yet, we are already hardwired to possess another side of self-interest, one that is motivated by strong relationships fostered by peace and harmony. Taking this into account serves to add a more sophisticated account of human nature and to the kinds of integration of the various value clusters that can be done in furtherance of social stability. Doing so does not amount to a simplistic analysis in

which we pretend to be pre-historic, upright apes living in a romanti-
cized setting of Eden. Instead, as De Waal puts it:

> We need not be under the illusion that aggressive tendencies will ever leave
> us, but neither should we neglect our heritage of reconciliation. In shifting the
> emphasis from the one to the other, we would in no way be crossing the
> boundaries of human nature. We would only be making use of what we have,
> and doing what we do best – adapting to new circumstances in our own self-
> interest.[54]

The anthropological record: hunter-gatherers

With this all-too-brief summary of the primate dispositions toward
power-aggrandizing, economizing, and ecologizing as mechanisms of
social stability, we are better able to understand the human primate
story. Because of our techno-symbolic capability, we are able to vary
our cultural adaptations significantly. Yet in doing so, the same three
traits continue to extrude. Of course, there is always a danger in
romanticizing a time we currently do not live in. Whether it is a
nostalgic yearning for a once-perfect past, such as the Garden of
Eden, or whether it is a future time of existential painlessness (for
Marx, a communist proletariat state), Nirvana, or salvation, human
beings risk brushing over the complexities in favor of the romantic
possibilities of peace and harmony.

For purposes of this chapter, the danger is to romanticize our human
(and primate) heritage to claim that, by nature, we are peaceful beings
whose lives have been complicated by modern technologies and ideol-
ogies. As we have already seen, primates fight over many things –
power, position, status, food, sex, and other disputes. So do human
beings. Indeed Lawrence Keeley argues that there is no such thing as a
purely peaceful hunter-gatherer. Hunter-gatherers raided and engaged
in vengeance and blood feuds. Given what we have already seen, this
should not be surprising. Conflict, even violent conflict, is something
that we live with. Hunter-gatherers may not have engaged in "organized warfare" in the sense of aligning significant forces of warriors to
go into a battlefield and the level of killing may have been far less than
in the so-called "civilized" twentieth century.[55] At the same time,
organized warfare and killing was probably relatively rare. Another
leading anthropologist has concluded that:

The accumulated specimens of fossil hominids currently available in the collections of museums and universities throughout the world reveal that *nonviolence and peace were likely the norm throughout most of human prehistory and that intrahuman killing was probably rare.*[56]

The question is how that conflict is managed and how the various value clusters interact in order to provide a sense of social harmony. David Fabbro has analyzed the characteristics of peaceful, hunter-gatherer societies and provides a sense of how human beings can use their techno-symbolic – or culture-making – capability to minimize the bloody manifestations of conflict. Fabbro concludes that the following attributes are absent in peaceful societies of hunter-gatherers: inter-group violence or feuding, internal (civil) or external war, a threat from external enemy group or nation, social stratification and other forms of structural violence such as sorcery or witchcraft, a full-time political leader or centralized authority, and a standing police and military organization. On the other hand, the following attributes are present: small and open communities with face-to-face interpersonal interactions, an egalitarian social structure, a normative ethic of generalized reciprocity, social control and decision-making through group consensus, and the enculturation of non-violent values.[57] In addition, other anthropologists note a positive correlation between gender equality and non-violence from ethnographic studies of the Semai, Chewong, Buid, and Piaroa. Warfare is associated with the rise of agricultural economies and their associated political states, as we shall see soon in more detail, rather than in hunter-gatherer societies.[58]

Fabbro's description shows that the institutions most conducive to war-making are absent in peaceful societies. This may have less to do with the cultural sensibilities of the societies *per se* than it does with the absence of competitors with whom to go to war. For instance, if no rival group is nearby, why would one develop a standing military organization? Nevertheless, other attributes do seem to lend themselves to using our linguistic capabilities to foster it. These are directly tied to the expression of the tripartite value clusters.

Perhaps the most notable characteristic is how power-aggrandizing is remarkably held in check. Fabbro's characteristics describe a decision-making process that is highly egalitarian and based on consensus and in fact, is directly contrasted with hierarchy and its associated status implications. The size of the groupings is small enough so that social enforcement mechanisms can be on the basis of collegial, inter-personal interaction. As has been noted elsewhere, such relationships draw on naturalistic sentiments of empathy, solidarity, and commu-nity, exactly the kind of emotions least likely to result in violence. On the other hand, as Raymond Kelly has pointed out, social substitut-ability arises when sizes of organizations increase. Social substitut-ability is the sense that a person is more of a replaceable component than a flesh and blood human being. The more one's humanity is stripped away, the easier it is psychologically to exterminate him. Face to face, egalitarian social structures, on the other hand, work best in small groups that inherently run contrary to social substitutability. So too is power-aggrandizing in that it is checked by the humanization of those over which power is exercised. Further, as noted elsewhere, political theories emphasize that one reason that democratic countries do not go to war with each other is because democracies require negotiation in order to achieve power. If two countries have cultures of negotiation, their leaders are more prone to be open to negotiate differences rather than to go to war over them. Fabbro's groups are examples of cultures of negotiations.

This leads to the second cluster of economizing where the ethics of reciprocity, generosity, and distributive justice dominate. Resources are neither hoarded nor accumulated, in part undoubtedly because of the difficulty of storing them. One's status and prestige is based on the generosity one has toward others rather than in the accumulation of goods. It would diminish one's place in the community to refrain from generosity as it would to not reciprocate for favors received. The finding of resources belongs to the group, allows the group to survive, and the ethic of going about that is based on a communal sense of sharing and well-being.

This economizing survival strategy is reinforced by ecologizing norms rooted in communal identity, largely reinforced by religious conceptions and practices. Religious belief itself has been shown to be an effective survival strategy and one that benefits individual believers as well.[59] This is not to argue which of these value sectors comes first – that is, whether economizing creates the religion, the religion creating political system, the political system creating the economizing func-tion, and so on. The point is not to determine which came first but that a series of activities are highly associated with one another and appear to be informed by each other.[60]

In short, the techno-symbolic capabilities of hunter-gatherers were able to fashion social structures in which the value clusters were in a kind of harmonious balance that limited violence. Of course, two hugely important caveats must be remembered. First, one of Fabbro's main characteristics of peaceful societies was that there was not an immediate threat to the community.[61] In other words, there was either enough distance or sufficiently good relationships with neighbors so that violence between groups was minimized. It is, after all, hard to get into a fight without someone else around to slug in the mouth. Geographic dispersement undoubtedly contributed to the conclusion of anthropologists that hunter-gatherers did not resort to organized violence.[62] Second, as Keeley has argued, there was raiding.[63] Yet, as Keeley himself notes, the level of killing even when raiding was present is far less than what occurs in agricultural or industrial societies.[64] Consistent with the discussion on primates, the point is not that conflict and even violence can be eliminated, but that it can be limited and channeled.

The agricultural/industrial dilemma

Whereas hunter-gatherer cultures tend to be small in size, egalitarian, and with modest technology, anthropologists have consistently shown that "war and organized aggression are associated with community size and cultural development".[65] Although larger collectives allow human beings to accomplish things they otherwise would not – construction of large public works, accomplishment of ambitious exploration, and advances in science and medicine – there is a cost that larger collectives carry with them the propensity for increased, more organized, and more deadly violence. As Michael Nagler has put it:

The shift from *oikos* networks to a regime of *poleis* in the ancient world and the codification of the nation-state in seventeenth-century Europe – both cases of large formal association – led in similar ways to less peace in their respective systems. I suggest that this development took place because they swept aside valuable modes of association that had evolved in their respective cultures while creating a framework for even larger polarizations.[66]

The standard anthropological explanation for this evolution is that once human beings shifted from a nomadic, hunter-gatherer lifestyle to a more sedentary, agricultural one, the conditions were set for the creation of surplus assets (food) that allowed for specialized agents (bureaucrats and soldiers) who both protected now critical, particular land, and who could use surplus labor to increase the land controlled and the assets derived from acquired real estate.[67]

In his popular book, *Guns, Germs and Steel*, Jared Diamond describes the sequence and rationale for this development. Diamond argues that until 11,000 years ago, a nomadic, hunter-gatherer lifestyle was the means of feeding human beings. Food production, identified by domesticating wild animals and growing crops, is a relatively recent phenomenon in human history. By concentrating on edible foods, human beings can ingest more "edible calories per acre".[68] That is, in an environment where edible foods comprised less than 0.1 percent of a given acre of land, agricultural cultivation increased the percent to 90 percent and thereby allowed for the feeding of ten to a hundred more people per acre than a hunter-gatherer lifestyle would. The domestication of animals, Diamond argues, further enhanced the productivity of a sedentary, agricultural lifestyle because the animals furnished a ready supply of meat, milk, fertilizer, and labor (e.g. pulling plows).

Two important developments arise from this new way of feeding. One is that there are more material things produced; there are surplus assets with which a community must deal. Second, there are more people. In particular, agricultural societies have higher birth rates because in a hunter-gatherer band, a mother would have to carry the child during tribal moves and this resulted in spacing of children about every four years. Sedentary societies, however, "can bear and raise as many children as they can feed" and have a birth rate of every two years, something that also produces more workers for farmland. Added to this is that storage of surplus assets is possible in sedentary societies as opposed to nomadic ones.[69]

More people and more food impacts organizational structure and also provides opportunities for "specialists" to appropriate the surplus produced by the society for their own gains. As we have seen, hunter-gatherer societies tend to avoid a great deal of organizational hierarchy and are "relatively egalitarian":

In contrast, once food can be stockpiled, political elite can gain control of food produced by others, assert the right of taxation, escape the need to feed itself, and engage full-time in political activities. Hence moderate-sized agricultural societies are often organized in chiefdoms, and kingdoms are confined to large agricultural societies.[70]

Diamond argues that not every human banded society needed to go through this laborious discovery of the advantages of agriculture. Human beings are practiced copycats and, with a model in hand, replicated some if not all of their neighbors' practices.[71] Literacy and writing, also possible with a sedentary lifestyle, also made possible increased learning for easier replication of successful practices. The result is what Diamond calls an autocatalytic process: "one that catalyzes itself in a positive feedback cycle, going faster and faster once it has started".[72] The autocatalytic process creates competitive advantages so that, as Diamond puts it:

[i]n a one-on-one fight, a naked farmer would have no advantage over a naked hunter-gatherer . . . [but] ten naked farmers certainly would have an advantage over one naked hunter-gatherer in a fight . . . [particularly when f]armers tend to breathe out nastier germs, to own better weapons and armor, to own more-powerful technology in general, and to live under centralized governments with literate elites better able to wage wars of conquest.[73]

The question is what this means for how society is organized and what that organization means for cycles of violence. On Diamond's account, the greater size of the community to be held together leads to more hierarchy, stability gained through coercion,[74] and the increasing unimportance of any particular individual (Kelly's notion of social substitutability).

Like our primate cousins, human beings lived in small bands for millions of years until agricultural technologies allowed for larger organizational settings.[75] Even with "tribes", which are larger and more settled communities, the number of individuals in a community is small enough for individuals to know everyone else by name and relationship. The limit of "a few hundred" is the limit for a group in which individuals can know most others, a fact verified in contemporary settings by schools, for instance, where principals can only know the names of students if the school's enrollment is relatively small. In tribes, people still know each other; in chiefdoms, comprised of larger groupings, people become strangers and more formalized processes are necessary to resolve conflicts. In tribes, decision-making remains informal, egalitarian, and communal, whereas in chiefdoms, decisions are more hierarchical and coercive. Not surprisingly, in chiefdoms, the acquisition of power becomes far more contested and the societies organized as chiefdoms have been shown to be more unstable than the smaller, informal bands and tribes.[76] When chiefdoms arose 7,500 years ago, "people had to learn, for the first time in history, how to encounter strangers regularly without attempting to kill them".[77] One way to do this was for the chief to hold a monopoly on the right to use force. As Diamond notes, the question as to why commoners allow for elites to dominate them in a ranked society is a perpetual question.[78] The answer, he argues, has been a mixture of four solutions:

(1) Disarm the populace, and arm the elite. (2) Make the masses happy by redistributing much of the tribute received, in popular ways. This principle was as valid for Hawaiian chiefs as it is for American politicians today. (3) Use the monopoly of force to promote happiness, by maintaining public order and curbing violence. (4) The remaining way for kleptocrats to gain public support is to construct an ideology or religion justifying kleptocracy.[79]

The first strategy is a power-aggrandizing one based on hierarchy. The second is one based on economizing. The third is something of a combination of the first two: assumed power and a sense of security through stability. These three strategies might be found in several primate populations. The fourth arises out of a communal sense, one that even taps into a human recognition of transcendence through religious belief or ideological commitment to a good extending beyond the particulars of an existential society. It is a quintessentially human development. Although rooted in an ecologizing commitment to community, great goods and great dangers arise in the development of religion and ideology. Diamond is not enthusiastic about it.

The spiritual beliefs of bands and tribes, Diamond argues, did not justify a divine right to leadership, the transfer of wealth to a central authority, the maintenance of peace between unrelated individuals, or patriotic, suicidal military charge. "Fanaticism in war", Diamond argues, "of the type that drove recorded Christian and Islamic conquests, was probably unknown on Earth until chiefdoms and especially states emerged within the last 6,000 years".[80]

Obviously, human beings now live in large, centralized organizations even though there are conflictual risks associated with them. Large societies do allow individuals to accomplish things they otherwise would not and in such societies, communal decision-making is simply unrealistic. Large-scale economic considerations also make centralized decision-making more efficient. Unlike small, banded societies, fights become those between strangers with few people knowing both parties and, in such cases, one sides with the parties one knows – an us – against the parties one does not know – a them.[81] But two problems result. First, the centralization of power also creates opportunities for the abuse of that power.[82] Second, as Kelly argues, once human beings cease to be persons with whom one has relationships, one can, particularly in large societies, perceive any particular person to be replaceable – or substitutable – by another. This can further lead to the exploitation of the commoner by those in power and it can also more easily justify violence against another group, the members of which possess no distinctive and endearing human traits.[83]

If this account of social development is accurate, the nation-state would seem to be prone to violence, which as Lawrence Keeley argues, is exactly the case. Although as already noted, he eschews the notion of a romantic, peaceful hunter-gatherer nomad, Keeley does conclude that, after adjusting for population numbers, the rate of killing in the so-called "civilized" twentieth century exceeded that of hunter-gatherer times by a remarkable factor of twenty. His research is not simply that more people were killed in warfare in the twentieth century – that would seem to be clearly true given the sizes of populations in the last one hundred years – but that the rate of killing exploded.[84] The century also manifested a remarkable series of ideological movements – particularly communism and fascism – that regularly and ruthlessly exploited governed populations and ignored human rights.

One reaction to such movements has been democracy, which for all its faults, attempts to replicate a balance of power by protecting citizens with basic human rights and providing them with the opportunity to participate in the decisions that govern them. Indeed a leading peace studies theorist, R. J. Rummel, notes that centralized, totalitarian governments demonstrate the worrisome problems just explained in chiefdoms:

Consider, by contrast, a centralized society with a totalitarian government. In the main, behavior is no longer spontaneous, but commanded; in its most significant outlines, what people are and what they do are determined at the center ... A management-worker, command-obey class division cuts across all society, and the system has all the characteristics of an organization (coercive planning, plethora of rules, lines of authority from top to bottom) needed to direct each member's activities. The consequence of the totalitarian model is to polarize major interests.[85]

On the other hand, Rummel argues, in democratic countries, the diversity of interests that a free person can have (religious, political, recreational, gender, age, race, region) create a set of cross-cutting interests which discourage violence, because violence may pit one interest a person has against that of another interest.[86] With studies indicating that democratic countries do not war with each other,[87] and on the basis of the naturalistic importance of relatively egalitarian decision-making with individual empowerment, democracy can be seen as an attempt to extrude naturalistic dimensions into a political system that is less likely to be at war with similar kinds of political systems.

Consistent with the tripartite division of value sectors, it is important to see how advocating for human rights and democracy is one alternative to maintaining an ecologizing sense of community and stability. The economic advantages of such large agricultural and industrial societies are such that they provide far more war-making capability, and also far more opportunity for social and economic disparity, traits that run against our relatively egalitarian human history.[88] To be clear, this is not to equate morally, democracy with its twentieth-century competition, fascism and communism. Indeed, as Bobbitt argues, democracy triumphed in the twentieth century, at least in part, because of its military prowess.[89] It also triumphed, I would argue, because of its moral superiority, a superiority derived by its capability of providing a greater sense of justice for its people and for its connection with the pacific characteristics rooted in our human nature. Democracy serves as its own reflexive check on power-aggrandizing. Through its frequent companion, the free market, it fosters economizing by enhancing trade. But as de Tocqueville argued in earlier US history, the dimension that keeps such an individualistic system from becoming selfish is a spiritual sense of an ultimate good that fosters self-interest rightly understood. This may be done with the consent of religious leaders, as Diamond seems to suggest, or it may be done to religion. Obviously, this is a deeply complex topic,[90] but the essential point is that at the heart of religion, spirituality and ethics is to stand apart from economizing and power-aggrandizing rather than being subservient to them. To the extent they are conflated, one loses the balancing that fosters harmony.

Post-industrial issues

If there is a sense of truth in the preceding account, one can view the twenty-first century with alarm. If disparity is not in accord with our basic social orientation, due to the increasing amount of economic disparity and the telecommunications capability of being able to observe such disparity, then resentment is a likely counterpart. If social substitutability thrives when human beings are interchangeable parts, then the market system, for all its other advantages, can tend to make economic activity faceless as well. If population size contributes to hierarchy and substitutability, then the sheer immensity of the world's population can dwarf any attempt to feel a sense of solidarity with others around the world.

At the same time, the ability of individuals and small groups to equip themselves with weapons of mass destruction makes the complexity upon which post-industrial society sits – its web-based, electronic models of communication – unstable themselves. Nation-states are awkwardly positioned to counteract such asynchronous threats, particularly vis-à-vis the empowerment of "disempowered" terrorists.

Such a scenario would seem to provide impetus for a consideration of the naturalistic traits that tend to produce more stability through justice and peace than through coercion and suppression. It requires attention to the meaning of justice, representation, and rights, as Bobbitt would suggest, but it also requires that representative institutions within each value cluster are attentive to the variety of value clusters that they themselves engage with. That is, the world is too complex only for governments to worry about power-aggrandizing, or corporations only to worry about economics, or religions only to worry about community.

The market-state challenge

Technology and representative taxation

Niall Ferguson argues that government financing has developed as a reaction to the need for the state to raise money, quickly, to fight wars. Ferguson notes that the most significant expense in fighting wars is not the payment of soldiers. The major expense is technologically driven improvements in war-making capability. Whether the technological breakthrough is that of a cannon, an aircraft carrier, a B-1 Bomber, or an intercontinental ballistic missile, such weapons impose massive costs on governments faced with war or the threat of war. Moreover, countries facing imminent threat of hostilities do not have a great deal of time to raise money to procure these expensive weapons. They must raise cash quickly in order to obtain the weapons needed in order to fight the war in question.[91]

The need for vast amounts of cash, and the speed with which they must be obtained, places pressures on government finance. Some funds may be raised through governmental businesses – that is, if governments have resources that produce a revenue stream such as a hydroelectric dam, those funds can be captured as well as the government selling or leasing assets in order to obtain cash or materiel. It is likely that these sources, however, will have significant limits, requiring governments to turn to taxation and the issuance of bonds.[92]

Even in coercively run societies, there are limits to the amount of taxes one can extract from citizens and still maintain levels of popular support necessary to make the government viable. According to Ferguson, if a state requires more funding from its citizens, as a historical matter, it alters the social contract with its citizens so that they obtain something in return. The "something", he argues, is representation in the government to oversee how the taxes collected will be utilized for the benefit of the population. Thus, the American Revolutionary slogan, "no taxation without representation", is a model for the extension of a fundamental right of representative government, according to Ferguson, that justifies the raising of taxes necessary to support war-making.

In a similar fashion, the government may float bonds in order to raise requisite cash by selling them to investors. The British model of debt financing, according to Ferguson, proved superior to other models in part because England funded debt repayment through allocation of tax funds. Investors, according to Ferguson, did negotiate contractual obligations from issuing governments, but this linkage of bond financing and taxation further pressured governments to solidify the tax system, which was done through the extension of democratic notions of government. Thus, although counterintuitive, the establishment of a principle of justice – here, taxation with representation, which provides an instance of the institutionalization of democratic self-governance – resulted from, on Ferguson's account, the rather base ambition of governments to win wars.

War, popular legitimacy, and constitutional government

Phillip Bobbitt makes an even more ambitious and unsettling argument that more explicitly connects contemporary notions of justice with the enhanced war-making capabilities of the nation-state. Bobbitt argues that law and strategy are interconnected. The strategies governments use lead directly to the kinds of constitutional formulations by which sovereign authority governs, and the way in which sovereign authority is constituted leads directly to the challenges that must be addressed in competition with other polities. In other words, in order to be more effective war-making units, governments gradually extend more rights protections and privileges to wider groups of people as a way to co-opt their participation in the actions, including war-making, of the government. The sequence of governmental evolution, at least in the West over the last 1,000 years, proceeds, according to Bobbitt, from princely states to kingly states to territorial states to state-nations to nation-states. Each incremental step of this revolution results from a challenge to the existing kind of government structure from a competing geopolitical body. This does not mean that the challenge to the government was ideological, but simply that a territorial state, for instance, was faced with war from other entities. To defend itself, a territorial state in which a royal ruler claimed authority over a certain geography and was considered as the embodiment of the territory – *L'état est moi* – simply had to command enough support to be able to raise the funds necessary to pay a mercenary army to face an opposing (likely also a mercenary) army.

However, if a ruler could harness an entire nation in support of the state, one might increase the war-making capabilities of the ruler. According to Bobbitt, this was, in fact, the strategy of Napoleon. Mercenary armies were expensive and, in part because of that, both relatively small and relatively unused in actual battle. They were better used as deterrents and in maneuvers rather than actual clashes. While highly trained, they were, however, vulnerable to a massive army, even if the members of that army were relatively untrained. An untrained army of 100,000 men would overwhelm even a well-trained and well-armed troop of, say, 5,000. Napoleon put together huge armies, which were able to overwhelm the smaller, mercenary armies of other European countries. His universal conscription, the *levée en masse*, proved militarily superior to a regime with a more limited claim on popular involvement. Napoleon was able to secure that popular involvement, at least in part, by the creation of The Napoleanic Code, which guaranteed certain rights, privileges, and legal systems and principles to the French people.[93] This is not to argue chronologically that Napoleon offered rights in exchange for conscription. French history is more complicated than that. It is, however, to note that Napoleon's ability to raise large armies coincided with an increased sense of ownership and participation in French political society.

Thus, just as Ferguson argued with respect to the military genesis of notions such as taxation with representation in order to secure the cash necessary to buy the technology necessary to fight wars, Bobbitt suggests that legal and constitutional guarantees provided the social contract that enabled Napoleon to win continuous, early nineteenth-century military victories. The important point is that popular participation and support can enhance the war-making capability of the state.[94]

Bobbitt uses this perspective to explain "The Long War" of the twentieth century. This war, which Bobbitt marks as beginning in 1914 and ending in 1989, featured a struggle between three alternative ways of proposing a relationship between government and individuals in which people in those societies would be better off under their regime.[95] With good reason, it is easy to dismiss fascism and communism as violating the rights of its citizens, but Bobbitt explains that fascism claimed to better protect people from the rapaciousness of the free market by delegating power to a ruling business and military class, and communism claimed to similarly provide a more just, humane way of providing equality and security of its citizens in a way capitalism and fascism could not. In competition with parliamentary democracy, these two systems simply did not win, in large part due to the fact that parliamentary democracy provides a militarily more effective way to compete geopolitically. Bobbitt argues that parliamentary democracy was able to defeat fascism and communism because of better technology (including nuclear weapons), better communications, and better economic productivity. The combination of these made clear to citizens in the Soviet sphere that western lives under capitalism seemed better than their lives under communist rule, a realization made possible by the communications that showed the economic differences between the two systems. To oversimplify, parliamentary democracy's extension of a variety of rights, objective legal systems, participatory governance, and economic freedoms allowed the West to be able to defeat both systems, one through direct military action and the other through sporadic war-making. More bluntly, republican notions of justice proved more geopolitically dominating.

I am not arguing that I necessarily believe Ferguson's and Bobbitt's historical account. Both accounts are intriguing, but leaving aside the question of whether their *quid pro quos* are chronologically on the mark, I relate them because they strike as rather depressing accounts of how liberal democracy and human rights emerged and triumphed on the world stage. If accounts this depressing can demonstrate a superiority of liberal democracy and human rights, then philosophically richer, normatively compelling reasons (for instance, that human beings have an essential dignity that ought to be respected through democracy and human rights) seem not only spiritually more uplifting, but more realistically grounded in nature and history. Foreshadowing Part Two's summaries of studies showing that corporate social performance at least does not harm and may in fact help corporate financial performance, good ethics may make political sense. They are, at least, a decent option.

Corporate conduct and the peace interest

Although neither Ferguson nor Bobbitt make the following argument, it is worth considering the unsettling logical extension of their framework that suggests that the extension of just business behavior enhances the war-making capability of the state. The more business organizations, the agents of free market capitalism, are perceived to be ethical, the more likely the system itself is likely to be perceived as just, thereby enhancing the popular buy-in of citizens for the system. Such buy-in enhances the war-making capabilities of the governments administering the market system, because the system is perceived to have struck a social contract just enough (1) to provide the cash necessary to fund major technological military capability and (2) to obtain the willingness of the population to sacrifice (militarily) on the system's behalf. There are reasons to believe, however, that a mindfully constructed set of corporate purposes can turn the justice-in-return-for-military-capability formula into one that institutes the justice while heading off violence, even under a realist conception of enhancing state power.

Given the destructiveness of weapons in the twenty-first century, especially weapons of mass destruction, it would seem that the only way to win a battle where these might be used is to do so without engaging the actual use of them. At some level, the chase to cut off the supply of materiel for WMD will be unsuccessful; instead, the only real way to get at the non-use of them is to get at the motive:

[E]thnoreligious bigotry is deeply entrenched. But even strutting demagogues require some sort of legitimization, however hypocritical, for their actions, and ethnoreligious bigotry seldom reaches the point of organized violence without some precipitating cause. In all too many cases, the demand for weapons is ultimately a surrogate for the demand for social justice. Therefore, although not the only factor at play, probably the single most important factor stoking the market from the demand side is the prevailing misdistribution of income, wealth, and ecological capital. What is striking in the world today are the gross and growing disparities in all three. Until these are frankly and fairly addressed, there is little hope of damping the desire of the dis-advantaged to seek the tools to rectify those disparities by violent means.[96]

Justice may provide societal buy-in, but it can also calm the reasons for resorting to the use of what has been developed.

Religion also plays a role in aphoristically recommending caution in the use of military capability. The fact that Pope Paul VI's "if you seek peace, work for justice" has become a bumper-sticker does not diminish its wisdom. Perceptions of being treated fairly may well encourage people to give allegiance to those institutions so treating them, but the absence of fair treatment also can trigger the resentment that leads to unrest. The forces that have been unleashed in globalization also unleash the capabilities of the disaffected to object to the system. Terrorists can use computers to disrupt communications. They can turn sophisticated aircraft into missiles. They may be able to take nuclear and biological substances to the heart of major cities. To sustain sovereign power may require addressing the inequalities that allow for extremists to capitalize on their frustrations. Regardless of whether attending to those frustrations is ethically wise, under a realist perspective, it simply may allow the liberal model to defend itself.

Business itself represents a "peace interest". Karl Polanyi argues that peace was kept in the nineteenth century in large part because business did not want there to be conflict.[97] The Rothschilds and later the Morgans also had demands when they purchased the securities. Those demands tended to favor business stability over warfare. The mark of twenty-first century capital has been its securitization so that a variety of individuals and institutions can participate in what in the nineteenth century was called *haute finance*. Securities markets and how they are structured in order to be perceived as just institutions may play a critical role in transforming capital developed for military capability into that which is not violently unleashed. Thus for economic, communal, and even political reasons, the capability built by financing creates its own friction for the use of it.

To my mind, it is a repulsive concept to believe that extending principles of justice should occur only to enhance killing capability. It may be true that a just regime is worth fighting for, yet the question is now to sustain justice principles in light of the threats faced in the twenty-first century. Our anthropological heritage suggests that we best foster peace by looking at economizing, ecologizing, and power-aggrandizing values, and integrating them in a way to try to thwart violence. Human history is replete with failures of attempts to do this. There are also successes. Today's time and season requires us to try yet again, this time with business interests more directly in the mix.

Corporations enter into this mix, but the current, convenient configurations of communitarianism and contractarianism do little to constructively contribute to this battle. Moreover, corporations need to play an active role in this effort from an evolutionary standpoint. The last part of this chapter is hardly inspiring. Championing virtues because of their military efficacy is, to my mind, a dreadful argument. The point, however, is that even from this cynical point of view, there are survival reasons for taking ethical principles seriously. Further, we are faced today with potential catastrophes not unlike those faced by The Forest Troop described at the outset of the chapter. As human beings, we possess the foresight to anticipate the catastrophe so we can change prior to the unleashing of horrific weapons. That realization can create a tipping point where it makes sense for our social institutions, like those of The Forest Troop, to change. It no longer makes sense to solve problems by violence or at least to primarily do so. It now makes sense to modify our social institutions to better our chances at survival.

The good news is that our human nature provides resources for that change by reintegrating the tripartite values in our social institutions. One of those institutions that could use some attention will be corporations. As Seabright writes, "[w]hat all stable societies have in common, though, is that the balance between reciprocity and self-interest holds even when unscrupulous individuals test its strength … The hallmark of the most successful of these [social] institutions is their ability to entrench a culture with a trust with a minimum of explicit enforcement."[98] Our theories of the firm are one such social institution that very consciously must grapple with the connection between self-interest and reciprocity and trust. And so, it is important to directly discuss theories of the firm and how they measure up to the tests of the twenty-first century.

Notes

1. Robert M. Sapolsky, *A Natural History of Peace*, FOREIGN AFFAIRS 114–16 (January/February 2006).
2. *Id.* at 120.
3. PAUL SEABRIGHT, THE COMPANY OF STRANGERS, A NATURAL HISTORY OF ECONOMIC LIFE 234–5 (2005). I am grateful to Bill Frederick for putting me onto this source and this specific quotation.
4. RAYMOND KELLY, WARLESS SOCIETIES AND THE ORIGIN OF WAR 5 (2000).
5. ANTHONY THOMAS, RHODES: THE RACE FOR AFRICA (1996).
6. See generally, FRED ANDERSON AND ANDREW CLAYTON, THE DOMINION OF WAR: EMPIRE AND LIBERTY IN NORTH AMERICA, 1500–2000 (2005).
7. Laurie Goodstein, *For Hindus and Vegetarians, Surprise in McDonald's Fries*, N.Y. TIMES A1 (May 20, 2001).
8. Farewell Radio and Television Address to the American People by President Dwight D. Eisenhower, January 17, 1961, at http://www.eisenhower.archives.gov/farewell.htm accessed August 1, 2006.
9. RONDO CAMERON, A CONCISE ECONOMIC HISTORY OF THE WORLD: FROM PALEOLITHIC TIMES TO THE PRESENT (2002).
10. ANDERSON AND CLAYTON, *supra* note 6, at 1,
11. ANDERSON AND CLAYTON, *supra* note 6, at 24.
12. ANDERSON AND CLAYTON, *supra* note 6, at 27 (emphasis in original, footnotes omitted).
13. ANDERSON AND CLAYTON, *supra* note 6, at 28, 38.
14. ROBERT L. HEILBRONNER AND AARON SINGER, THE ECONOMIC TRANSFORMATION OF AMERICA: 1600 TO THE PRESENT 25 (4th edn. 1998).
15. CAMERON, *supra* note 9, at 130–2.
16. WALTER MEAD, POWER, TERROR, PEACE AND WAR: AMERICA'S GRAND STRATEGY IN A WORLD AT RISK (2004).

17. See THUCYDIDES, THE PELOPONNESIAN WAR (1982).

18. MICHAEL T. KLARE, RESOURCE WARS: THE NEW LANDSCAPE OF GLOBAL CONFLICT 31 (2001).

19. IMMANUEL KANT, PERPETUAL PEACE A PHILOSOPHICAL SKETCH (1795).

20. MONTESQUIEU, THE SPIRIT OF THE LAWS 5, 6 (1748).

21. F. A. HAYEK, THE FATAL CONCEIT: THE ERRORS OF SOCIALISM 38–47 (1988).

22. SAMUEL HUNTINGTON, THE CLASH OF CIVILIZATIONS AND THE REMAKING OF WORLD ORDER 21 (1996). Huntington is profoundly skeptical of anything like a universal civilization emerging, instead insisting that peoples around the world are defining themselves according to their traditions, language, and religions. Free market economics will not gain universal acceptance: "The Davos Culture", with emphasis on individualism, market economies, and political democracy, claims the allegiance of fewer than 1 percent of people outside of the West.

23. AMARTYA SEN, IDENTITY AND VIOLENCE: THE ILLUSION OF DESTINY (2006).

24. JOSEPH NYE, THE PARADOX OF AMERICAN POWER: WHY THE WORLD'S ONLY SUPERPOWER CAN'T GO IT ALONE (2002).

25. HENRY KISSINGER, DIPLOMACY 102 (1994); see Thomas W. Dunfee and Timothy L. Fort, *Corporate Hypergoals, Sustainable Peace and the Adapted Firm*, 36 VANDERBILT JOURNAL OF TRANSNATIONAL LAW 563 (2003), connecting Kissinger's identification of moral sympathies to business analogues.

26. PHILLIP BOBBITT, THE SHIELD OF ACHILLES: WAR, PEACE AND THE COURSE OF HISTORY 61–2 (2002).

27. *Id.* at xxii.

28. *Id.* at xxiii–xxix. Bobbitt notes that the US Constitution carried with it the seeds for the Civil War, the European Treaty of Westphalia in 1648, Vienna in 1815, and Utrecht in 1713, and also set the stage for later conflicts.

29. See KISSINGER, *supra* note 25 at 102.

30. STANLEY MILGRAM, OBEDIENCE TO AUTHORITY (1974).

31. See e.g. JEFFREY IAN ROSS AND STEPHEN C. RICHARDS, BEHIND BARS: SURVIVING PRISON (2002).

32. See David Fabbro, *Peaceful Societies: An Introduction*, 15 JOURNAL OF PEACE RESEARCH 67 (1978); see also KELLY, *supra* note 4; Kent Flannery, *Prehistoric Social Evolution,* in RESEARCH FRONTIERS IN ANTHROPOLOGY 3 (Carol R. Ember and Melvin Ember, eds., 1995).

33. See HAYEK, *supra* note 21. In justifying development of protection of property, contract enforcement, and other market mechanisms, Hayek

argued that the good of these cultural artifacts is that they help us to survive and there is something to be said about that. Normatively, I think this is unsatisfying, but I am willing to live with that test for purposes of this particular argument.

34. WILLIAM C. FREDERICK, VALUES, NATURE, AND CULTURE IN THE AMERICAN CORPORATION 263–74 (1995).

35. See *id.* See also Paul R. Lawrence, *The Biological Base of Morality?* in BUSINESS ETHICS QUARTERLY, RUFFIN SERIES #4 BUSINESS, SCIENCE AND ETHICS 59 (R. Edward Freeman and Patricia H. Werhane, eds., 2004). See also Timothy L. Fort, *A Deal, a Dolphin and a Rock: Biological Contributions to Business Ethics,* in BUSINESS ETHICS QUARTERLY, RUFFIN SERIES #4 BUSINESS, SCIENCE AND ETHICS 81 (R. Edward Freeman and Patricia H. Werhane, eds., 2004).

36. FREDERICK, *supra* note 34, at 70–3. Frederick asserts that takeovers are sometimes the result of ego rather than based on economic sense.

37. *Id.* at 161.

38. See SEABRIGHT, *supra* note 3, at 49, 51.

39. FRANS DE WAAL, PEACEMAKING AMONG PRIMATES (1990).

40. See *id.* at 75.

41. See *id.* at 52–3.

42. See *id.* at 1–2.

43. See *id.* at 2.

44. See *id.* at 11, 33 (noting that chimpanzees engaged in a long kiss have probably just recently confronted each other).

45. See *id.* at 16.

46. See *id.* at 42.

47. See *id.* at 125.

48. See e.g., Jutta Kuester and Andreas Paul, *The Use of Infants to Buffer Male Aggression* 91–92 cited in Signe Preuschof and Carol P. van Schaik, *Dominance and Communication: Conflict Management in Various Social Settings* 77 in NATURAL CONFLICT RESOLUTION (Filippo Aureli and Frans B. M. de Waal, eds., 2000).

49. De Waal, *supra* note 39, at 270–1.

50. See De Waal, *supra* note 39, at 231.

51. See De Waal, *supra* note 39, at 270–1.

52. See De Waal, *supra* note 39, at 141.

53. See De Waal, *supra* note 39, at 171–2, noting the DNA similarities among chimps, humans, and bonobos on the one hand and gorillas and orangutans on the other.

54. See *id.* at 271.

55. LAWRENCE KEELEY, WAR BEFORE CIVILIZATION (1996), noting rates of death in the twentieth century as opposed to "pre-civilized" times.

56. Leslie Sponsel, *The Natural History of Peace: A Positive View of Human Nature and its Potential*, in A NATURAL HISTORY OF PEACE 103 (Thomas Gregor, ed., 1996) emphasis in original.

57. Fabbro, *supra* note 32, as cited in Sponsel, *supra* note 56, at 108.

58. Sponsel, *supra* note 56, at 106.

59. See e.g. LOYAL RUE, RELIGION IS NOT ABOUT GOD (2005).

60. See generally BOBBITT, *supra* note 26.

61. See Fabbro, *supra* note 32.

62. See Sponsel, *supra* note 56 at 103.

63. See generally KEELEY, *supra* note 55.

64. See generally KEELEY, *supra* note 55 at 93.

65. See Sponsel, *supra* note 56, at xvii, citing various studies.

66. Michael Nagler, *Ideas of World Order and the Map of Peace*, in APPROACHES TO PEACE: A READER IN PEACE STUDIES 378 (David P. Barash, ed., 1999).

67. See e.g. JONATHAN HAAS, THE ANTHROPOLOGY OF WAR (1990); see also JARED DIAMOND, GUNS, GERMS AND STEEL 86 (1999), arguing that food production was the "indirect prerequisite for guns, germs, and steel".

68. See DIAMOND, *supra* note 67, at 86–8. The process by which human beings learned to concentrate on these few edible foods is itself an interesting story as told by Diamond. He argues that as nomads, human beings had a difficult job in locating the foods that were edible and tasty. When human beings found such foods and gathered them to return to a home camp, the natural result was that the seeds of such edible foods would be transplanted at the camp latrines as humans relieved themselves. Gradually noticing the increased number of (fertilized) edible plants gave rise to the domestication of them.

69. DIAMOND, *supra* note 67, at 89. "In practice, nomadic hunter-gatherers space their children about four years apart by means of lactational amenorrhea, sexual abstinence, infanticide, and abortion."

70. DIAMOND, *supra* note 67, at 90.

71. DIAMOND, *supra* note 67, at 108. A major dimension of Diamond's book is to demonstrate that one of the competitive advantages of agriculture was almost entirely incidental. Agricultural societies also "breathe nastier germs". *Id.* at 195. Because they live close to their own germs (i.e. excrement), because they closely associate with domestic animals who serve as intermediaries for many kinds of germs, and because their own populations are more dense, increasing urbanization creates the perfect setting for more lethal forms of infection. *Id.* at 205–6. In a large population where this increase occurs on an ongoing, yet relatively slow fashion (slow in terms of how it plays out within the population), human beings develop resistance to those germs. Yet, when human

beings with such immunities encounter societies where this process has not occurred, the encountered society can be almost entirely eliminated. This, Diamond argues, is exactly what happened when Europeans, where agriculture and domestication of wild animals were particularly present, encountered populations in the Americas. *Id.* at 21. Thus, Cortez, "armed" with smallpox, was able to conquer millions in Mexico with only about 600 men, Pizzaro conquered the Incan Empire with less than 200 men, and the native population of Hawaii dropped from 500,000 in 1779 to 84,000 in 1853 after Captain Cook's men introduced typhoid, influenza, syphilis, and gonorrhea. *Id.* at 21–5.

72. DIAMOND, *supra* note 67, at 111.
73. DIAMOND, *supra* note 67, at 195.
74. See Flannery, *supra* note 32.
75. See DIAMOND, *supra* note 67, at 270–3.
76. See Flannery, *supra* note 32.
77. See DIAMOND, *supra* note 67, at 270–3.
78. DIAMOND, *supra* note 67, at 273–6.
79. DIAMOND, *supra* note 67, at 278.
80. DIAMOND, *supra* note 67, at 278–82. Diamond does not use the "us" – "them" terminology.
81. See DIAMOND, *supra* note 67, at 286–7.
82. DIAMOND, *supra* note 67, at 288.
83. See KELLY, *supra* note 4.
84. See KEELEY, *supra* note 55.
85. R. J. Rummel, *Political Systems, Violence, and War* 254–5, in APPROACHES TO PEACE: AN INTELLECTUAL MAP (W. Scott Thompson and Kenneth M. Jensen, with Richard N. Smith and Kimber M. Schraub, eds., 1991).
86. *Id.* at 354–5.
87. See e.g. SPENCER R. WEART, NEVER AT WAR, WHY DEMOCRACIES WILL NOT FIGHT EACH OTHER 3 (1988).
88. See Peter J. Richerson and Robert Boyd, *Complex Societies: The Evolution of a Crude Superorganism*, 10 HUMAN NATURE 253, 269 (1999), noting our Pleistocene brain is not equipped to deal with social inequality.
89. See BOBBITT, *supra* note 26, at 24.
90. For a more extended analysis, see TIMOTHY L. FORT, PROPHETS, PROFITS AND PEACE (2007).
91. NIALL FERGUSON, THE CASH NEXUS: MONEY AND POWER IN THE MODERN WORLD, 1700–2000 (2001).
92. *Id.* at 177–80.
93. See BOBBITT, *supra* note 26, at 5.

94. See BOBBITT, *supra* note 26, claiming that Napoleon's defeat in Moscow resulted from the fact that the Tsar's legitimacy was not based on a contract to protect the Russian people, so that he could leave Moscow abandoned and burned. Napoleon's methods assumed some level of social contract protection (a social contract if not instituted by Napoleon, at least taken advantage of by him and extended as well) between the ruler and the people, so that when Napoleon was able to destroy the popular support for the wars of the ruler, the society would surrender, and in defeat provision his invading army. When that did not happen due to the abandonment of the city, Napoleon's army was exposed to the fact that it did not have the additional kind of popular support that could maintain extended supply lines, popular support that might have been available through additional cash, requiring additional buy-in from the citizenry. At the other end of the continent, Napoleon's defeat at Waterloo ran up against the opposite problem of an England which matched its military capabilities to its popular support.
95. See BOBBITT, *supra* note 26, at 24–64.
96. R. T. NAYLOR, WAGES OF CRIME 131–2 (2002).
97. KARL POLANYI, THE GREAT TRANSFORMATION: THE POLITICAL AND ECONOMIC ORIGINS OF OUR TIME (1944, 2001).
98. See SEABRIGHT, *supra* note 3, at 65.

3 | *Tales of the firm*

S EVERAL years ago, I consulted with a family-owned firm that any
ethicist would love. The company was the leader of its industry, it
treated its employees extremely well and it was deeply engaged in
the well-being of its community. The example of it as a deeply engaged
citizen of its community is one that I also saw replicated in my law
practice in the rural Midwest ranging from car dealers to banks to
insurance firms to doctors. These businesses could be dismissed as the
nostalgic residue of small communities left behind in a global age. Yet
big companies too, sometimes, see their employees as human beings
with creative intelligence and their communities as neighbors rather
than assets to be leveraged. Moreover, some business people see their
work specifically as a way to dampen conflict. For instance, Greek and
Turkish Cypriot businesses have engaged in dialogue for the peace
settlement of Cyprus's conflict through economic cooperation.
Businesses were active in modeling peace agreements in El Salvador.
Tourism interests in Israel and Palestine work together to promote the
region's tourism through cooperation; similar work fostering interethnic
cooperation occurs in Nigeria, Northern Ireland, and Sri Lanka.[1]

These kinds of companies practice a theory of the firm not typically
addressed today by the profit-only approach to business. As we saw in
Chapter 1, this is not necessarily surprising because the law is open to
different ways of running a business. There is no one way to do it, yet it
seems that when it comes to business education, the profit-only model
is dominant and that one way is considered "appropriate". The irony of
insisting that the duty of managers is shareholder profitability is that it
threatens to eliminate any other duty. The examples from the previous
paragraph indicate that there are other ways of running a business and
utilizing its capabilities.

In an influential article, posthumously published, Sumantra Ghoshal
argues that business schools do actual harm in emphasizing that managers cannot be trusted. More broadly, "by propagating ideologically

inspired amoral theories, business schools have actively freed their students from any sense of moral responsibility".[2] Ghoshal argues that unlike the physical sciences, in social science, theories tend to become self-fulfilling, and the only reason to cast shareholders as principals and managers as self-centered agents is because the assumption allows for attractive mathematical modeling. While I share many of Ghoshal's views, I am not so concerned with making the case for what businesses should do as a matter of debating contemporary theories of the firm. Instead, just as the last chapter tried to see what human beings do by looking at our anthropological history, in this chapter, I want to try to look at something of an anthropological history of the firm. Just as in the last chapter, I wanted to show that human organizations have the capability of changing by integrating the three value sectors, in this chapter, I want to show how theories of the firm also have some malleability. In fact, social forces are pushing corporations to develop ethical cultures in a way that seems more along the line of my small Midwestern firms I admire. The good news is that the business practices of these firms – my nostalgiac firms, the companies practicing today's notions of ethical cultures, and those directly enmeshed in zones of conflict – operationalize a viable theory of the firm that is different from the profit-only model. Their approach provides hope for a conception of the firm that fosters sustainable peace.

In other words, I want to show that the predominant theories of the firm link to the values I discussed in the previous chapter. Contemporary theory can be enhanced by seeing those linkages. To make this argument, the first part of this chapter sets out a generally accepted way of differentiating among different conceptions of the firm. I suggest that this contractarian-communitarian divide accurately describes an aggregate theory of the firm, but conflates concession and entity models in its treatment of communitarianism. In the second part of this chapter, I introduce a critique of the contractarian-communitarian bifurcation in two respects. The first respect argues that corporate models rise and fall in cyclical fashion with neither (what I would characterize as) contractarianism or communitarianism winning out. What wins out is the entity approach: one consistent with the market-state model described by Bobbitt. The final part of this chapter then suggests implications for war and peace from the perspective of this account of corporate governance in legal history, particularly with respect to how effective the models may be in responding to twenty-first century challenges.

The communitarian versus contractarian argument

The contemporary corporate governance debate tends to oscillate between communitarian and contractarian notions. In probably the most authoritative analysis of the debate, a Sloan Foundation-funded study written by Michael Bradley, Cindy Schipani, Anat Sundaram, and James Walsh bifurcated the debate in just this way.[3] This article, to my mind the best extant summary of current corporate governance approaches, contrasts between contractarianism and communitarianism. Contractarians believe that firms are places where interested parties contract with each other in order to achieve their goals and purposes, with responsibilities to shareholders. Communitarians see the firm as part of a wider community, with responsibilities to a range of stakeholders. Germany and Japan, for Bradley *et al*, represent modern notions of communitarianism and the UK and US represent contractarianism. As the authors conclude their study, they wistfully look for a model that will "enact communitarian sentiments in a contractarian world".[4]

Although an understandable division of corporate characterizations, the differentiation between "communitarian" and "contractarian" approaches to corporate governance has caused significant problems in understanding the moral nature of the firm. While the article argues that "[s]tripped of their complexities, the debates in much of the scholarship on corporate governance can be distilled to one fundamental issue: whether the corporation should be viewed as a 'nexus of contracts', negotiated among self-interested individuals or as a 'legal entity', with rights and responsibilities as a natural person",[5] the communitarian position, as described by Bradley *et al*, conflates different kinds of corporate form: a concession-based model and an entity-based model.

The contractarian view holds that the best way to handle the inherent conflicts of interest among various corporate constituents is to rely on voluntary agreements and market forces.[6] This conflict, they argue, has become particularly acute in large public corporations where there is a separation of ownership and management; the conflict between managers and owners in particular, and among other constituents as well, has become more problematic. In the merger era of the 1980s, the law and economics literature extended the insights of Ronald Coase from his application of them to entrepreneurs to that of public corporations. The Coase approach, that the entrepreneur/owner is the centerpiece of the firm who negotiates contracts with all the firm's stakeholders and who has the sole right to sell or disband the business, translates to a primacy of shareholders in a public corporation. The contractual model also makes shareholders into another set of stakeholders who are in the midst of negotiating the contracts that create the firm.[7] Efficiency dictates that some transactions are better handled internally and others externally so that, for instance, within a firm a hierarchy may be the most efficient way to organize the employees of a firm whereas a market may well be most efficient in accessing capital and supplies.[8]

In this contractarian approach, Bradley *et al* argue, the firm is not an entity, but the locus for the contracts that bind individuals to transactions that produce wealth for them in the self-interested ways. Those negotiations occur with labor, capital, and other stakeholder groups. Moreover, in the United States, each state offers a home for incorporation and certain embedded legal governance standards with it that differ from other states, so that there is a competitive, contractual market for incorporation as well.[9]

In such a contractual schema, the primary moral need is transparency so that the various contractors can have the information to effectively and fairly negotiate on the basis of actual facts and their own self-interested preferences.[10] Such knowledge enhances efficiency as well as protecting autonomy-based interests of negotiators.[11] If governance rules are aligned to promote efficiency and transparency, to assure competitive markets (through antitrust laws) and protect property rights, then markets themselves will self-correct and produce an efficient market where individuals can make informed choices as to what they should do to further their own self-interest in the economy.[12]

As Bradley *et al* note, taken to its logical conclusion, there are some interesting implications of the contractarian view. Shareholders become the most important, protected group of stakeholders not because of moral preferences, but because, as residual claimants, they are the group that has the incentive to maximize the total economic value of the company.[13] Other stakeholder groups do not have "the incentive to increase the value of the firm beyond the point that the payment of their fixed claim on the firm is assured".[14] If shareholders are prioritized, the contractarian view claims that, assuming "perfect market conditions", the stakeholder groups are also better off because economic value generally will increase that, in turn, provides the wealth for side payments to a wider group of stakeholders.[15]

In contrast, the stakeholder approaches to business typically emphasize the impact of corporate behavior on individuals and argue that individuals, endowed with inherent dignity and human rights, should be considered and protected. It might seem, then, that corporations are monolithic "things" that need to be sensitized to the consequences of their actions. Yet, the contractarian view emphasizes that the corporation, in some sense, does not exist. Individuals within the corporation make decisions, pollute, pay taxes and so forth. Individuals make moral choices. In a sense then, the nexus of contracts view allows all individuals, stakeholders and shareholders, to interact with the corporation as they see fit in order to extract the agreements beneficial to them.[16] Individuals are those to be sensitized to the consequences of their choices and because a contractarian approach emphasizes the individuals interacting with the firm, it provides a real mechanism for consideration of moral choices. In fact, if the firm does not even exist, then we misplace our energies to ask the firm to be socially responsible.

The contractarian view is typically challenged by several arguments. One is that the assumption that individuals can freely and knowledgably contract with respect to the corporation is an impossible, ideal world. The inability to contract could be because of incompleteness, asymmetry of information, fraud, various transactions costs, and jurisdictional differences. Thinking of the corporation in terms of perfect markets does make, as Ghoshal argues, for elegant mathematical modeling, but perfect information for such contracts does not exist. Moreover, third parties are also affected and while some may be able to protect themselves in the market, other more vulnerable groups may not. In other words, even with perfect information, the negotiating position of the parties may be so different as to negate the possibility of actual bargaining. Added to these critics, communitarians argue that the corporation is a social organization with social responsibilities that go beyond economic efficiency.[17] It does have a life beyond the specific interactions of the individuals in it. It has a history, a tradition, and a culture.

The communitarian alternative is a more amorphous collection of approaches to business and as a result, treatment of it suffers. For instance, it is tempting to argue that a communitarian view of business is based on philosophical commitments to a socialized understanding of human nature, but the primary sources of contemporary business ethics critics come from an individualistic, albeit not materialistic, sense of human nature. Such approaches tend to focus on the impact of the corporation on individual human beings and detail the moral worth of such individuals that require protection.[18] In this view, corporations may not have moral intentions, a prerequisite for ethical behavior in Kantian theory, but they do have consequences for which they should be accountable.[19] Because the law accords corporations with legal status as a person in a variety of ways,[20] they can reciprocally be treated as persons for purposes of business accountabilities in the actual actions they take. In short, the heart of the moral critique of contractarianism comes from outside any communitarian school of thought.

To be sure, there are scholars who critique contractarianism as not recognizing the social dimensions of human nature. Those who start from a more socialized view of human nature tend to emphasize the interactions that occur within the workplace itself. Thus, scholars such as Robert Solomon, Edwin Hartman, and Thomas Morris stress the virtues that arise in the workplace and how those virtues intersect with our social human nature. Yet these theorists too are cautious about being associated with communitarianism. They emphasize that businesses become communities in their own right, but being a community does not necessarily mean that one embraces communitarianism as will be discussed shortly.

These two views of ethical business behavior, predominant in the field, tend either to explicitly reject any association with a communitarian paradigm or to at least cautiously distance themselves from it. Neither autonomy-based business ethics nor Aristotelian-based virtue ethics really goes down the same path as either contractarianism or communitarianism. This suggests that there is a theory of the firm, perhaps not specifically articulated as such, that exists in addition to contractarian and communitarian ideals.[21] One of the arguments I wish to make in this book is that within this third alternative conception, there is a way to integrate the leading approaches to business ethics (again, which are neither contractarian nor communitarian) in a form I call Business as Mediating Institution. That approach, which is the essence of Chapter 7, recognizes the social nature of human beings and the ethical duties that arise from understanding the consequences of individuals' actions, and so differs from a contractarian approach. Neither does it go so far as to endorse a communitarian approach, because it does not associate the corporation with larger social and political entities of the state and nation. Instead, it looks to corporations as being communities in their own right and in a way that has been documented to take on characteristics of relatively non-violent organizations. It is exactly in this way that corporations can contribute to Peace Through Commerce.

The communitarian paradigm is more associated with a more generalized notion of business behavior arising out of sociology, law, and management literature; From sociology, the work of Amitai Etzioni; in law stretching back to the E. Merrick Dodd in the famous 1930s Berle–Dodd debate; and in management, from earlier works of Ed Freeman (who bridges the aforementioned business ethics approach and the management corporate social responsibility model) and Max Clarkson. Communitarians do see a wider set of corporate obligations than do contractarians. Etzioni is generally considered the founder and paradigmatic spokesperson for the communitarian approach. As characterized by Bradley *et al*, the communitarian paradigm takes a holistic approach to human nature, conceives of the firm as a social, political, historical, and economic entity whose legitimacy is based on cooperation and justice rather than competition and liberty. Managers of firms should exercise a multifiduciary duty to stakeholders, rely on trust as a method of social control, and should promote a sense of distributive justice.[22]

The communitarian–contractarian bifurcation can be extended geopolitically as well. Bradley *et al* distinguish between German and Japanese systems, which tend to be more communitarian because of firms' attention to the well-being of national society, and the Anglo-American system, which tends to be more contractarian because of firms' attention to their own contractual self-interest.[23] What becomes apparent in these differentiations, however, is that the communitarian regimes, as described, essentially conflate community with nation. That is, Etzioni's sense of communitarianism runs parallel to concerns over the contributions of corporations to the nation-state, particularly that of the United States.[24] Similarly, the German system of companies' management for the *volk* traces to Hitler's Germany and continues today.[25] That is not to necessarily disparage corporate responsibility in Germany (or anywhere else); it is, however, to highlight that the sense of corporate responsibility, as statutorily prescribed, connects to the well-being of the nation-state. The same is true of Japan.[26]

Bradley *et al* certainly are right to contrast their view of human nature as those emphasizing methodological individualism and self interest of contractarianism while noting that communitarians emphasize how communities mold individuals in collectives.[27] Yet, as Mark Granovetter argues, both of these extremes tend to dehumanize the individual. The communitarian model describes an oversocialized view of human nature and the contractarian model provides an undersocialized view. Our communities do form our moral character but we also have the ability to transcend community norms through our own efforts and judgments.[28] To describe human beings as wholly formed by communities demeans the ability to transcend and exercise independent judgment and choice; to describe human beings as wholly independent of relational influence and commitments makes us into atoms devoid of a social nature, something contrary to all empirical studies of human nature.[29] Neither version is particularly attractive, which is one reason why, when Bradley *et al* compare communitarianism and contractarianism, they rightly note that adherents of each view paint a scary picture of the implications of the other's perspective.[30]

In fact, the notions of corporate responsibility are far more complex than a simple communitarian–contractarian approach and appropriately so. Human nature is mixed. We are social creatures who have the gift of independent thinking. No one person is likely to embody only one set of the communitarian–contractarian dichotomy. Neither is any corporation. Certainly, the nexus of contracts approach defines both a way in which businesses organize a significant portion of their affairs and also provides a model suitable to economic theory in which insights as to improvements in financial theory or accounting theory and the like might be developed. At the same time, contracts are a step into relationships. Even if one were to eschew communitarian insights, businesses frequently do not fill contracts by computer order forms, but instead send human beings out to person-to-person meetings to develop relationships based on human interaction and trustworthiness. In some cultures, the signing of a contract without an elaborate stage of relationship-building is unthinkable. But as soon as one starts contracting on relational rather than purely transactional terms, a host of human issues based on solidarity, affection, and the like enter the relationship – whether within the workplace, between company and customer, or between supplier and company, and so on – and so the nexus of contracts takes on a communitarian component.[31] Not cutting off a supply contract because one knows if the company did the supplier might go bankrupt, or not firing a poorly performing employee because the manager knows that the employee is going through a tough personal time, are examples of what Granovetter calls concrete patterns of social relationships that are too varied to be predicted in advance, but which suffuse any human organization, including the corporation.[32]

In short, the contractarian versus communitarian debate describes certain poles of corporate characterization, but the positions only partially illuminate the complex nature of corporations. As Rogene Buchholz and Sandra Rosenthal describe it:

> [T]he creativity of the individual can be contrasted with the conformity represented by the common perspective, but not with community. That which both founds and is founded upon this activity of ongoing adjustment is a community, and in its historical rootedness it develops its own particular organs for the control of the process. The ability to provide the means of mediating within the ongoing dynamics of adjustment constitutes a community of any type as a community.
>
> This adjustment is neither assimilation of perspectives, one to the other, nor the fusion of perspectives into an indistinguishable oneness, but can best be understood as an accommodation through accepted means of mediation. Thus a community is constituted by, and develops in terms of, the ongoing communicative adjustment between the activity constitutive of the novel individual perspective and the common or group perspective, and each of these two interacting poles constitutive of community gains its meaning, significance, and enrichment through this process of participatory accommodation or adjustment.[33]

The conflation of concession and communitarian theories obscures the ways in which corporations might act as independent agents in contributing to more global stability. If the firm is essentially a parallel communitarian construct of the state, which the descriptions of Japan and Germany seem to suggest and which even US-based communitarians such as Amitai Etzioni seem to suggest, then the firm and the state probably do not differ sufficiently for there to be a role of the firm separate from the state. The firm becomes close to a mercantile model, exactly as Bobbitt describes Japanese corporate governance and which historically fits well in Germany. The aggregate approach (the name in legal theory for the contractarian model), in this portrait is an individualistic alternative to such a mercantile communitarianism.

Yet, if the corporation is a community, even a geopolitical entity in its own right, then it may have collective, communitarian sentiments that both dangerously challenge contemporary geopolitics and also act as something of an additional balancing wheel to the contemporary geopolitical landscape. That notion is more akin to what has historically been referred to as a real entity approach. If a corporation is an independent community, it also is more open to the voice of its internal constituents and it is an institution that can more readily engage public issues. It is an approach which can help to connect the nostalgic models I have noted in my experience to those companies engaging in resolving conflict around the world to large companies that attempt to make public concerns part of their corporate culture.

Of course, in practice, real entity, contractarian, and communitarian notions of the firm are mixed up. They exist in some form in all firms and courts rule in favor of one aspect or the other depending on the particularities of a case. Yet, it is important to see these differences, to embed them in legal history, so that we can see that the three differing conceptions provide room for a corporate governance model that avoids the models that are prone to business enhancement of governmental violence. Instead it is important to demonstrate how *today's corporate interests* tip the relationship between business, government, and peace *toward peace and stability and away from nationalistic and economic violence.*

Legal history and corporate governance

Conceptual models: cyclical transformations

Reuven Avi-Yonah provides a historical understanding of how corporations have been transformed.[34] Avi-Yonah argues that there have been four central transformations throughout a history of the corporate form stretching back to Roman law. The first was the establishment of the corporation as a legal person in Roman law, in which differentiations between the three legal alternatives of real, aggregate, and artificial versions of the corporation are already present. Those organizations established as corporations were non-profit organizations with purposes directed toward a public good. The second transformation moved corporations to for-profit status. This transformation took place from the mid-fourteenth into the nineteenth century, including the transformation within American law from corporations being chartered for purposes limited to public goods such as bridge-building or ferries to that of for-profit corporate purposes. In the third transformation, corporations went from being closely held institutions to widely held, and the final transformation was that of national corporations to multinational enterprises.[35]

Within each of these transformations, Avi-Yonah finds the three legal alternative theories in existence: as an aggregate of individuals (the Aggregate Theory), as a creation of the state (the Concession Theory), and as an independent entity with its own institutional identity (the Entity Theory). The Aggregate Theory matches up reasonably well with the contractarian approach, although Aggregate Theory, at least as applied, seems more open to the variety of non-economic values that may be brought to bear in a particular firm.[36] In the Aggregate Theory, the interpersonal governance dimension tends to preserve the role of individuals within the organization and to be open to their voices. In theory, this may be true of the Aggregate Theory as elaborated in the contractarian approach, but the difficulty is that in very large organizations, the capability of any one voice having an impact is much smaller than it would have been in a small institution. Moreover, in smaller institutions, an aggregate of individuals may be able to discuss various kinds of non-economic issues as relevant to the practices of their organization, but in large organizations, it is likely that the only common denominator bringing people together is economic. With less ability to bring to bear one's moral viewpoints, with a larger number of people to consider, and with the differences among moral perceptions that require a fair amount of energy to discuss, process, and implement, the Aggregate Theory may be applicable to large and small organizations alike, but it has a starkly different character when it comes to notions of moral maturity and self-regulation.

The Concession Theory argues that corporations are creations of the state and subject to whatever terms the state chooses to allow corporations to enjoy. It matches up reasonably well with the communitarian model. In the famous *Dartmouth College* case, for instance, Chief Justice Marshall wrote: "A corporation is an artificial being, invisible, intangible, and existing only in contemplation of law. Being the mere creature of law, it possesses only those properties which the charter of its creation confers upon it, either expressly, or as incidental to its very existence."[37] In this view, corporations are, if not agents of the state, at least creatures of the state and subject to a variety of laws the state imposes on them. The state can modify those laws and create new kinds of business organizations with different tax, liability, and other attributes. Moral responsibility in such a conception of the corporation need not necessarily preclude the kind of individual impact of moral maturity and self-regulation, but the emphasis shifts more to a compliance notion of obedience to the laws of the parent – the state – as opposed to that of self-regulation. The make up of the public good is likely to be very similar for the state and the communitarian model. The same problems of size afflict this approach as well. How does one internalize obligations to 300 million people? How does one find a sense of voice and consequence even in a corporation of 10,000 employees (and who knows how many shareholders)?

Finally, in the Entity Theory, corporations are deemed to have their own legal personhood allowing them to own property, sue and be sued, make campaign contributions, and enjoy some aspect of First Amendment protections. Typically, they are also given limited liability protection, allow for free transferability of interests (shares), enjoy centralized management, and have perpetual life. As persons in the eyes of the law and in the eyes of much of the public, corporations have moral responsibilities and an enduring identity beyond that of the collection of individuals that comprise them.

The tendency, of course, in arguing that two models (here contractarianism and communitarianism) are flawed is to default to a third alternative as something that will integrate the good parts of the other models and avoid the bad. That is very much the course I would like to take, but the Entity Theory is frankly scary. It is scary because corporations looking out for their own, independent self-interest (something apart from either its national community or its aggregation of individual interests) can be completely unhinged with any notion of moral responsibility. To the extent the Entity Theory has any sense of moral responsibility and moral maturity, it will be indirectly accessed through national societies and individuals, but to institutionalize it requires corporations to take some independent effort in their own right. The problem is that it is unclear whether they will bother to do that and, if they do, how they will go about it. Perhaps the saving grace is that corporations are so important to societies and to individuals, that theoretical models (while making for nice framing) never will wholly capture what society, individuals, or corporations themselves expect of the organization. That is, the fact that courts, legislatures, and commentators mix all these models up may pragmatically provide resources regardless of the adoption of any one model for corporate governance. Because Entity Theory is more of an open book than the Aggregate or Concession Theories, it may be in a position to best pick and choose the kinds of responsibilities that define its moral responsibilities. History, perhaps then, more than philosophy may provide a better vantage point for today's theory of the firm.

Just as with the communitarian–contractarian differentiation, however, the Aggregate-Concession-Entity characterization provides analytical vantage points, but also risks over-simplifying what occurs in corporations. For instance, Avi-Yonah notes that Chief Justice Marshall used all three views of the firm in his decisions. In *Bank of the United States vs. Deveaux*, Marshall used the aggregate view to uphold federal jurisdiction in a suit between members of the Bank of the United States, all Pennsylvania residents, and the tax collector of the State of Georgia. Georgia wanted to collect a tax on the Savannah branch of the bank and the bank refused to pay. The Bank wanted the case heard in federal court through diversity jurisdiction. Marshall said that the corporation, as a "mere legal entity", could not be a citizen suing in federal court except as "a company of individuals".[38] Marshall viewed the case as members of the corporation "suing in their corporate character", but the essence of diversity protection under the Constitution applied because of the citizenship differences among various individual litigants.[39]

This aggregate view, however, took a back seat ten years later, according to Avi-Yonah, in the *Dartmouth College* case, where, as previously noted, Marshall stressed the fact that the corporation is a creation of the state – the Concession Theory.[40] In Dartmouth College, he viewed the corporate charter establishing the corporation as a contract between the founders and the state and therefore protected under the Contracts Clause. Hearkening to the Concession Theory, Marshall argued that the corporation was a "creature of the law" with incorporation terms as allowed by the state, but in further arguing that the terms of corporation could not be interfered with, he also hinted at the Entity Theory in that the corporation took on its own enduring identity.[41]

Avi-Yonah notes that Marshall came to a full rendering of the Entity Theory in 1827, eight years after *Dartmouth College* and eighteen years after *Deveaux*.[42] In *Bank of the United States vs Dandridge*, Marshall dissented from Justice Story's holding that corporations were held to a different standard of evidence than individuals because corporations are not capable of acting in the absence of some written authority. In the case, a cashier, Dandridge, had executed a bond and the defendant argued that it had not been approved by the Board of Directors as required by the charter. The legal question concerned the type of evidence necessary to determine the authority of Dandridge. Story held that corporations and individuals were subject to the same standards. Marshall dissented, however, arguing that corporations were distinct from its members and must transact business "according to its own nature".[43] In other words, corporations took on a life and characteristics of their own apart from the collection of individuals comprising them.

Avi-Yonah suggests that one could explain Marshall's differing opinions according to the subject matter of the case.[44] Both the extension of diversity jurisdiction (*Deveaux*) and the powers of state chartering (*Dartmouth College*) favored governmental authority. The entity view of *Dandridge* cuts against this, but Avi-Yonah notes that during this sequence, limited liability was increasingly given to corporations in the 1830s, a historical development that undermined the aggregate and concession conceptions in favor of the Entity Theory. At the same time, general incorporation laws spread as well, a development which lessened the ability of a state to pass judgment on the relative merits of a particular incorporation and its members in favor of a generalized permission to conduct business in corporate form. This too lessened state oversight (Concession Theory) and Aggregate Theory in favor of the Entity Theory. Thus, one set of reasons that Marshall could have an evolving view of the nature of the corporation is because of specific historical developments and topics.

Avi-Yonah, however, does not leave the possible explanation at that. Instead he argues that the controversy concerning corporate form is one that is both endemic and also passes through certain stages whenever there has been a transformation of the law with respect to corporations. For instance, he notes that all three theories of the firm existed in Roman legal principles to the Industrial Revolution era to the antebellum period to a contemporary emphasis on multinational, global corporations. Indeed, each of these time periods witnessed an important transformation as to the character of the corporation as follows:

1. The establishment of the corporation as a legal person
2. From non-profit to for-profit corporations
3. From closely held to widely held corporations
4. From national corporations to multinational corporations.[45]

Within each of these transformations, Avi-Yonah argues, one witnesses a progression from the Aggregate Theory to the Concession Theory to the Entity Theory.[46] Indeed, one could argue that a high water mark of the contractarian view of corporations emphasizing a new version of the Aggregate Theory occurred during the hostile takeover crisis of the 1980s in which the primacy of the shareholder was championed and that courts, for instance *Revlon*[47] and *Paramount*,[48] decided in favor of the Entity Theory in which corporations are independent beings with responsibilities to various corporate constituents. During this same period, corporate constituency statutes were enacted that also reinforced the notion of corporate responsibility to a variety of stakeholders.[49] Further, the 1990s saw the advent of "reflexive" statutes and decisions that mandated that corporations become their own institutions of legal compliance, if not justice, in order to comply with the Federal Sentencing Guidelines[50] and *Burlington Industries* kinds of sexual harassment procedures,[51] a trend that continued after the turn of the century with the similar approach of Sarbanes-Oxley.

But, of course, these legal endorsements of the entity approach do not fully explain the corporation's obligations given that shareholders can effectively challenge managers for ignoring shareholder interests and that states, through regulatory affairs, do change the character and nature of corporate obligations regularly. Markets punish corporations for not prioritizing shareholder interests, but they can also punish corporations for not taking moral considerations into account. The Aggregate-Concession-Entity framework does provide analytical vantage points from which one can view certain approaches to corporate behavior, but corporations are a mix of all of these. Moreover, in Avi-Yonah's helpful summary of the transformations that have occurred, there is an important evolutionary note. The transformation from one kind of legal entity to another does not make previous forms extinct. Thus, while the Industrial Revolution saw a transformation from non-profits to for-profit organizations, non-profits still exist. While the antebellum period saw the transformation from closely held to widely held corporations, closely held corporations still exist. While the contemporary era has seen a transformation from national companies to multinational companies, national companies still exist.

Implications

Avi-Yonah's account of the three models of governance demonstrate a historical summary of the ways corporations can be categorized. He draws cases primarily from the US, but by linking aggregate-concession and entity to ancient formulations, he shows that these models have cross-cultural salience. The argument that these models are always present, in some form, in conceptions of the corporation also demonstrate the complexity of governance regimes. No one regime is fully entrenched; they vary within and across countries. The current US and UK may be relatively more aggregate than the German, Japanese, or French models, but even in Anglo-American law, the aggregate approach has never really held full sway. French, Japanese, and German models may be more concession-based, but they too, as Bradley *et al* have reported, adapt aggregate forms as well.

The difficulty with the concession and aggregate approaches is not that they are unreal. They clearly are quite real. They have existed in history and they exist today. But they are joined by entities that have an institutional identity beyond individuals while also different from state agency. Further, both approaches poorly encourage a sense of moral maturity that would lead a corporation to consciously adopt the kinds of policies and programs that might independently contribute to sustainable peace. The concession approach aligns the corporation with the nation-state with an implicit obligation to be loyal to the country of its origins. Moral responsibility is essentially legal responsibility plus what is patriotically good for the country. These two aspects may be good; but are they enough in a global environment where a threat to stability is not the balance of power fashioned by nation-states, but by terrorists with grievances from perceived injustices?

The aggregate approach fosters freedom, but does not attend to the gaps where those outside of the market can effectively negotiate contracts. Moreover, the aggregate approach shears the corporation of moral responsibility because it denies any conscious moral agency of the firm. It is, simply, a locus of intentioned individuals, who do have moral agency. The disjunction, however, shelters individuals from the consequences of their moral agency in part because, and also resulting in, a tremendous collective action problem.

Avi-Yonah's argument that the entity approach tends to prevail suggests that it is worth paying more attention to the self-standing attributes of corporations apart from what they are endowed with by the government and beyond what individuals wish to achieve in forming and maintaining a company. Simply speaking descriptively, the real Entity Theory also does exist and it is quite real. It has the conceptual capability to transcend nationalistic policy-making because multinational companies do transcend borders and because these companies have an identity beyond their nation. It also has the ability to address the collective action problem insofar as it recognizes that corporations have policies, histories, and identities that not only characterize firms, but also which lead firms to behave in one way as opposed to another. Because of its policies, history, and identity, BP Amoco looks and acts differently from Exxon Mobil.

What this suggests is that the ways in which real entities formulate their policies and develop their corporate cultures matter a great deal. The emphasis on corporations developing such cultures in a way that lead beyond legal compliance, but also ethical cultures, is precisely what laws now call for and which are at the heart of contemporary academic scholarship on corporate responsibility. This emphasis on corporate culture is exactly what is called for in preventing the spread of the components of weapons of mass destruction to terrorists. Corporate culture is an attribute of a corporation that goes beyond the sum of the individual members of the organization, but it is not the same as the nation-state. It is something unique to each company. The recognition that culture is essential to ethical behavior is a recognition of the necessary reality of the entity approach. This does not mean that the kinds of cultures that exist in companies are sufficient to create ethical behavior. Nor is it to say that the calls that have been made for culture and the guidelines government has provided for how a corporate culture that encourages ethics is optimally developed are efficacious. In short, there is a recognition that corporate culture is essential to ethical business behavior and that such behavior is a good thing for corporate governance. But just how a real entity approach actualizes this idea is something else. The next section demonstrates both the reliance upon the idea of culture as well as showing how that idea has its own difficulties. Seeing both of these points is important to set the stage for how companies can create these cultures through an integration of the three value sectors. The resources for that integration already exist, but the integration itself has not occurred.

The market-state, business, and weapons of mass destruction

Just as plants and animals must adapt to changing conditions, competitive pressures challenge business as well. The same is generally true of cultures and traditions too. Today, one of the significant challenges facing businesses, cultures, and nations is globalization, particularly with respect to the illicit behavior that has come with porous borders. More specifically, it has been argued by Raymond Baker that capitalism has an "Achilles Heel".[52] That vulnerability is one of illicit commercial (and other) behavior that is hard to control because markets, technology, and communications overwhelm traditional border-protected ways for nation-states to regulate behavior. Baker, citing instances of executive complaints around the world, says that "lawlessness has permeated global commercial and financial affairs far more extensively than is commonly perceived".[53] Dirty money, Baker argues, flourishes not only because of porous borders, but also because of inequality and poverty. The inability to enforce sovereign laws creates opportunities for those in disparate (and sometimes desperate) circumstances to cash in. Drawing on Adam Smith, Baker argues that today "the well-being of society can be overridden for the advantage of another part of society, but brutalizes our practice of capitalism in a way completely unimagined by seminal thinkers".[54] And so Baker concludes that "illegality contributes to inequality. Inequality is worsened by usurped philosophy. And perverted philosophy maxims underpinning capitalism serve to excuse rank illegitimacy and severe inequality."[55]

Moises Naim, editor in chief of *Foreign Policy*, makes a similar point in his book *Illicit*.[56] He shows how global crime has soared, creating economic power that has political weight. Analogizing to the return of smallpox we thought eradicated, Naim shows that slavery is thriving in "the form of coerced sex, domestic work, and farmwork by illegal immigrants".[57] Similarly, the drug trade flourishes "despite the declared war on drugs, the largest deployment of money, technology, and personnel that humankind has ever devoted to stopping drugs from moving across borders".[58] So too does money laundering and tax evasion flourish.[59]

Perhaps more worrisome, Naim notes that the international weapons trade has gone underground since the end of the Cold War. Rather than being the province of governments and a few large companies, there is now also a huge market for small arms, AK-47s rifles, and rocket-propelled grenades. Thousands of merchants sell these to fuel wars around the world.[60] And of course, the most fearsome weapon is nuclear. Graham Allison, in his book, *Nuclear Terrorism*, notes that "[o]ver half of the KGB's suitcase of nuclear weapons are unaccounted for".[61] Osama bin Laden's spokesman, Suleiman Abu Gheith, said after September 11 that al-Qaeda had the right to kill four million Americans, half of them children, and to exile that number[62] to avenge US actions in the Middle East. Globalization opens the door for the means to acquire the WMDs that would accomplish Abu Gheith's ambition. I do not want to argue, as some protestors of globalization might, that globalization caused terrorists' complaints. That argument strikes me as simplistic. Yet, there is a point that an aggrieved party (however that grievance arose) has the possibility to extract horrific revenge.

It may be that there is no direct causal proof of a link between equality and violence,[63] but it may not be wise to wait to establish the proof. The only "causal" proof is likely to be found in an archae-ological sifting through the ruins of a destroyed city.[64] Regardless of whether issues of perceived injustice, poverty, and inequality causally lead to catastrophic violence, it is worth acting to try to mitigate the risk of such causality. If nation-states have increasing difficulty in controlling affairs within their own borders, if globalization creates market opportunities for corporations to match buyers and sellers, and if there is a demand and supply for arms and for dual use technology that can be used for weapons, including WMDs, then it would seem that, increasingly, what stands in the way of the procurement of such weapons are the businesses that could sell them. Since governments may not be able to constrain them, it may be up to business to exercise its own self-restraint. This places a significant burden on businesses to be aware of the laws that do affect such sales and to follow them on their own. In addition, laws governing things such as arms sales are haphazard, again throwing the prophylactic of avoiding dangerous arms sales onto businesses themselves. Moreover, selling these weapons and components may well be a value-maximizing proposition and one that is not illegal. This Achilles Heel of the free market is real and it threatens everyone.

Arms sales and exports

Depending on one's perspective, arms sales comprise a tremendous source of economic activity. In 1995, the United States spent $277.8 billion, or 32 percent of all global expenditures on military items.[65] That is a tremendous sum of money, but it amounted to only 3.8 percent of gross national product.[66] The government does provide other arms sales and exports supports. The US facilitates exports of armaments to other countries through foreign military sales from the government to other governments, through direct commercial sales, and through foreign construction sales. With foreign military sales, the US government purchases the equipment and sells it directly to a foreign government.[67] Direct commercial sales, however, are between US companies and a relevant agency of a foreign country and are subject to approval by the US State Department. In some cases, State Department decisions can be overridden by the US Senate.[68]

The transfer of arms, of course, is subject to regulation, in this case two key laws: the Foreign Assistance Act of 1961[69] and the Arms Export Control Act of 1976.[70] The Foreign Assistance Act mandates that any arms transfer by the United States must "promote the political independence of states and the individual liberties of their citizens that in turn serve to secure world peace and the attainment of the United States foreign policy and security objectives".[71] They should also allow states to improve their security, promote social, economic, and political progress, and lead to universal regulation and reduction of armaments. In authorizing the transfers, the President is limited by prohibiting transfers where there is consistent, gross violation of human rights. The Arms Export Control Act has similar kinds of provisions.[72]

Lucien Dhooge reports that the global trade in arms declined in the ten years between 1985 and 1995 from $52.8 billion to $31.9 billion.[73] As of 1995, five countries – the United States, United Kingdom, Russia, France, and Germany held 86 percent of the world market.[74] Weapons orders worldwide stood at $42.1 billion in 2000 and declined to $37 billion in 2004; between 1997 and 2004, these same five countries held 78 percent of the market, with other European countries making up another 14 percent of world sales. The United States had nearly $9.6 billion, or 42 percent of all arms deliveries to developing nations, Russia had $4.5 billion or 20 percent; and France had $4.2 billion, or 18.7 percent of all such arms deliveries.[75]

There are international agreements that attempt to place some control on the sale of this weaponry. This is particularly true of controls on missiles, and biological and chemical weapons.[76] Putting aside the question of how well these really work, for conventional weapons, the only agreement is the Wassenaar Arrangement on Export Controls for Conventional Arms and Dual-Use Goods and Technologies. This agreement aims to promote transparency of such sales, promote national policies that do not create the capabilities that can undermine stability, reinforce international agreements related to weapons of mass destruction, and cooperate to prevent the acquisition of dangerous dual-use technology items for military use. There is, however, no institution created to enforce these objectives, deferring to national laws to achieve them.[77]

The efficacy of national enforcement of restrained accumulation of such weaponry and technology, however, has been harshly criticized.[78] For instance, while the United States laws include human rights standards for arms exports, as previously noted, the countries receiving most of the military equipment from the US are those that have questionable human rights records. Middle Eastern countries figure prominently in this assessment with Saudi Arabia, Israel, and Egypt receiving collectively the largest amount of arms transfer, all while being subjects of allegations of human rights abuses. In East Asia, Singapore and Indonesia receive large transfers and also are targets of human rights critics. A similar story has been recounted in Europe with transfers to Turkey, as well as in Latin America with respect to Columbia, Peru, and Mexico.[79]

There are efforts to attempt to mitigate the potential, grim results of arms exports, such as advocated by the Commission of Nobel Peace Laureates.[80] The Code promulgated by this commission aspires to govern all transfers of arms "including conventional weapons and munitions, military and security training, and sensitive military and dual-use technologies".[81] The Code requires that no transfers are to be made until a recipient demonstrates that the materials will not contribute to "grave violations of human rights";[82] these are "defined as genocide, summary execution, forced disappearances, torture, and other forms of cruel, inhuman, or degrading treatment or punishment and detentions in violation of international standards".[83] They are also required to design and implement procedures for assuring the investigation of such abuses and also to encourage the function of human rights, including humanitarian emergency assistance, democratic rights of elections, free speech, association, and assembly; civilian control over national security and military forces, and show that their states spend more on health and education than on their military. They must also endorse principles of non-proliferation, comply with UN sanctions on targeted countries, and must be used only for self-defense, not upsetting regional stability, and not allowing any terrorist organizations to make use of its territory.[84] This Code has not been passed by the United States. However, in 1998, the EU accepted a regional Code of Conduct on Arms Exports covering all conventional arms.[85] Furthermore, in 2001 the United Nations launched the Program of Action (POA) to Prevent, Combat and Eradicate the Illicit Trade in Small Arms and Light Weapons in All Its Aspects.[86]

Transfers of conventional arms and the criticism of them may be the easier ones to track. It becomes much more difficult to track dual-use technology simply because materials that might otherwise be an innocent business transaction can, in the wrong hands, become a component of a device with devastating potential. The Nobel Code clearly contemplates that its restrictions apply to dual-use technologies and the concern has also been recognized by the President's Advisory Board on Arms Proliferation Policy. Unfortunately, the laws affecting exports have been described as a "frightful labyrinth".[87] Some reasons for this are that several different agencies are responsible for issuing licenses and regulation for exports, there is no central legislation – most export legislation comes as an amendment to other laws – and, on occasion, the legislation simply lapses. Different congressional committees exercise overlapping jurisdiction and, of course, regulatory requirements differ among nations as well.

So much for the aspirational regulation. Legally, things are not much more enforced or enforceable. For instance, during the writing of this book, the Export Administration Regulations (EAR) lapsed, were temporarily extended, nearly lapsed, and were temporarily extended again by Presidential order. I have no idea what the state of the law will be by the time the reader actually is looking at these words, but the fact that this ambiguity existed immediately after the 9–11 attacks – when one would think laws on such things would be tightened – is an indication of how porous regulation is.[88]

Three executive departments control licensing of exports: Commerce, State, and Treasury. The Department of Commerce controls approximately 3 percent of US industrial exports through the EAR. These regulations control commodities, technology, and software that are in the US or are of US origin and located outside of the US except for technology that is deemed "publicly available". A second regulatory agency is the Department of State, which enforces the International Traffic in Arms Regulations. Finally, the Treasury Department, through the Office of Foreign Asset Control, enforces economic sanctions such as freezing of assets, bans on investing in a country, and embargoes.[89] It may well be that a comprehensive legislation will be enacted, but this inconsistency makes it very difficult for a business which *wants* to contribute to better security to have any idea what it should do.

The result is a system of laws that is complex with no centralized place to look for existing laws, and market pressures to respond to export opportunities presented by globalization. There may be a significant market opportunity for computer technology in an emerging country whose markets are now open due to globalization, but finding out if the technology can be licensed, for instance, could sink in the ambiguity of regulation. Not only might a company lose a market opportunity by waiting for clearance, but even if it tried to figure out what clearance to obtain, it may be unsuccessful. All the market opportunities, then, would drive the licensing of the technology regardless of government approval, yet the technology could pose risks to security. Even a well-intended company is in a trap.

This confused state of affairs may not have much impact on a firm uninterested in complying with the laws in the first place. Such a firm may well try to get around whatever laws exist even if they are crystal clear. But firms who want to know what to do are left in the lurch, and then there are others in between these two poles that may have paid attention to the laws if clear and clearly enforced, but without such clarity, default to profit-making decisions.

Achilles Heel and tales of the firm

Each of the three theories of the firm is challenged by these issues. An aggregate approach would seem to have great difficulty to refuse seizing on the profit opportunities presented if no external (state) agency effectively enforced a prohibition against such sales. Individual owners and managers, of course, may take quite seriously potential harms associated with their product and may act to do their best to ensure that their firms pay careful attention to potential consequences. The aggregate approach, relying on the nexus of contracts of participants, is open to the influence of individuals in exercising judgment. That is true as long as the individual has significant enough power vis-à-vis the rest of the firm to have an impact. The larger the firm, the fewer individuals may have such impact and in such cases, if personal moral views are put to the side and bottom line profitability becomes the prime driver of business decisions, the aggregate model seems most at risk for succumbing to illicit market temptations.

A Concession Theory would obligate an agent of the state to comply with its laws, particularly when there is a national security interest. But if those laws aren't enforced, then even an agent of the state may not know how to benefit the national community. Moreover, if the business organization is unsure of to which nation-state it belongs (is Daimler-Chrysler German or American?), the Concession Theory has problems generating the framework for avoiding illicit sales.

An entity view may be the best potential to resolve these issues, although that may simply be the least worst solution. Entity corporations have an independent interest in existing in their own right apart from individuals and apart from the state. They can generate moral norms apart from the individual and aggregate approaches and without state direction. They can do so out of self-interest, but a self-interest that is attentive to what is necessary for the firm to continue to exist. Sales of illicit arms to individuals bent on destroying the market system would hardly seem to be in the self-interest of a company. And so, a company may well see that regardless of the extant policies on the topic, there is something they should do to ensure that arms do not get into the hands of those who could subvert the company's interest.

Of course, companies may not do so. What differentiates between whether they are likely to generate norms that protect against illicit behavior or not is the extent to which they develop moral maturity through their corporate cultures, a maturity which, as maturity does, balances competing interests. The balancing of those interests would need to be, it seems, toward an overarching objective of peace and security. The culture answer, in fact, seems to be exactly where the law points corporations today, perhaps in recognition of the fact that governments cannot mandate the kinds of compliance that may be necessary to adequately protect stakeholders from harms. The culture answer also necessitates a consideration of how this positive corporate culture can be achieved. Moreover, the culture answer is exactly the answer sought for a slew of contemporary business ethics questions.

Corporate compliance systems and their problems

This ambiguity and vagueness of the export controls in particular, and to a lesser extent the arms control transfers, creates a true dilemma for businesses. On the one hand, there is every reason to expect that increasing attention will be provided to the control of technologies that could be utilized to produce or contribute to the production or delivery of weapons of mass destruction. Because of the various aspects of such technologies, it is reasonably clear that compliance with regulations will require awareness of many people in the organization. Thus, there will be a demand for greater awareness and training of all people in the organization and, to that end, the compliance issue is similar to many other aspects of contemporary compliance programs ranging from sexual harassment to general compliance with federal laws through the Federal Sentencing Guidelines to Sarbanes-Oxley.

Commentators have already begun to look at what may make for an effective corporate compliance program for companies with respect to export controls. For instance, John Liebman notes the challenges in the "soft underbelly of corporate compliance programs: the so-called 'cultural issue'".[90] As Liebman points out, a formal compliance program does not ensure success; both Enron and Arthur Andersen had programs that should have prevented off-balance sheet partnerships and document-shredding.[91] One key problem for compliance, he notes, is that small companies are typically not even aware of the application of export control regulations, so that one way to assure compliance is through a "big sibling" arrangement, where larger companies are accountable for the compliance of their smaller subcontractors. With larger companies, one can predict that those companies that have recently experienced a major restructuring, such as through a merger, acquisition, or consolidation, risk problems in integrating cultural norms. This is, he notes, because of differences in supervisory practices, auditing practices, operating strategies, regulatory approaches (adversarial or submission), and risk tolerance. Liebman's approach addresses issues such as whether compliance personnel are penalized for voluntary disclosures, which could stifle communication, rewarding compliance personnel who support profit centers, and with bonuses from a general bonus pool in order to demonstrate how good compliance performance is good for the company.[92]

In addition, a special task force headed by former Senator Sam Nunn and now-World Bank President Paul Wolfowitz was commissioned by Hughes Electronics to compile a report of industry best practices for ensuring corporate compliance with the spirit and letter of export controls. The task force identified twelve central characteristics.

1. An emphatic, written management commitment, frequently reiterated, stressing the importance of the program to national security and to the company, with senior management actively involved in the program, with adequate resources, and evaluations of the effectiveness of the program. This should include evaluating the program through audits, encouraging internal disclosure, punishing repeated failures, and modifying the program;

2. A compliance council chaired by a senior executive with appropriate senior export personnel and corporate and business level units, meeting at least quarterly, with additional working groups, appropriate records and direct reporting to the board of directors;

3. Hiring of export compliance personnel of the right quantity and quality and appropriate location to work effectively, and looking out for potential conflicts of interest between profitability and compliance;

4. The creation of an export instruction manual that is widely circulated and with a procedure for regular updating;

5. The creation of an export compliance intranet site with information to assist in interactive employee training (and testing), a place for employees to ask questions, mechanisms for updating the information, effective encouragement to use the site, and provisions for computer security;

6. Training and education of employees with all employees given some initial overview training, intermediate training to all export personnel, advanced training to all key compliance personnel, training tailored for particular levels, and training that is recursive and documented;

7. Licenses requirement identified by defaulting to the judgment of the best-qualified personnel (the key compliance personnel), planned and standardized rather than reactive license applications, automated procedures in place in advance to screen exports against the government list of controlled items with multiple layers of review but one central contact with government agencies, high-risk areas with focused separate controls, and maintenance of good relationships with government agencies;

8. Implementing license authorizations with written plans, personnel training, export logs, transmittal and acknowledgment of license conditions, self-assessment and monitoring;
9. Handling of foreign nationals issues by identifying foreign nationals, screening them for licensing issues, submitting licensing requests, and developing a physical and information security plan in advance;
10. Extensive record keeping with interaction with government and foreign entities;
11. Audits done by experienced personnel, some internally to business and corporate units and some externally, with the results reported to business units in question and to the board of directors, and aggressive follow-up procedures; and
12. Handling suspected violations through senior management, unconstrained avenues of reporting without fear of retaliation, internal procedures for handling reports, procedures for external reporting and appropriate discipline for non-compliance.[93]

This kind of list has significant value because it delineates factors by which management can demonstrate the seriousness with which it takes compliance. Strict attention to problematic behavior is, of course, a sensible approach, but there are at least two major problems. First, there is an issue of whether strict compliance measures are efficacious. Do they work? Top-down compliance models can be too unidimensional. Although the Nunn–Wolfowitz best practices acknowledge the good of protecting national security, the approach is driven by a power dynamic of making sure that everyone recognizes that top level management is watching and will enforce the rules necessary to be in compliance with export control laws. As will be detailed in Chapter 6, however, researchers have found that programs tend to be most successful when they go beyond a compliance approach. That is, demanding that members of an organization comply with the law typically is not motivating enough for them to undertake the pro-active steps necessary to achieve desired results.[94] Effective corporate compliance systems draw on more than refined rules. They draw upon other elements of the three value sectors previously described. That is, they draw upon the economic alignment of values and incentives so that individuals tend to be most in compliance when they are rewarded – or at least not punished – for taking steps to foster compliance.[95] To that end, both Liebman and Nunn–Wolfowitz point out essential aspects of compliance programs. Nunn–Wolfowitz stress the need to not punish those who are forthcoming about potential violations[96] and Liebman emphasizes both how bonuses should be linked to compliance performance as well as noting how it is exactly the disconnect between evaluation of performance and changes in the supervisory system in a corporate transition that can make for compliance problems.[97] Thus, one can readily obtain a consensus that effective compliance programs tend to emphasize the power dynamic inherent in increased, high-level management attention and to integrate economic rewards with desired behavior.

In addition, however, those programs that work seem to draw deeply on a sense of pride and emotion in good programs. Johnson & Johnson drew on a corporate culture seeking to do good in addition to one that had the aforementioned management attention and incentive alignment. Similar accounts are reported in companies such as Timberland,[98] Merck,[99] and Cummins Engine.[100] Such efforts still attend to the identification of clear rules that govern the corporation and to the alignment of incentives, but they also instill a notion of communal pride, identity, and aspiration which creates an atmosphere in which attending to duties is more likely to occur (because it is viewed as being important to one's own identity) and when there is a crisis, to be able to draw on that capability to address it directly.

More needs to be said about such programs and will be in the following chapters, but an essential reason for why it is important to note the interplay of all the value sectors is because of the increasing reliance on non-public institutions to provide public goods of cooperation.

At the beginning of the twenty-first century, it is to be hoped that informal private networks that cross international lines – for example, the large multinational corporations developed in the twentieth century, or the extensive social networks developed by overseas Chinese in East Asia and the United States, or global nongovernmental organizations – will supply the links necessary to prevent the growing divergence of the three models [Anglo-American, German, and Japanese] of the market-state.[101]

Thus, it would seem that time's arrow points toward governments (and perhaps markets) asking corporations to take on the maturity to be organizations that foster ethical cultures. Such cultures are institutions with traditions of certain ways of doing business. The culture approach hopes for businesses to instill a goal of attention to the public goods of avoiding putting illicit arms in the hands of the wrong people, an opportunity provided by the market and rationalized by a short-term version of value-maximization. This may not work. It seems to be, however, how governments look at the way to solve the problem of the times when corporate activities could contribute to social ills. Governments ask companies to develop cultures that point its workers away from such ills. Government's delegation of this responsibility itself reflects a shift away from a communitarian/concession approach to the firm. It also is inconsistent with an aggregate/nexus of contracts approach because it asks for more than individual effort and more than attention to government obedience; it asks for corporations to be independent entities. And so, the entity approach seems to be winning out again, continuing the sequence identified by Avi-Yonah, even on issues of corporate responsibilities.

This may not work. In arguing that the entity approach seems to be the historical choice is not to claim that it is necessarily a good thing. It does strike me as being less worse than the alternatives. But there are some things that the entity firm will find hard to accomplish. One of those is whether companies will actually take up the challenge of developing cultural traditions to contribute to public goods (or at least not contribute to social ills). A second is that some things are simply likely to be too remote for anyone to be able to control.

For instance, a 2004 *Wall Street Journal* article demonstrated how a Pakistani nuclear ring avoided export laws. The writers demonstrated how innocent products – such as parts for an Apple IMac computer or aluminum tubes for tanker trucks – could be purchased and then re-assembled to build components for a Malaysian factory to build components for Libya's secret nuclear weapons program. Stricter controls, in this case often by European countries, simply led to the purchase of smaller components for subsequent re-assembly.[102] At some level, it is virtually impossible to know what sales might lead even to weapons of mass destruction. That is true insofar as governments go and it is also true insofar as companies as entities go. Yet it is what we have to work with and although the Entity Theory has historically won, it is also amorphous enough to be open to contemporary definition of how companies can go about building such cultures and traditions. Setting out a way that can occur is the topic of Part Two.

Firms reducing conflict

To some degree, all businesses are enmeshed in conflict, particularly given the reach, consequence, and even strategies of terrorism. Some businesses are more directly involved such as private security companies, which are akin to mercenaries, contracting to provide military services. In some instances, such as Iraq, private security forces are direct targets.[103] In other cases, business and politics are enmeshed in quests for power where there is no real dividing line between governmental and economic. Such is the case, for instance, in Russia where an executive of a major Russian company, Inteko, was attacked with an axe just as the company was opposing a governmental plan to transform collective farmland into agribusiness.[104] On the other hand, I have already alluded to the fact that companies already engage in helping to resolve conflict around the world. Those companies undertake this from a theory couched in entity terms. Put otherwise, it is an institutional engagement (and so beyond aggregate/contractarianism) and independent of state obligation (and so beyond concession/communitarianism). This is the model of the firm that can act as an instrument of peace.

Stephen Ladek, in his solely authored work and also in conjunction with co-authors Kathy Getz and Jennifer Oetzel, has shown how multinational corporations can develop strategies for responding to violent conflict in the places where they do business. They include a range of actions from philanthropy, independent audits and certifications, training, lobbying, negotiations, withholding payments, public condemnation, providing support to peacekeeping missions, and global multilateral agreements.[105]

Similarly, World Bank studies demonstrate what the private sector can do in providing infrastructure in post-conflict countries.[106] This study shows that investment into conflict areas begins with telecoms followed by electricity generation and then investment in transportation and water. In a widely noted study, Paul Collier shows that when the main export product of a country is a commodity, the risk of civil war increases. Similar causes concern the domination of a single ethnic group as well as poverty.[107]

On the positive side, features such as democracy and absence of corruption seem to lessen the likelihood of violence. Dean Bapst, among others, has shown that democratic countries do not go to war with each other.[108] Elliot Schrage argues that an unintended consequence of Sarbanes-Oxley is that it offers protection against corruption, something that seems to be a partner with violence.[109] Our biological heritage includes forces for peace as well as for war. What is important is how our institutions are configured to integrate our multiple values in a way that fosters peace over war.

While theories of the firm are not directly implicated in causing violence, they are insofar as the question runs to how they can positively be a force for peace. That is, corporations may not cause war (although there may be such examples), but could they contribute to peace? The interesting phenomena is that when challenged with the tests of the day – spread of WMDs, illicit money laundering, slavery, and so on – it seems that governments ask for corporations to develop institutional cultures that are different from a purely value-maximizing approach. Thus, considering whether theories of the firm promote these cultures becomes important. Moreover, it seems that of the three theories of the firm, the Entity Theory has a better chance of developing the culture that could address issues of peace. For better or worse, it seems to be the best theoretical conception of the firm available for this role of the company.

The efforts to create corporate cultures that can address an issue such as WMD proliferation suggests that success depends upon more than legal regulation. It also depends upon more than clearly articulated policies. It requires these aspects as well as the actualization of organizational dynamics that form corporate cultures. To date, neither the laws nor the elements of ethical corporate cultures have been sufficiently integrated to provide a model that could, in fact, lead to the positive contributions businesses might make to sustainable peace. The challenge is to recapture a theory of the firm that integrates law with larger dimensions of culture-forming forces. I have identified those sources as rooted in our nature. The aggregate/contractarian model of the firm dwells on one of these dimensions, but the challenges of the twenty-first century, including WMDs and other illicit trade, require a much greater engagement with firms and the people in them seeking the good. The concession/communitarian model recognizes the state interest in security and government seems to recognize that this may best occur through the development of corporate culture. But is corporate culture the answer to these vexing questions of violence and peace just as it is for so many other questions of business ethics? It is a real entity solution that approaches the answer to this, for better or worse, and it seems to be what we have to work with.

The next chapter provides a metaphor for that approach in the form of Honest Brokers. It is exactly that combination that creates the corporate cultures most likely to address the Achilles Heel of the free market as well as today's other business ethics challenges. Part Two then attempts to describe the leading approaches to current business ethics from the perspective of law, normative ethics, and social scientific dimensions. As we shall see, these aspects need to be integrated and then additionally integrated with the affective aspects described in Chapter 7 in order to create corporations that can become instruments of peace.

Notes

1. INTERNATIONAL ALERT, LOCAL BUSINESS, LOCAL PEACE: THE PEACEBUILDING POTENTIAL OF THE DOMESTIC PRIVATE SECTOR 29 (2006).
2. Sumantra Ghoshal, *Bad Management Theories Are Destroying Good Management Practices*, 4 ACADEMY OF MANAGEMENT LEARNING AND EDUCATION 75, 76 (2005).
3. Michael Bradley, Cindy A. Schipani, Anant K. Sundaram, and James P. Walsh, *The Purposes and Accountability of the Corporation in Contemporary Society: Corporate Governance at a Crossroads*, 62 LAW AND CONTEMPORARY PROBLEMS 9 (1999).
4. *Id.* at 86.
5. *Id.* at 9.
6. *Id.* at 34.
7. *Id* at 35.
8. *Id.*; see also OLIVER WILLIAMSON, MARKETS AND HIERARCHIES, ANALYSIS AND ANTITRUST IMPLICATIONS (1975).
9. See Bradley *et al*, *supra* note 3, at 36.
10. See Bradley *et al*, *supra* note 3, at 36.
11. See Bradley *et al*, *supra* note 3, at 36.
12. See Bradley *et al*, *supra* note 3, at 36.
13. See Bradley *et al*, *supra* note 3, at 37.
14. See Bradley *et al*, *supra* note 3, at 37–8.
15. See Bradley *et al*, *supra* note 3, at 38.
16. See Bradley *et al*, *supra* note 3, at 36–8.
17. See Bradley *et al*, *supra* note 3, at 38–42.
18. PATRICIA H. WERHANE, PERSONS, RIGHTS, AND CORPORATIONS (1985).

19. *Id.* at 34–40, quoting Peter French, *The Corporation as a Moral Person*, AMERICAN PHILOSOPHICAL QUARTERLY, 16, 210 (1979).

20. In 1909 the US Supreme Court recognized the corporate entity as a 'person' for all purposes under the US Constitution and Bill of Rights except for the Fifth Amendment right against self-incrimination. Southern Railway Co. vs. Greene, 216 US 400, 417 (1909). Thus, the corporation can own property, make campaign contributions, institute lawsuits, and so on.

21. See e.g. Edwin M. Hartman, *The Commons and the Moral Organization*, 4 BUSINESS ETHICS QUARTERLY 253 (July 1994); Robert C. Solomon, *The Corporation as Community: A Reply to Ed Hartman*, 4 BUSINESS ETHICS QUARTERLY 271 (July 1994).

22. See Bradley *et al*, *supra* note 3.

23. See Bradley *et al*, *supra* note 3, at 50–77.

24. See Timothy L. Fort, *The First Man and the Company Man: The Common Good, Transcendence and Mediating Institutions*, 36 AMERICAN BUSINESS LAW JOURNAL 391, 410–11.

25. See Bradley *et al*, *supra* note 3, at 52–3.

26. See Bradley *et al*, *supra* note 3, at 57–61.

27. See Bradley *et al*, *supra* note 3, at 41–3.

28. Mark Granovetter, *Economic Action and Social Structure: The Problem of Embeddedness*, 91 AMERICAN JOURNAL OF SOCIOLOGY 481, 485 (1985).

29. *Id.* at 487.

30. See Bradley *et al*, *supra* note 3, at 43.

31. IAN MACNEIL, THE RELATIONAL THEORY OF CONTRACT: SELECTED WORKS OF IAN MACNEIL (2001). MacNeil pioneered the differentiation between relational and transactional contracts.

32. See Granovetter, *supra* note 28, at 493.

33. Rogene A. Buchholz and Sandra R. Rosenthal, *Toward a New Understanding of Moral Pluralism*, 6 BUSINESS ETHICS QUARTERLY 263, 268 (1996).

34. Reuven S. Avi-Yonah, *Aggregate, Artificial, or Real? The Cyclical Transformations of the Corporate Form*, 30 DELAWARE JOURNAL OF CORPORATE LAW 767.

35. *Id.* at 770–1.

36. Partnerships, for instance, are classic examples of business organizations that are comprised of an aggregate of individuals. With individual partners liable for each other's actions, individual rights to control of the entity, termination of the partnership on the death of one of the partners, and unlimited liability, legal rules recognize that this kind of business organization is one totally dependent on the identity of the

particular human beings who have contracted together to create a business organization. Because of the emphasis on individuals, there can be a larger sense of corporate purpose than might exist in corporations.

37. The Trustees of Dartmouth College vs. Woodward, 17 US (4 Wheat.) 518, 636 (1819).
38. Bank of the United States vs. Deveaux, US (5 Cranch) 61, 64–5, 86–7 (1809).
39. *Id*. at 87–8.
40. Trustees of Dartmouth College, 17 US at 636.
41. *Id*. at 642.
42. Avi-Yonah, *supra* note 34, at 788–9.
43. See Bank of the US vs. Dandridge, 25 US (12 Wheat.) 64 (1827).
44. Avi-Yonah, *supra* note 34, at 789–90.
45. Avi-Yonah, *supra* note 34, at 770–3.
46. Avi-Yonah, *supra* note 34, at 770–3.
47. See Revlon vs. MacAndrews and Forbes Holdings, Inc., 506 A.2d 173 (1986).
48. See Paramount Communications, Inc. vs. time, Inc. 571 A.2d 1140 (1989).
49. The following statutes permit directors to consider the interests of non-shareholder constituencies in any appropriate context: Conn. Gen. Stat. 33-756(d) (1997), mandating consideration of non-shareholder constituencies; Fla. Stat. ch. 607.0830(3) (Supp. 1999); Ga. Code Ann. 14-2-202(b)(5) (Supp. 1998); Haw. Rev. Stat. 415-35(b)(1)-(4) (1997); Idaho Code 30-1702 (1996); 805 Ill. Comp. Stat. 5/8.85 (West 1993); Ind. Code 23-1-35-1(d) (1995); Iowa Code 491.101B (1991); Me. Rev. Stat. Ann. tit. 13-A, 716 (West Supp. 1998); Mass. Gen. Laws Ann. ch. 156B, 65 (West Supp. 1998); Minn. Stat. 302A.251(5) (Supp. 1999); Miss. Code Ann. 79-4-8.30(d) (1998); Nev. Rev. Stat. 78.138(3) (1994); N. J. Stat. Ann. 14A:6-1(2) (West Supp. 1998); N. M. Stat. Ann. 53-11-35(D) (Michie 1997); N. Y. Bus. Corp. Law 717(b) (McKinney Supp. 1999); N. D. Cent. Code 10-19.1-50(6) (Supp. 1997); Ohio Rev. Code Ann. 1701.59(E) (Anderson 1993); Or. Rev. Stat. 60.357(5) (Supp. 1999); 15 Pa. Cons. Stat. 515 (1995); Wis. Stat. 180.0827 (1992); Wyo. Stat. Ann. 17-16-830(e) (Michie 1997).

    The following statutes permit directors to consider the interests of non-shareholder constituencies in the context of transactions for corporate control: Ala. Code 10-2B-11.03(c) (1994); Ariz. Rev. Stat. 10-2702, 10-1202(c) (1996) (sale of assets); Ark. Code Ann. 4-27-1202(C) (Michie 1996) (sale of assets); Colo. Rev. Stat. 7-106-105(7) (reverse splitting of shares), 7-111-103(3), 7-114-102(3) (1998) (authorization of dissolution after issuance of shares); Ky. Rev. Stat. Ann.

271B.11-030(2)(b), 271B.12-020(3) (Banks-Baldwin 1989) (sale of assets); La. Rev. Stat. Ann. 12:92(G) (West 1994); Mo. Ann. Stat. 351.347 (West 1991); Mont. Code Ann. 35-1-815(3), 35-1-823(3) (1997) (sale of assets); N. H. Rev. Stat. Ann. 293-A:11.03(c), 293-A:12.02(c) (Supp. 1996) (sale of assets); N. C. Gen. Stat. 55-11-03(c), 55-12-02(c) (1990) (sale of assets); R. I. Gen. Laws 7-5.2-8 (1992); S.C. Code Ann. 33-11-103(c), 33-12-102(c) (Law. Co-op. 1990) (sale of assets); S. D. Codified Laws 47-33-4 (Michie 1991); Tenn. Code Ann. 48-103-204 (1995); Tex. Bus. Corp. Act Ann. art. 5.03 (West Supp. 1999); Utah Code Ann. 16-10a-1103(3) (1995); Vt. Stat. Ann. tit. 11 A, 11.03(c), 12.02(c) (1997) (sale of assets); Va. Code Ann. 13.1-718(C) (Michie 1993); Va. Code Ann. 13.1-724(C) (Michie Supp. 1998) (sale of assets); Wash. Rev. Code 23B.11.030(3), 23B.12.020(3) (1994) (sale of assets).

50. US Federal Sentencing Guidelines for Organizations (the "Guidelines") U.S.S.C. section 8A1.2.

51. Burlington Industries vs. Ellerth, 524 US 742, 747–9 (1998), announcing a new standard for analyzing employer liability by dividing liability into two categories based on finding a hostile work environment and then determining whether a tangible employment action occurred.

52. RAYMOND W. BAKER, CAPITALISM'S ACHILLES HEEL: DIRTY MONEY AND HOW TO RENEW THE FREE-MARKET SYSTEM (2005).

53. *Id.* at 15.

54. *Id.* at 16.

55. *Id.* at 16.

56. MOSES NAIM, ILLICIT: HOW SMUGGLERS, TRAFFICKERS AND COPYCATS ARE HIJACKING THE GLOBAL ECONOMY (2005).

57. *Id.* at 13.

58. *Id.* at 14.

59. *Id.* at 13–16.

60. *Id.* at 14–15.

61. GRAHAM ALLISON, NUCLEAR TERRORISM: THE ULTIMATE PREVENTABLE CATASTROPHE 10 (2004).

62. *Id.* at 12.

63. See WOODROW WILSON CENTER FOR SCHOLARS REPORT: PREVENTING THE NEXT WAVE OF CONFLICT 32 (Carla Koppell with Anita Sharma, 2003).

64. ALLISON, *supra* note 61, at 10–14.

65. Lucien J. Dhooge, *We Arm The World: The Implications of American Participation in the Global Armaments Trade*, 16 ARIZ. J. INT'L J. COMP. L. 577, 583 (1999) citing ACDA reports.

66. *Id.* at 583.

67. *Id.* at 589.
68. *Id.* at 590.
69. *Id.* at 591, citing Foreign Assistance Act of 1961, at 22 U.S. C. Section 2151–2430i (1994).
70. *Id.* at 591, citing Arms Export Control Act of 1976, at 22 U.S. C. Section 2151–2799aa-2 (1994).
71. *Id.* at 591.
72. *Id.* at 594, citing statute at Section 2304(a)(2).
73. *Id.* at 610.
74. *Id.* at 610, citing WMEAT at 19, 37.
75. The Grimmett Report, *Conventional Arms Transfers to Developing Nations, 1997–2004*, Report for Congress, US Congressional Research Service, Library of Congress (August 29, 2005).
76. Dhooge, *supra* note 65, at 600 listing multiple treaties.
77. Dhooge, *supra* note 65, at 600–1 citing Wassenaar Agreement.
78. Dhooge, *supra* note 65, at 614–38 for a summary of these criticisms.
79. Dhooge, *supra* note 65, at 620–55.
80. Commission of Nobel Peace Laureates, International Code of Conduct on Arms Transfers (1995), cited in Dhooge, *supra* note 65, at 683.
81. Commission of Nobel Peace Laurcates, International Code of Conduct on Arms Transfers (1995), cited in Dhooge, *supra* note 65, at 683.
82. Nobel Commission at Article 3(A), quoted in Dhooge, *supra* note 65, at 684.
83. Dhooge, *supra* note 65, at 684, footnote 901.
84. Dhooge, *supra* note 65, at 684–5.
85. *European Union Code of Conduct on Arms Exports, Council of the European Union*, Publication 8675/2/98 (June 5, 1998).
86. *Report of the United Nations Conference on the Illicit Trade in Small Arms and Light Weapons in All Its Aspects*, UN Document A/CONF.192/15 (2001).
87. Cecil Hunt, *Coping with the US Export Controls, 2003 Export Controls and Sanctions: What Lawyers Need to Know*, Practising Law Institute 857 PLI/Comm 597 (December 2003 and January 2004) [hereinafter cited as Hunt, Coping]; see also, Cecil Hunt, *Overview of the US Export Controls* (2003) [hereinafter cited as Hunt, Overview]; see also Anne Q. Connaughton, *Exporting to Special Destinations and Persons: Terrorist-Supporting and Embargoed Countries, Designated Terrorists, and Sanctioned Persons*, 857 PLI/Comm 255 (2003).
88. In August 2001, President Bush issued Executive Order 13222 declaring a national emergency with respect to national security because of the expiration of the Export Administration Act (EAA) of 1979 as amended. The EAA had not been renewed and so President Bush extended the

emergency with respect to national security and the EAA on August 17, 2001, August 14, 2002, August 7, 2003, and August 5, 2005. See 69 FR 48763, found at http://web.lexis-nexis.com/universe/document?_m=b4234a6337d14b0a047c8eeacd7a1ed5 (accessed August 4, 2006), and 70 FR 45273, found at http://web.lexis-nexis.com/universe/document?_m=99f)7883b2785d80e558f81a0eda617c& (accessed August 4, 2006).

89. According to Hunt, the activities subject to the Export Administration Regulations (EAR) are exportation, re-exportation, the release of software or technology to a foreign national, intangible exportation such as posting technology or software on the web or transmission by fax, and any involvement of a US national in a transaction not otherwise prohibited but which the participant knows to have a "proliferation link". A controlled export is one that impacts national security, nuclear technology, missile technology, chemical and biological weapon technology, and other terrorist issues. Foreign countries are also identified according to the threat they pose, so that if there is a match between a threatening country and a controlled export, a license is required. Certain prohibitions prevent contact with users regardless of what one is exporting, while others further prohibit activities that might assist in other prohibitions, such as financing, employment, freight forwarding, and service contracts. Other prohibitions prevent the shipping of an export through a country that has been deemed to be a threat (so that for example a nuclear reactor, shipped to Japan, cannot make a port call in North Korea). Licensing for software and technology is vague. Although there is a prohibition against the export of technology if it is to be used for the "development, production, or use" of a controlled item, but if the technology is "publicly available", then the prohibition does not apply. Enforcement of the EAR can come through the Department of Commerce in an administrative capacity through a denial order; in addition, a criminal investigation can be initiated by a US attorney's office. See generally Hunt, Coping; see also Hunt, Overview for a general description of the export control laws.

90. John R. Liebman, *Export Compliance Counseling: The Role of Corporate Culture* 857 PLI/Comm 597 (December 2003 and January 2004).

91. *Id.* at 600.

92. *Id.* at 605.

93. Nunn and Wolfowitz, *Nunn-Wolfowitz Task Force Report: Industry Best Practices Regarding Export Compliance Programs* (July 25, 2000), at http://usexportcompliance.com/Papers/nunnwolfowitz.pdf.

94. See e.g. Lynn Sharp Paine, *Managing for Organizational Integrity*, HARVARD BUSINESS REVIEW (March/April 1994), arguing that more aspirational values such as integrity serve to focus employees on doing good things rather than simply obeying the law.
95. *Id*. See also L. K. TREVINO AND K. A. NELSON, MANAGING BUSINESS ETHICS: STRAIGHT TALK ABOUT HOW TO DO IT RIGHT (1995).
96. Nunn–Wolfowitz, *supra* note 93, at 34–5.
97. Liebman, *supra* note 90.
98. The Timberland Company established its Social Enterprise Department in the 1990s to incorporate community service into company operations and offer employees year-round opportunities to volunteer. Timberland's Path of Service program gives employees forty hours per year of paid leave to volunteer in community work. See www.timberland.com/corp/index.jsp?clickid=topnav_corp_txt.
99. See e.g. DAVID BOLLIER, MERCK AND COMPANY (The Business Enterprise Trust: Stanford, CA, 1991) 5. Merck's corporate culture for serving people through medical advances leads to incidents like its donation of over $1 billion of Mectizan to treat river blindness in the poorest, most remote regions of Africa. Even though Merck management knew there was little economic promise for this medicine, once they understood its capacity to cure severe human suffering, they felt ethically obliged to develop it, at substantial cost to Merck.
100. See e.g. DAVID BOLLIER, AIMING HIGHER: 25 STORIES OF HOW COMPANIES PROSPER BY COMBINING SOUND MANAGEMENT AND SOCIAL VISION (The Business Enterprise Trust: Stanford, CA, 1996). Cummins Engine Foundation made contributions to pay architectural fees for the construction of aesthetically pleasing public buildings such as schools and a library in its home base of Columbus, Indiana.
101. PHILLIP BOBBITT, THE SHIELD OF ACHILLES: WAR, PEACE AND THE COURSE OF HISTORY 675 (2002).
102. David Crawford and Steve Steclow, *How the Pakistani Nuclear Ring Managed to Skirt Export Laws*, WALL STREET JOURNAL (March 23, 2004) at A1.
103. See *The Day the War Turned* GQ, February 2006 p 106 (detailing the death of four private contractors who were ambushed).
104. Peter Finn, *Russian Case Shows No Holds Barred in Business and Politics*, THE WASHINGTON POST (January 16, 2006) at A1.
105. Ladek, Getz, and Oetzel, The role of Multinational Enterprise in Responding to Violent Conflict: A Conceptual Model and Framework for Research, December 05 (unpublished manuscript on file with author); see also, Getz and Ladek, The Role of the Private Sector in Responding to Violent Conflict (unpublished manuscript on file with

author); and Ladek, The Role of the Private Sector in Responding to Violent Conflict (unpublished manuscript on file with author).

106. JORDAN SCHWARTZ, SHELLY HAHN, AND IAN BANNON, THE PRIVATE SECTOR'S ROLE IN THE PROVISION OF INFRASTRUCTURE IN POST-CONFLICT COUNTRIES: PATTERNS AND POLICY OPTIONS (World Bank Social Development Papers; Conflict Prevention and Reconstruction #161, August 2004).

107. PAUL COLLIER, ECONOMIC CAUSES OF CIVIL CONFLICT AND THEIR IMPLICATIONS FOR POLICY (World Bank Papers, June 15, 2000).

108. Dean Bapst, A Force for Peace, INDUSTRIAL RESEARCH 55 (April 1972).

109. Elliot J. Schrage, *Corruption's New Nemesis*, THE WASHINGTON POST (November 15, 2005) at A25.

4 | *Honest Brokers*

T HIS chapter serves as a bridge between the idea that businesses can do something to contribute to sustainable peace and how companies can actually do this through an approach I call Total Integrity Management. Total Integrity Management is a way to blend the three value clusters of economizing, power-aggrandizing, and ecologizing into a coherent approach that builds business culture and which also happens to coincide with the three contributions business can make to sustainable peace. This chapter is largely the bridge that links Peace Through Commerce via Total Integrity Management by first proposing some metaphors that can be built upon.

The tone of this chapter changes. The previous two chapters have engaged in some abstract conceptual thinking about the history of business, politics, peace, anthropology, and theories of the firm. The basic conclusion is that we have three dimensions of our nature – power-aggrandizing, economizing, and ecologizing – and these play out in our social settings. Integrating them is a way to reach peace and stability. Our nature is such that we do have the capability of changing our social institutions. Those include our business institutions. Thus, the theories of the firm show ways firms have been thought of and how the Entity Theory both tends to historically emerge in business development, but also stands the best chance to make businesses into instruments of peace. That can be done through corporate culture, particularly in integrating three approaches to corporate responsibility: legal, managerial, and spiritual. These three approaches flow directly from our nature and also link to the contributions businesses can make to sustainable peace. This chapter starts that process by trying out some more accessible metaphors of the firm, metaphors less obscure than aggregate, concession, and entity or contractarian, communitarian, or value-maximizing. I want to start with a metaphor of Honest Brokers.

A personal metaphor: Honest Brokers

Diogenes may have searched long and hard for an honest man, but he may have had a more difficult time finding an Honest Broker. Or at least so it seems in reading about business shenanigans over the past few years. But as the previous chapters suggest, as easy as it is to take potshots at corporate misconduct, the key to global stability may just lie in the recovery of the idea of how businesses can be Honest Brokers. Not only might that restore trust in businesses themselves, the likelihood of violence may be reduced if businesses mindfully implement a straightforward set of ethical practices.

This doesn't just mean complying with the latest legislative attempt to rein in corporate miscreants. But it does mean that complying with just laws is a good first step. It doesn't just mean that one should practice good ethics only if it pays. But it does mean that recognizing the alignment of the times when doing well by doing good is a solid second step. In addition, to be law-abiding citizens and recognizing the long-term connection between good ethics and good business, the key to ethical business behavior, the key to restoring trust in business, and indeed, the key to unlocking the potential for businesses to contribute to a more stable global environment, is to tap into a set of hard-wired, aspirational commitments to the good that are as much part of human nature as are the darker sides all too frequently documented in the press.

In today's charged political climate, it may seem odd to turn to politics for examples of Honest Brokering, but Honest Brokering is essential for good democratic government and examples abound of individuals filling this role. Growing up during the 1960s in central Illinois, no one was held in greater esteem in our house than Senator Everett Dirksen. If my siblings or I were giving a speech at school or at church, we were forced to listen to an old 33 LP record of Dirksen speaking the words to "God Bless America" so that we would remember to enunciate our syllables properly. Dirksen verbally massaged each vowel and each consonant in such a rich, deep, soothing, baritone voice that even a school kid had fun listening to and trying to imitate.

Dirksen was beloved in our household for reasons other than his vocal chords. He was a solid, commonsensical, Main Street politician. It was Dirksen who originated the expression, "a billion here and a billion there and soon you are talking about real money". If Ev Dirksen believed in something, it was probably worth believing yourself. In the 1970s, my house followed the Dirksen family tree and became fans of his son-in-law Howard Baker. Baker's calming thoughtfulness was, in many ways, even more appealing to us.

Both Baker and Dirksen demonstrated all three kinds of Honest Brokering. There was never a whiff of scandal about them. They had a reputation for being gracious and fair to friends and opponents alike, even when in the midst of disagreement with them. Thus, people came to them to help sort out difficult issues. And they possessed a sense of prioritizing the common good over personal or partisan self-interest.

For instance, as the Minority Leader of the US Senate, Dirksen had plenty of opportunity to oppose the enlargement of government on many fronts and he did so regularly. But as is well-known, when it came time for the showdown votes for the landmark 1964 Civil Rights Act, the bill was bogged down by a filibuster of southern Democrats and President Lyndon Johnson couldn't get them to budge. Johnson turned to Dirksen to see if he could get enough Republicans to join with liberal Democrats to end the filibuster. After modifying the bill, Dirksen delivered, the filibuster was killed, and the Civil Rights Act became law.

Dirksen didn't have a significant constituency favoring the bill. His Illinois political base was in the overwhelmingly white Downstate and suburban parts of Illinois where the Civil Rights Act was, at best, not something people were passionately supporting. But Dirksen, referencing Lincoln, thought the legislation was simply the right thing to do. So although it didn't do much of anything to help him politically, he was the central figure in getting the legislation passed.

Dirksen's Honest Brokering became something of a family tradition when, a decade later, Baker sat as the ranking Republican on the Senate Watergate Committee and intoned one of the most famous phrases in Congressional investigator history: "What did the President know and when did he know it?" The phrase, it seems, has been borrowed by just about every subsequent Congressional investigation. Baker's question aimed to get at the heart of the facts, political implications to the side, in order to know what the right thing to do was. Like Dirksen, Baker prioritized a moral good above what self-interested partisan benefits might be at stake.

Dirksen's and Baker's actions imprinted the idea of Honest Brokering on me, but it does not mean that Republicans have a corner on the role. One can point to a number of Dirksen's and Baker's colleagues and successors on the Democratic side of the aisle just as well. For instance, Paul Simon, another Illinoisan admired during my upbringing springs to mind as a Democratic example of an Honest Broker. He too never had the whiff of scandal around him. He was renowned for the respect with which he treated others and could be looked to to help settle problems. And he saw common goods that transcended self-interest in partisanship such as in the need to have the courage to oppose what he called a culture pandering. In fact, he thought it was exactly the lack of courage among the leadership of nearly all contemporary institutions to prioritize the moral and the common good above that of expedient self-interest that was essential for democracy. The point is that even in the midst of competitive politics, there are times and places for looking at the public good over personal interest.

I'd be willing to bet that if readers stopped for thirty seconds, they would be able to think of an example in business, too, of an Honest Broker. In fact, in my MBA ethics classes, I give students an assignment where they are to identify something they saw in business that they thought was good and then to justify why it was good. In nearly every case, the students end up writing about someone who filled the role of an Honest Broker. The person was a person of unimpeachable integrity, who helped to resolve a workplace conflict, or who stood up for a higher principle (assurance of quality for instance), even though it would have been more expedient to ignore a product problem.

A goal-setting metaphor: Peace Through Commerce again

The concept of moral maturity that I have already referred to is an overlooked aspect of the business world today because of our fascination with conflicts of interest. If a journalist or prosecutor can find a conflict a person has in doing their job, trouble awaits. It seems that to be ethical, one is only to do one thing; considering anything else is an unethical conflict of interest. The problem is that life is a conflict of interest. Adults manage conflicts of interests. Adults learn to prioritize, to sublimate their own well-being for that of their children, spouses, neighbors, and friends. Sometimes, they rightly prioritize their own self-interest. Sometimes they sublimate their short-term self-interest for a longer-term interest in the well-being of their community. What

Aristotle called *phronesis*, or judgment and wisdom, is a skill developed by a morally mature person to know how to prioritize among the conflicts of interest that we daily face.

One of our contemporary ethical problems in business is that our large, bureaucratic, corporate organizations do not place people in situations where they can learn to manage conflicts of interest – or other moral issues for that matter – particularly well. Research shows that we cognitively connect our actions with consequences when we are in relatively small organizations. As I showed in Chapter 1, the moral cognition for these groups are surprisingly small, as tiny as 30 and no larger than 150. In those sizes of groupings, we understand the moral consequences of our actions, whereas in large institutions it seems that our actions don't matter. If they don't matter, not only might one run the risk of getting away with something, but one also loses a sense of joy for doing something good. Both run directly counter to the development of moral maturity that prioritizes ethical responsibility over narrow self-aggrandizement. And without them, the standard left to evaluate ethical behavior tends to fall on the very thin soil of conflicts of interest.

Unfortunately, as already noted, we don't encourage corporations to act with moral maturity. We ask them to act like toddlers. One doesn't expect a toddler to act like a citizen, one expects them to follow their primal instincts until those are hemmed in by parental discipline. That is not a far cry from what we ask corporations to do: pursue short-term profitability as long as one stays out of legal trouble. Now one could say that corporations, as artificial organizations, do not possess the moral intentionality of human beings, but this ignores the fact that institutions do develop maturity, through their cultures and traditions, and are able to navigate times and places where it is necessary to place a common good ahead of short-term gratification.

For instance, regardless of how one feels about the outcome of the 2000 US Presidential election, the remarkable thing about it is that it did not engender armed conflict. That option wasn't even remotely on the table because of the confidence in the maturity of the democratic and dispute resolution processes that have developed in the United States. Those processes navigated our national dilemma imperfectly, but with a thoughtfulness that wouldn't be found in an immature democracy. Similarly, there are companies that have established, thoughtful institutional practices that consider what it means to be a citizen of the country.

So how does being an Honest Broker connect to less violence and more stability? As I have explained in the first three chapters, it does so in three ways governed by a mindful commitment to linking ethics and peace.

First, a corporate Honest Broker is accountable to the laws of a society and insists on accountability within its own corporate boundaries. A good amount of corporate scandals are simply violation of the law. Countries that have an established rule of law, dispute resolution processes, and respect for contractual and property rights tend to be less violent. I have shown that studies have demonstrated that countries more prone to bribery are also more prone to resolving disputes by violence, so to the extent companies refuse to engage in bribery, a practice outlawed in every country and condemned by every religion, a company not only avoids scandals, it contributes to an environment where there is order, stability, and peacefulness. Companies are well-versed in developing control systems to avoid illegality and they must do so if they are to have the trust of society. Doing that mindfully and with the consequence that doing so correlates with reducing the likelihood of violence in a society, seems to be a no-brainer in terms of an organizational institutionalization of Honest Brokerage that is readily achievable.

Second, a company that is an Honest Broker has a record of engagement with its constituents that engenders a trustworthiness of reliability. Organizational theorists sometimes call this building social capital. By treating others fairly, one earns their trust. This is the essence of what typically goes under the name of corporate citizenship. Companies that win recognition as good citizens are good stewards of the environment, treat local communities with respect, listen to their concerns as well as those of their shareholders and customers, and respect the rights and voice of their employees. In giving employees a voice on how to better run an organization, something that quality management programs insist upon, for instance, one also equips individuals in the corporation with an aspect of self-governance. Many management approaches, such as quality management, emphasize the development of employee voice in order to achieve higher quality and greater profitability. Might the workplace training of how to exercise voice have a positive, albeit unintended spillover effect in improving democratic political processes? There is capital, social and economic, to be gained through responsible corporate citizenship. Mindfully building internal and external dimensions of corporate community with an eye on what else it might lead to – a more stable and secure society – provides even more impetus for engaging in the fair treatment of others.

Third, businesses do what businesses do best: provide economic development and the jobs that go with it. Numerous studies show connections between poverty and violence. When businesses provide jobs, economic differentiation (i.e. not just mining resources, but adding value to them), and train managers in state-of-the-art management techniques, they contribute to conditions that favor peace over violence. That is, they do so if they provide this development in a way that supports the rule of law, including avoidance of corruption, and if they treat others fairly and justly. If they are viewed as exploitative and domineering, multinational corporations may sow the seeds for resentment and the violence that can come with it. In short, when businesses act as Honest Brokers, they can marry economic productivity with peace-making.

Finally, like an individual, companies can aim for a common good that transcends individual self-interest. That is, the human spirit desires achieving common goods as well as satisfying material wants. Such passion can engage great motivation.

My favorite, admittedly cheesy, example of this draws on my background of being a graduate of the University of Notre Dame and, for the eleven years prior to coming to George Washington University, teaching at the University of Michigan. For many reasons, I have always thought that the Notre Dame–Michigan game was the best college football rivalry in the country, but beyond the historical excellence of the programs' traditions, there is little doubt that the schools have the two best college songs. It's worth attending the game just to listen to the bands play all day long. The schools have a neat tradition of first playing the other's song before playing its own. When they play the other's song, they follow the first two characteristics of being an Honest Broker. They abide by the rules. They play the right notes, the right time signature, right key signature, right rhythm – they do everything "right". There is something to be said for that. They also build a sense of respect for politely playing the song. The fans whose song was just played aren't going to boo their own song and the fans whose band just played aren't going to boo their own band. So there is polite applause and there is something to be said for that too. But when they play their own song, it takes on an entirely different character because it is played with passion, pride, and identity. At that point, it transcends the particulars of the written music and takes on a profoundly inspiring transcendent character.

Companies are like that too. No, they don't have their own fight song. But some companies make a commitment to the well-being of the world they exist in so much part of their corporate mission that it inspires the people who work there. It is an important reason why they work there. There is a moral good to be achieved by being at that company aside from the self-interested notions of salary, promotion, and profit. Understanding that ethical actions might reduce the likelihood of violence is as powerful an existential reason for being ethical in business as one can imagine. Connecting that vision to daily work life raises the stakes for Honest Brokering, making business ethics a contributing force for the establishment of justice that drains the swamp of discontent that can spawn violence. It leads to Peace Through Commerce.

A managerial metaphor: Total Integrity Management

People are inclined to think of ethics as being something concerning dilemmas. In fact, ethics are often about difficult dilemmas. But dilemmas are dilemmas because there is no clear answer to them; if there was a clear answer, they wouldn't be dilemmas. They would be something else. Yet, being something else doesn't mean that ethics aren't still involved. Aristotle said that most ethical actions we take are not related to intractable dilemmas, but the habits that we have cultivated. Sometimes we don't even think about them because they are so much part of our nature that they don't require a formal reasoning process.[1] The most effective way to prevent ethical misconduct is through prevention, not via dilemma-solving. Preventing dilemmas requires regular attention to ethical issues so that consideration of ethics is natural. Regular consideration produces the spontaneous understanding of what to do, even when a crisis does occur.

Quality is a particularly helpful analogue in this regard. As quality management has taught, a company does not assure that it provides quality products and services by an end-of-the-line quality check. By then, it is too late to do anything about a defect. One is faced with a dilemma: swallow the costs of this defect and start from scratch or send out a defective product or service to our customer. There is no good answer. The right answer, as various quality programs show, whether Six Sigma or total quality management (TQM), is to build quality into each part of the business process. It is only by regular attention to quality that one gets quality.

The same thing is true for ethics. If the first time a company considers ethical questions is, to take the case of the Exxon Valdez, when oil is in the water, it is too late. There is no good answer about what to do about millions of barrels of oil in the water. The right answer is what kinds of processes would have prevented oil from ever getting into the water in the first place. Thus, just like quality, one produces ethical corporate culture by regularly attending to ethics, not just when things are dilemmas.

There is an alternative way of looking at these issues. In doing so, companies practice an analogue to quality management. One might characterize it as Total Integrity Management. Total Integrity Management builds and is based on trust: Hard Trust, Real Trust, and Good Trust. Or to put it in terms of a formula:

Total Integrity Management$^2 = (L_{C/J} + (R_K + J_R + U)) \times M^3$

Where

Hard Trust $= L_{C/J}$

Real Trust $= R_K + J_R + U$ and

Good Trust $= M^3$

The formula stands for the idea that Total Integrity Management is the result of complying with the law (Hard Trust), provided that the law is just ($L_{C/J}$) plus the product of "The Philosopher's Formula"[3] (Real Trust), which assesses how stakeholders are treated in terms of their Rights (R_K) plus Justice (J_R) plus Utilitarianism (U), all of which is multiplied by Music, Mediating Institutions, and More Mediation (M^3). Of course, this needs further elaboration and is meant tongue-in-cheek. If one could really come up with a number that reflects what is ethical, most people would think that something has been missed. Isn't ethics more complex than a number? And, of course, they would be right. Quantifiable numbers are very helpful, but they rest on foundations. Ethics are those foundations. Those foundations are more complex than can be simplified into a numerical equation. Still, given the proclivity of business professors as well as law-and-economics legal scholars to speak in formulae, and because this formula does roughly approximate the dimensions ethicists use to evaluate ethical business behavior, it is worth using it as a way to summarize what ethical business behavior is a result of.

Proposing for businesses to contribute to peace may seem to be a stretch, particularly since businesses may not be held in as high esteem as they once were just a few years ago. These anecdotes, however, suggest that corporations may have a positive face that could be helpful. Earlier, we saw the results of a Pew Study demonstrating that corporations are held in relatively high regard. So is there any reason for business to change what it is currently doing? Perhaps not, yet, there is a danger that the esteem in which they are held could be damaged by misbehavior. For instance, an American Enterprise Institute study in 2003 reported that only 16 percent of Americans believe that corporate executives have high ethical standards; this is down from the 25 percent of the public who thought executives had such standards and were honest in 2002.[4] Calls to rein in the excesses of executive behavior – from Jack Welch's and Richard Grasso's compensation packages to Dennis Tyco's $2 million birthday party for his wife – have left executives, in the words of a headline from *The Economist*, humbled. Rather than dealing with interviews and hobnobbing, *The Economist* pointed out, executives must resume more routine duties, such as interacting with employees to maintain their motivation.[5] Businesses themselves have undertaken focused efforts to improve their reputations and to restore trust in themselves as executives and in corporate behavior. This rebuilding of moral stature can be labeled Real Trust. Real Trust is connected to the creation and maintenance of social capital, particularly in terms of reputation, goodwill, and reliability. It is about being a good citizen in a community by being fair and ethical. It is also where most academic work in the field of corporate responsibility located in management schools tends to focus both normatively and descriptively.

Governments take a role in trying to ensure the public's trust of business by getting tough to prevent this kind of misconduct from recurring. Particularly with respect to corporate scandals, a good deal of attention focuses on tougher conflicts of interests policies, such as the Sarbanes-Oxley Act. A central component of Sarbanes-Oxley calls for clear codes of conduct, more rigorous reporting standards, independent boards of directors, personal accountability of executives for the accuracy of corporate records, and stiffer fines. At stake is not simply moral reprobation, but actual criminal conviction.[6]

Similarly in Europe, the importance of consumer privacy protection resulted in the EU Privacy Directive that mandates that companies follow strict laws to assure protection of the customer. In short, even if businesses don't see that their reputation might be helped by attending to stakeholder interests, government frequently forces them to do so.

Legal solutions, whether in the US or elsewhere, are important weapons in the battle against corporate corruption, in part because they set out the standards a corporation must live up to in order to be a law-abiding citizen. They are markers of ethical responsibility. Rules and the strict enforcement of them do create a kind of trust, one that can be called Hard Trust. Having a clear articulation of applicable standards assists making those affected by the standards accountable for their actions. If they duck that accountability, they can be convicted of a crime or lose a civil lawsuit. This specification of standards for appropriate business conduct is where the attention of legal scholars focuses.

Yet compliance with the law does not address the totality of ethical issues in business. Hard Trust interacts with Real Trust and must further be supplemented by Good Trust. Good Trust goes beyond both Real Trust and Hard Trust by not only responding to social expectations of what a person or company should do, but gets to the passionate commitment to ethical behavior as part of one's identity. It is, in essence, almost a spiritual predisposition, which can be manifested religiously and non-religiously. That spiritual component is an ineliminable dimension of our human nature and is at the heart of ethical behavior. It is an attitude or predisposition of approaching issues with a mind toward acting responsibly. This approach is one that predominates discussion of responsibility within theological circles and, in a surprising twist, appears in some popular, secular management theory.

Part Two suggests that the time has come to integrate these various approaches to corporate responsibility. Such an integration need not identify any one approach as predominant, but rather as integrated dimensions of trust-building regimes. Without Real Trust and Good Trust, even the clearest legal standards can become no more inspiring than a no-trespassing sign. That is, without an understanding of why one is a good citizen by not trespassing and why refraining from trespassing is good for one's identity, the sign simply means that one gets in trouble by trespassing.[7] Similarly, addressing issues of corporate malfeasance can be helped by codes of conduct and tough standards prohibiting conflicts of interests, but executives need to come to grips with the notion that, left to itself, a rules-based approach asks companies and the individuals working for them to be as morally mature and as ethically responsible as three-year-olds. Ethical business behavior is much more complex than rule-making and rule-following; it is about exercising informed, wise judgment on difficult (and sometimes not so difficult) issues on a regular, daily basis.

People trust business when they know the company faces stiff sanctions for violating a law. Moreover, these three approaches also represent important description approaches for the field of business ethics. To use a personal example, I serve on the editorial boards of three key journals: *Academy of Management Review*, *Business Ethics Quarterly*, and *American Business Law Journal*. In reviewing papers for publication, it is remarkable how little scholars from one discipline know about the others. That does not even include more mainline legal scholarship found in law reviews nor the theological/spiritual literature. In Part Two, I wish to use the Total Integrity Management formula as a way to capture and to integrate the various approaches to corporate responsibility with an eye toward how their integration can lead to the development of ethical corporate cultures. These cultures are the key for an entity model of the firm that can bring Peace Through Commerce. Showing how Peace Through Commerce can be pursued via Total Integrity Management is the topic of Part Two.

And so, a variety of metaphors can give us a different feel for what businesses are. They can become Honest Brokers where they have their own moral standing as entities that avoid scandal, treat others graciously and fairly, and aim for a transcendent common good. That good can be captured by the metaphor of Peace Through Commerce where businesses provide economic development, attend to rules of law, and aim for aesthetic/spiritual goods. In doing so, they will make themselves into more trustworthy institutions. Each of these attributes of Honest Brokering and of Peace Through Commerce is a kind of trust. Hard Trust is about complying with the law and, as Chapter 5 shows, there is an abundant supply of legislation and legal scholarship on this point. Real Trust is about how business integrates moral duties efficaciously into its works and, as Chapter 6 shows, there is an abundant supply of managerial scholarship on this point. Good Trust is about freeing the human spirit to aim for transcendent goods at work and, as Chapter 7 shows, there is scholarship on this point too. These three trusts can be integrated by Total Integrity Management, an approach which not only makes for more trustworthy business entities, but also for making corporations into instruments of peace.

Notes

1. See ARISTOTLE, NICHOMACHEAN ETHICS (Martin Ostward, trans., 1962); ROBERT SOLOMON, ETHICS AND EXCELLENCE: COOPERATION AND INTEGRITY IN BUSINESS (1993); and TOM MORRIS, IF ARISTOTLE RAN GENERAL MOTORS (1997).
2. While I must confess to having great affection for the acronym of Total Integrity Management, my wife characterizes it as disturbingly narcissistic, so I'll keep it written out.
3. William Frederick coined this in his 1995 book, see WILLIAM FREDERICK, VALUES, NATURE AND CULTURE IN THE AMERICAN BUSINESS CORPORATION (1995).
4. American Enterprise Institute study, see *Humbled; Chief Executives*, THE ECONOMIST (December 20, 2003) at 109.
5. *Id.* at 110.
6. Sarbanes-Oxley Act of 2002, Pub. Law No. 107–204, 116 Stat. 745 (codified as amended at 15 U.S.C. §§ 7201–7266 (2005) and in scattered sections of 18 U.S.C., 28 U.S.C. and 29 U.S.C.). Criminal provisions related to disclosures in financial statements are codified in section 404, 15 U.S.C. 7262 (Supp. II 2002).
7. This idea, with appropriate references, will be expanded upon in Chapter 6.

PART TWO

Total Integrity Management

5 | *Hard Trust*

I n Part One, I suggested that there were three contributions business could make to sustainable peace in a Track Two fashion. Peace Through Commerce comes through corporations fostering economic development, submitting to external evaluations of their actions (rule of law kinds of issues), and building of affective dimensions of community. Those dimensions do not come out of thin air. They come from values deeply rooted in our biological and even pre-biological nature: economizing, power-aggrandizing, and ecologizing. They also extrude into business life in a different way. Each represents an approach to defining corporate responsibility. From schools of management, one finds normative and strategic arguments for how ethics can be integrated into business. From law schools and legal scholarship, one finds constraints to rein in egregious behavior. From aesthetic and spiritual perspectives, one finds challenges for connecting moral excellence and personal meaning in work. Unfortunately, these three approaches to business ethics rarely interact with each other. Not only is the twenty-first century a time and season for business to contribute to sustainable peace, it is also a time and season for these approaches to be integrated. Part Two of this book suggests that integrity is indeed a metaphor for the twenty-first century for four reasons.

First, as its root suggests, integrity is a holistic concept and so integrating various approaches to business ethics is a way to build upon strengths of each of the approaches. Second, like quality, ethics is best approached as a way to prevent problems rather than wrestling with intractable dilemmas. Thus, just as total quality management proposed an integrative way to solve quality problems, so too could Total Integrity Management do the same for business ethics. Third, integrity and trust are buzzwords in business today and for good reason. They express a set of behaviors, attitudes, and sentiments necessary for business legitimacy and sustainability. While they may need refining, business people like to talk about them. The three kinds of trust are, of course, derived from our nature and pointed in the direction of Peace Through Commerce suggesting a fourth timely reason for discussing them: there is a needed payoff at this time of our history. And so, Total Integrity Management is a way to think about business ethics holistically, historically, and hopefully. This chapter begins with some baseline considerations of the law, Hard Trust.

Basic rules of Hard Trust

Laws aren't so bad

Laws get a bad rap. No one much likes them. Almost always when I begin a presentation, I tell a joke about lawyers. People love to hear lawyer jokes. Other than talking about the weather, I sometimes think it may be the most common icebreaker for conversations. People may not have read a single word of Shakespeare, but they know "first, let's kill all the lawyers" (yanking the quote a bit out of context). Once I had a student actually upset about my telling lawyer jokes (her husband was a lawyer and she thought such jokes were offensive), but the reaction to this effort to stifle lawyer jokes with political correctness seems not to have worked, particularly given the bewildered reaction by her classmates.

Public antipathy about law-related professions extends beyond lawyers. Law-makers, mainly politicians, receive public ridicule. The law-making function of other professions frequently becomes the butt of comedy. How many movies about teenage shenanigans use a strict, fussy school principal or teacher as the foil for a plot focused on getting around stuffy rules, protesting them, or simply ignoring them altogether?

I suspect that it is not simply lawyers, politicians, or school principals that people dislike. Rules themselves are unpopular. Rules restrict us. Written for a broad group of people, they always are too broad and demand exceptions that threaten to undermine the perceived fairness of the rule itself. Rules always have to be interpreted, which creates more exceptions and complaints about how these exceptions and interpretations are made. They limit what we'd like to do even when they protect us from objectionable things others may do to us.

The problem is that laws are crucial. And they are much better than the alternative. Were it not for laws, we would be subject to the whims of the powerful with no checks against them. This is not only true in a repressive regime; it is even so in a democratic country. When I practiced law, for instance, a public official of a small governmental body – a very fine person – called me to complain that she had been unfairly criticized in the newspaper. The official was very offended and wanted the complaining citizen to be put in jail for slander. This was wildly out of character for the public official; she would have never dreamed of such a thing had it not been for her position. Of course, I explained that the First Amendment to the Constitution protects the citizen. She knew this, but it was the first time this protection had been applied in a way to "harm" her. She chafed at my answer, but grudgingly agreed that it was right. The interesting thing about her reaction is how easy it is for a ruler to want to use their power to "get back" at a citizen. Even the small amount of power she had had skewed her judgment. It was also testament to the importance of a law that protected citizens and restrained an official. Laws, at least drawn from democratic principles and processes, check power.

They also create order. As noted in Chapter 2, human beings do live in ordered societies. Laws limit the extent to which that order is based on hierarchy and brute force and influence. The law, of course, often fails at this. Laws can be twisted by those with power too, but laws are an expression, admittedly imperfectly, of what a society values. At least in large societies, where informal decision-making is not possible, laws are a step in the right direction of checking power of the powerful.

In my example of the public official, there are two other noteworthy points. First, the First Amendment that protected the cranky citizen is important because it protects voice. Voice is a crucial element of laws that head in the right direction of good laws and sustainable peace. Second, the protection of voice in corporations has a long way to go compared with that of democratic society. It will become a significant, recommended trait of Hard Trust.

Hard Trust is about how to make sure that people do what they are supposed to do. It is "hard" because there is a coercive enforcement mechanism. Most people would not consider this as "trust" because there is no sense of one person being dependent on another person, or parties relying on each other in a mutually beneficial way. These kinds of trust are more along the lines of the following chapter's discussion of Real Trust. Yet legal duties are very important to creating behavior that cause people to trust business. If a customer or an employee knows that a company's failure to follow safety standards or fair employment practices could result in a lawsuit, the consumer or employee can rely more on the company. This is true even if the company's executives do not care much about these stakeholders. A third party, typically but not always government, requires the company to pay attention to these constituents whether the company wants to do so or not. As a result, there is a level of public trust in business.

In a slightly different way, the rise of the Internet along with non-government organization (NGO) advocacy groups make public opinion an effective weapon against corporate misbehavior. Spoil the environment and watch how an NGO like Greenpeace responds. Moreover, even with associations and companies, rules and policies abound. A few years ago, I taught a course on ethics for the National Association of Securities Dealers (NASD). One of the first things I did was attempt to summarize the basic rules for securities dealers under the rules of the NASD. I filled about seventy Powerpoint slides with just the *headings* of NASD's rules in an exceptionally small font. No one can know that many detailed rules. Yet, to gain the trust of the public, securities dealers are held accountable for following them. It provides a level of trust in the markets. Obviously in this example, rules will not be enough because no one can create rules for every subject and also because at some point, a large maker of rules can neither be made sense of nor absorbed. At the same time, rules do make sense in a mobile world where people of all kinds of different cultures, many with different backgrounds, need to know what the rules are for their particular company and industry.

Hard Trust is, in one sense, about (a) business law and (b) public regulation of business. Both are immense subjects. Business law entails a bewildering number of ways that the legal system holds business accountable for its actions. This includes, for instance, basic rules of contract, property, and tort law. Businesses may be able to claim they are not responsible for, say, a product defect, but no matter how hard they try, courts may well still hold them liable for a defective product or an implied warranty. Regulation, from environmental to consumer protection to minimum wage laws, to name just a few, also provide minimum floors for public trust in business.

Obviously, many laws may apply to a particular business. Securities dealers have rules very different than the farmers who used to be my clients when I practiced law. Table 5.1 lists a representative sampling of these laws, which include securities issues, workplace safety, consumer safety, and antitrust laws. Such laws typically attempt to counteract

Table 5.1. Hard Trust: legal aspects

Legal Rule	Relevant Duty	Examples
Fiduciary Duties	Duty of Loyalty	Conflicts of Interests
		Lawful Directives
	Duty of Care	Attention to Business
	Business Judgment	Constituents Wrigley and Paramount
Federal Sentencing Guidelines	Establishment of Compliance	Codes of Conduct
		Audit Plan
		Written Compliance Structure
		Handbook/Personnel Policies
	High-Level Supervision	More Senior The Better
		Prevention and Detection Program
		Divisional Responsibility
	Non-Delegation to Questionable Persons	Past Lawbreakers
		Screen for Future Lawbreakers
	Steps to Communicate Standards	Bulletins, Newsletters, Posters
		Direct Policy Distribution
		Seminars and Training
	Steps to Achieve Standards	Monitoring
		Auditing
		Ombuds-like Reporting
		Ethics Questionnaires
	Consistent Enforcement and Discipline	Suspension, Pay Changes, Firing, etc.
	Reasonable Response After Detection	Size
		Likelihood
		Prior History
Sarbanes-Oxley	Personal Liabilities and Accountabilities of CEO and CFO	Certification of Reports
		Establishment of Internal Controls
		Evaluation of Effectiveness of Controls
	Conflicts of Interest	Executive Compensation Rules
		Disclosure of Insider Trading: 2nd Day Rather than 10th Day
		Blackout on Trading by Officers and Directors Re Pension Plans
	Audit Committee Authority and Independence	Disclose (or Explain Why Not) Committee has One Financial Expert
		Comprised of Independent Directors
		Rotation Requirement for Primary Audit Partner

Table 5.1. Hard Trust: legal aspects (continued)

Legal Rule	Relevant Duty	Examples
	Disclosure Requirements and Independence	Real-Time Disclosure
		Off-Balance-Sheet Clarification Requirements
		Internal Control Report Signed by Auditors
	Whistleblower Protection and Legal Ethics Rules	Protection of Whistleblowing Employees
		Responsibility of Attorneys to Report Non-Compliance
	Code of Conduct and Ethics	Executives and Directors, but also Throughout Company
Other Regulatory Examples	Securities Beyond SOX	SEC; Other Federal; State
	Consumer Safety	FTC; Other Federal; State
	Workplace Safety	OSHA; Other Federal; State
	Environmental	EPA; Other Federal; State
	Antitrust	Justice; State
	Intellectual Property	PTO; Other Federal; State
	International	Varies Per Jurisdiction
Self-Regulation and Policies	Associational Rules	NASD and NYSE Examples
	Corporate Policies	Internal Rules of Organization Such as Receipt of Gifts (GM)

corporate misbehavior such as by checking securities fraud, unsafe working practices, unsafe products, and collusion. The range of these laws is vast, but critically important, and require corporations to address regulatory issues throughout the workplace rather than simply at the level of the General Counsel.

This chapter cannot go into all of these various laws. Certainly, businesses have to attend to the requirements of the laws applicable to the specific industry. Two kinds of laws, though, are worth delving into a bit more. One pertains to the general duties of managers and the other requires an in-depth analysis of a reflexive approach.

Basic duties

Perhaps the most important duty is the fiduciary obligation managers owe to the shareholders of the corporation. While some people argue that managers should owe duties to other corporate constituents, no one really challenges the idea that managers have primary duties to the owners of the organization. In large part, most of what the turn-of-the-century scandals were about was this breach of fiduciary duty. Rather than looking out for the interests of shareholders, executives from Enron, Worldcom, and Global Crossing were more interested in their own personal well-being, even at the expense of the shareholders. Two kinds of managerial duties are important.

The first is the duty of loyalty. The duty of loyalty represents the agency issue in corporations. Managers are agents of the shareholders and so have a duty to carry out the lawful commands of those principals. They are not to use their position for their own benefit, but rather are to prioritize the interests of their boss, the shareholders. A huge amount of scholarship addresses how to make sure that agents don't "shirk" their duties.[1]

Conflicts of interest are the classic example of the duty of loyalty. Directors who serve on boards while also running companies doing business with the company pose a conflicts of interest problem. Refusal and approval by non-interested directors are typically the solutions mandated in order to overcome such conflicts problems. Executives profiting from inside information, particularly at the expense of employee-investors, such as through a pension plan funded by company stock, is another example. Bribery is another instance of a conflict of interest. Individuals use a position for their own gain rather than for that of the company. Yet another example lies in employees leaving a company to work for a competitor. In doing so, they take with them knowledge developed at their old company and sometimes they also take with them protected secrets. These then lead companies to require signing of non-compete contracts.[2]

To repeat a central point of Chapter 1, within business schools, one frequently hears an admonition that the duty of managers is to maximize shareholder value. Legally, however, this duty is more accurately stated as managers have the duty to carry out the lawful directives of shareholders. Profitability will almost always be one of those directives; however, shareholders can also have other non-financial objectives. Family businesses are examples of this, where one of the objectives could be the ongoing employment of family members. In addition, a closely held business might have goals of being active within the community.

More complexly, when corporations go public, they may sometimes do so with a statement of how the corporation goes about its work. Thus, when Johnson & Johnson went public in the 1940s, it issued its aforementioned *Credo* which prioritizes its obligations to various constituents beginning with consumers and then to employees, suppliers, and community before ending with the shareholders.[3] Similarly when Timberland went public, it also declared how it played the game.[4] As a result, in their treatise on corporate law, Daniel Fischel and Frank Easterbrook state that it does not violate any notions of corporate governance if the *New York Times* pursues a goal of journalistic excellence in addition to shareholder profitability.[5] In other words, if shareholders wish their corporation to pursue non-financial objectives, managers should do so. In corporations without such mission statements and with thousands or even millions of shareholders, the only common denominator of shareholder interest may be financial. Yet it is important to recognize that, under contemporary American governance rules, the duty is broader than to maximize financial results.

I realize that I have already made this argument, but it so infrequently gets internalized, I want to emphasize that legally, the situation is more complex. Managers are not to simply maximize profitability, they are to carry out the lawful directives of shareholders. Although in the classic case of *Dodge vs. Ford*,[6] the Court held that even Henry Ford as CEO of Ford Motor Company had to place the interests of shareholders ahead of his own personal desires to provide better pay to employees and lower cost vehicles to customers,[7] a later case, *Shlensky vs. Wrigley*,[8] held that the owners of the Chicago Cubs could refuse to play night baseball games even if the shareholders would profit by them doing so.[9] In that case, the Court said that as long as there was a plausible connection between a corporate activity and a business strategy, even one that connected with a non-shareholder goal (in this case, family entertainment provided by playing day baseball), it could be justified. The Business Judgment Rule allows for managers to utilize discretion of what might be in the long-term interest of shareholders. In these situations, the legal duty of managers is to put the interests of shareholders first, but courts acknowledge that managers have significant leeway in determining how the shareholders are best benefited. More theoretically, economists such as Milton Friedman go further in arguing that a managerial direction to spend corporate funds on philanthropic initiatives would be the same as theft unless the charitable purpose contributed to economic value for the shareholders.[10]

The second major legal duty is the duty of care. The duty of care is concerned with the attention directors provide to the management of the company. Directors are expected to devote the same attention to corporate efforts as they would to their individual financial affairs. This applies to arguments about excessive CEO compensation insofar as directors don't rein in exorbitant pay. In the wake of the corporate scandals, directors are increasingly being held to higher standards of duty of care in order to make sure they are doing their jobs. What was once thought of as an easy job, being a director potentially subjects one to significant liability, particularly if rigorous attention is not paid to one's duties.

The duty of loyalty and the duty of care are well-established legal constraints regulating the behavior of directors of corporations. They stand for the notion that managers lose a range of freedom when accepting employment with a company. At the same time, they don't completely forfeit their discretion. Specific laws pertaining to conflicts of interest, bribery, and the corporate constituency statutes are attempts to specify the balance of discretion and duty. Complicating that balance is an ambivalence people feel about corporations. While corporations provide many benefits, there is also a long-standing expectation that companies are to be citizens too and to pay attention to public goods. And so, while in theory there is an argument that corporations should focus solely on shareholders, there is also a sense that corporations should benefit society. This explains why there is continued support for corporations to make contributions to social goods as well.

A reflexive model: the Federal Sentencing Guidelines[11]

Consistent with Chapter 3's attention to demands that corporations develop cultures that institutionalize legal compliance, several legal mechanisms ask companies to do the same on a variety of issues. While Sarbanes-Oxley (SOX) gets the most attention, the more comprehensive formulation of these reflexive approaches is the Federal Sentencing Guidelines. Because these Guidelines are exactly the kinds of laws that Hard Trust uses today to establish the incentives to create real entity corporate cultures, it is worth detailing their history and content.

The "old" organizational Sentencing Guidelines

Organizational criminal liability and the 1991 Sentencing Guidelines

An organization is vicariously liable for the criminal acts of its employees and agents done within the scope of their actual or apparent authority and with the intent to benefit the organization.[12] Thus, an organization is liable when it knowingly and intentionally authorizes an agent to act illegally on its behalf (i.e., actual authority) or where a third party reasonably believes that the agent was expressly authorized to take the action resulting in criminal violation (i.e., apparent authority).[13] In federal court, criminal liability is imposed regardless of the agent's position within the organization.[14] Moreover, criminal liability may be imputed to an organization even where the organization received no actual benefit from the criminal conduct; the agent must only intend to bestow some benefit, however minimal, on the organization.[15] Even if an organization expressly prohibits the illegal conduct and uses its best efforts to prevent any wrongdoing, it may still be held criminally liable for its agents' illegal acts.[16] Although an organization may not be imprisoned, it can be fined, sentenced to probation, ordered to make restitution, required to issue public notices of conviction and apology, or to forfeit assets.[17]

During the 1980s, Congress perceived that judges were too lenient in sentencing dangerous criminals and that "glaring disparities" in sentencing could be "traced directly to the unfettered discretion the law confers on those judges and parole authorities [that implement] the sentence."[18] To have more predictable and determinate sentencing, Congress passed the Sentencing Reform Act of 1984 (the Act). Under the Act, Congress created an independent agency of the federal judiciary (the Commission) to develop sentencing guidelines and policy statements for judges to use when sentencing defendants convicted of federal crimes. The Act's primary purpose was to limit federal judges' discretion in handling indeterminate sentencing under the guise of ensuring that the "ends of justice" were properly and equally satisfied.[19]

In 1991, the Commission promulgated rules for the sentencing of organizations convicted of committing federal felonies and Class A misdemeanors, which are located in Chapter 8 of the Sentencing Guidelines.[20] With respect to organizational crime, the Commission adopted a "carrot and stick" approach. The Guidelines reward organizations that create an "effective compliance program" to prevent and detect violations of the law through mitigation of proscribed fines or sentences and by severely punishing organizations that are involved in, condone, or tolerate criminal activity.[21] As originally adopted, the Guidelines define an "effective program to prevent and detect violations of law" as a "program that has been reasonably designed, implemented, and enforced so as to prevent and detect the instant offense".[22] The 1991 Guidelines provide that the "hallmark" of an effective program is "that the organization exercises due diligence in seeking to prevent and detect criminal conduct by its employees and other agents".[23] "Due diligence" requires "at a minimum" that the organization adopt a compliance program and that it:

(1) Establishes standards and procedures which are "reasonably capable of reducing the prospect of criminal conduct"
(2) Appoints "high-level personnel" to oversee the program
(3) Ensures that authority in the program is not given to those that have "a propensity to engage in criminal conduct"
(4) Communicates the program's requirements to all employees and agents
(5) Ensures compliance through monitoring and auditing
(6) Enforces the program through "appropriate disciplinary mechanisms"
(7) Once a violation has occurred, updates the program to ensure effectiveness.[24]

An organization's failure to satisfy these seven minimum requirements results in increased sanctions for criminal misconduct. As the Commission's chairperson explained: "These guidelines provide incentives for voluntary reporting and cooperation but punish an organization's failure to self-police."[25] An organization that incorporates all seven requirements, self-reports, cooperates, and accepts responsibility for the illegal conduct of their employees may receive up to a 95 percent reduction in their federal fines.[26] In contrast, organizations that fail to comply with these requirements may be subject to a 400 percent increase in their federal fines.[27] The fines imposed on an organization for violating federal law can be substantial. In 2001, the average fine for organizations was $2,154,929 (ten times greater than in 1995) and the median fine was $60,000 (twice the amount in 1995).[28]

Even more important than sentence reduction, the presence or absence of an effective compliance program can determine whether

Table 5.2. Federal Sentencing Guidelines fines

Size	Add 5 Points	More than 5,000 Employees (or Unit Thereof) and High-Level Participation or Condoning of Action
	Add 4 Points	More than 1,000 Employees (or Unit Thereof) and High-Level Participation or Condoning of Action
	Add 3 Points	More than 200 Employees (or Unit Thereof) and High-Level Participation or Condoning of Action
	Add 2 Points	More than 50 Employees (or Unit Thereof) and High-Level Participation or Condoning of Action
	Add 1 Point	More than 10 Employees (or Unit Thereof) and High-Level Participation or Condoning of Action
Prior History	Add 2 Points	Organization (or Separate Line) Committed any Part of Offense Within 5 Years of Criminal Adjudication of Similar Misconduct or Civil Adjudication of 2 or More Similar Misconduct
	Add 1 Point	Organization (or Separate Line) Committed any Part of Offense as Determined in Civil Adjudication of 1 Similar Misconduct
Order Violation	Add 2 Points	Offense Violated Judicial Order (other than probation) or if Organization Violated Condition of Probation By Engaging in Similar Misconduct
	Add 1 Point	Offense Violated Condition of Probation
Obstruction of Justice	Add 3 Points	Organization Willfully Obstructed Justice
Effective Program	Subtract 3 Points	Offense Occurred Despite Effective Program, but No Subtraction if High-Level Personnel Involved (and Unit had more than 200 Employees) and Further if Organization Unreasonably Delayed in Reporting the Offense to Government Authorities After Learning About it
Self-Reporting and Cooperation	Subtract 5 Points	Before Imminent Threat of Disclosure of Investigation, Reasonably and Promptly Reported, Fully Cooperated, and Accepted Responsibility
	Subtract 2 Points	Fully Cooperated and Accepted Responsibility
	Subtract 1 Point	

*Table 5.3. Federal Sentencing Guidelines
offense level fine table*

Offense Level	Amount
6 or less	$5,000
7	$7,500
8	$10,000
9	$15,000
10	$20,000
11	$30,000
12	$40,000
13	$60,000
14	$85,000
15	$125,000
16	$175,000
17	$250,000
18	$350,000
19	$500,000
20	$650,000
21	$910,000
22	$1,200,000
23	$1,600,000
24	$2,100,000
25	$2,800,000
26	$3,700,000
27	$4,800,000
28	$6,300,000
29	$8,100,000
30	$10,500,000
31	$13,500,000
32	$17,500,000
33	$22,000,000
34	$28,500,000
35	$36,000,000
36	$45,500,000
37	$57,500,000
38 or more	$72,500,000

or not prosecutors will initiate criminal proceedings against an organization. For example, from approximately 2000 to 2004, of the 377 organizations sentenced under the Guidelines, only 16 had any type of compliance program.[29] From 1993 to 2001, 812 organizations were sentenced under the Guidelines, but only three of those organizations received a sentence reduction for having an effective compliance program.[30]

The impact of the 1991 Guidelines

The Guidelines have led to significant changes by corporations. Compliance programs are now standard practice, with over 90 percent of large corporations having an ethics code.[31] The Ethics Officer Association, founded in 1992 with only a handful of members, now has over 1,000 members.[32]

Despite the widespread use of compliance programs, critics have challenged their effectiveness as a regulatory measure for several different reasons. The primary basis for many of these criticisms is the fear of cosmetic compliance: firms adopting only the appearance of a compliance program. According to one analysis, the adoption of these codes are commonly viewed by employees "as public relations vehicles or 'just a piece of paper'".[33] Other studies found that these "codes" were "unrealistic and failed to address practical management issues" and, thus, were largely ignored by employees.[34] According to Paul Fiorelli, a member of the Commission's Advisory Group, since the adoption of the Guidelines organizations developed "token" or "paper" compliance programs by merely "checking the boxes" to comply with the seven minimum requirements of the Guidelines.[35]

William Laufer identifies the "paradox of compliance", where a moral hazard problem results from firms using compliance programs simply as insurance against prosecution. Due to this "insurance", firms take less care to prevent wrongdoing, which may result in more wrongful behavior.[36] Laufer also identifies a problem of "reverse whistle blowing".[37] Under the Guidelines, firms receive leniency for working with prosecutors and providing them with information. However, this often results in senior managers providing prosecutors with information to implicate lower-level managers and protect the senior managers from liability (as well as preventing a more thorough investigation of the crime). Although that may be fair when the lower level manager is to blame, it creates problems when the firm has a culture of encouraging (and perhaps even rewarding) such wrongful behavior from its employees.

The reverse whistle blowing phenomena identified by Laufer shows how, in practice, the Guidelines are being used in a manner that goes directly against their intended purpose. The Guidelines were, in part, a recognition that illegal corporate behavior typically cannot be fully explained by the "character flaws" of one individual committing the offense.[38] The Guidelines were enacted to recognize organizations' culpability in encouraging and influencing employee misconduct.

There is also a general concern that the compliance programs adopted in response to the Guidelines are inefficient. That is, they create costs for firms that are not justified by the benefits they provide society.[39] For example, firms that genuinely seek to comply with the law must adopt the required compliance program – regardless of the other methods they use to ensure ethical behavior – to ensure they receive sentencing mitigation under the Guidelines if something does go wrong.[40] For other firms, simply forcing them to adopt a compliance program creates significant costs, but does little to prevent misconduct if implemented improperly.

Simply adopting a compliance program with the aforementioned seven factors does not assure a successful program; instead it depends on how the company approaches the program. Paine[41] argued that firms could adopt either a compliance-based or an integrity-based approach. Under a compliance-based program, firms typically over-emphasize threat of detection and punishment for misconduct, which can be counter-productive if employees view the program as simply a tool to achieve leniency from prosecutors and to protect top management from blame.[42] An integrity-based approach, on the other hand, seeks to develop legitimacy with the employees and focuses on internally developed organizational values. Under this approach, obeying the law "is viewed as a positive aspect of organizational life, rather than an unwelcome constraint imposed by external authorities".[43]

The sum of these criticisms is the idea that it is not simply the adoption of a compliance program that matters, but the culture of the organization that is the most important determinate for influencing employees' behavior (either positively or negatively). Although a good deal of ink has been spilt on the Enron case, a brief review and analysis is useful to demonstrate both the importance of corporate culture and the problems with the 1991 Guidelines.[44]

As is well known, Enron filed bankruptcy in December 2001 with debts over $100 billion amid allegations that it artificially boosted profits totaling over $1 billion. Enron, however, had a model code of ethics[45] that likely satisfied the seven requirements of the Guidelines. The vision statement in Enron's code of ethics was "RICE", which stood for "Respect, Integrity, Communication, and Excellence".[46] Enron's code "prohibited its employees from having financial or a management role in Enron's special purpose entities unless the chairman and the CEO determined that such participation would not adversely affect the best interests of the company".[47] However, Enron's directors waived the company's code of ethics in June 1999 to allegedly permit Enron's former CFO, Andrew Fastow, and former Enron employee, Michael Koppers, to run and financially benefit from Enron's special purpose entities.[48] In fact, three times in a twelve-month period, Enron's board of directors waived the code of ethics to permit transactions with its special purpose entities.[49] More importantly, the values of the vision statement appeared to be exactly opposite of the true culture that existed there.

Enron had developed a culture of pushing the law to the limit and encouraging the discovery of loopholes to benefit the firm. As one commentator on Enron's culture notes, "law and rules were viewed as hindering innovation, creativity, and the entrepreneurial spirit rather than being a necessary foundation for them".[50] For example, Enron's special purpose entities pushed the limits of technical compliance with the General Accounting Principles (GAP), which permitted Enron to mislead investors and creditors by avoiding disclosure of certain assets and liabilities.[51] Likewise, at all levels of the organization, employees were apparently rewarded for the results they achieved, without concern for how those results were achieved. Furthermore, conflicts of interests were seemingly practiced at the upper levels of management who did little to discourage such practices at lower levels. For example, in 1997, Enron acquired a company co-owned by the son of Chairman Kenneth Lay.[52] In addition, employees claim they were encouraged to use a travel agency operated by Lay's sister.[53]

The payouts for success – however it was achieved – were tremendous. For the most part, Enron removed seniority-based pay scales and replaced them with a twice-yearly, performance-based bonus system where all employees were ranked against each other.[54] A single committee of twenty managers that required unanimous consent did the performance reviews. This caused employees to fear raising any concerns about company practices because upsetting just one committee member could mean a poor performance review.[55] Enron's reward system gave significantly higher payouts to the top individual performers, which worked against teamwork and encouraged individuals to refuse to share information, and in some cases, resulted in employees stealing information from each other.[56] Likewise, it created tremendous pressures to continually improve earnings, as that was what was rewarded. This encouraged managers to push the boundaries of accounting practices further and further every year.[57]

A checks-and-balances system was either absent or seriously flawed. One commentator noted that Enron was missing "adult supervision".[58] New employees, some straight out of undergraduate business programs, could make multi-million dollar decisions without approval. In other cases, recent MBAs were appointed to the risk-management group and were expected to review proposals written by the same senior managers that wrote their performance evaluations.[59] In addition, the risk and control group reported to Skilling and not the board of directors.[60]

Fiorelli facetiously asked, "Assume that Enron successfully emerges from bankruptcy. Should it qualify for reductions from federal criminal fines because it had an 'ethics' program?"[61] The Enron example clearly shows the limits of the 1991 Guidelines approach. For example, even with a model code of ethics, how the organization rewards employees and controls risks can have a negative, and significantly stronger, impact on employee behavior. As Laufer argues, the presence of a compliance program may actually lead some firms to further encourage a culture that supports wrongful behavior.[62] The next section considers the reaction of the Sentencing Commission to such problems.

The Amendments to the Sentencing Guidelines

The ad hoc advisory group and the call for an increased focus on ethics

Enron and the various other ethics scandals at the start of the century led to a closer look at compliance programs. In January 2003, Deputy Attorney General Larry D. Thompson issued a Memorandum to all US attorneys requiring them to "determine whether a corporation's compliance program is merely a 'paper program' or whether it was designed and implemented in an effective manner".[63] If the compliance program was merely a "paper program", Thompson instructed US Attorneys to strongly consider this factor in evaluating whether to initiate criminal prosecution against an organization.[64]

Prior to that, in 2002, in response to the ten-year anniversary of the Guidelines, the Commission formed an ad hoc advisory group (the Advisory Group) to review the general effectiveness of the Guidelines for organizations.[65] The Sarbanes-Oxley Act also suggested such a review. The Commission conducted numerous public hearings as part of this review.

During the hearings, various commentators urged the Advisory Group to include "ethics" as a requirement under the Guidelines. Dov Seidman, Chief Executive Officer of Legal Research Network, stated, "by requiring only that an organization promote a culture that encourages a commitment to compliance with the law, I believe the advisory group short … you can't have a culture of compliance unless you also have a culture of ethics".[66] Seidman went on to state his concern that if ethics was not addressed, then the Guidelines would "foster the same type of corporate cultures that allowed individuals to seek out loopholes in the law".[67] Similarly, Bill Lytton, former counsel to Presidents Reagan and Bush, testified that the overarching goal in amending the Guidelines should be to "provid[e] and foster [an] atmosphere where people who want to do the right thing are encouraged to do it and people who don't want to do the right thing are found out and prevented from doing it".[68] Stuart Gillman, President of the Ethics Resource Center, testified that the Guidelines must "encourage organizations to foster ethical cultures, to ensure focus on the intent of legal and regulatory requirements as opposed to mere technical compliance that can potentially circumvent the intent or spirit of law or regulation".[69]

After these hearings, the Advisory Group concluded that the "effectiveness of compliance programs could be enhanced if, in addition to due diligence in maintaining compliance programs, organizations also took steps to build cultures that encouraged employee commitment to compliance".[70] As a result, the Commission modified the Guidelines to require organizations to specifically establish a "compliance and ethics program".[71] To have an "effective compliance and ethics program" an organization must both "exercise due diligence to prevent and detect criminal conduct" and "otherwise promote an organizational culture that encourages ethical conduct and a commitment to compliance with the law".[72]

In its commentary, the Advisory Report stated that:

organizational culture, in this context, has come to be defined as the shared set of norms and beliefs that guide individual and organizational behavior. These norms and beliefs are shaped by leadership of the organization, are often expressed as shared values or guiding principles, and are reinforced by various systems and procedures throughout the organization.[73]

One such value is "law compliance",[74] however, the Advisory Report sends conflicting messages on what they require beyond compliance. In one place, the Advisory Report notes their "emphasis on ethics and values" and states that it is consistent with an emphasis on "honest and ethical conduct" found in the Sarbanes-Oxley Act of 2002, and recent changes to the listing requirements of the New York Stock Exchange and Securities and Exchange Commission regulations.[75]

On the other hand, the new Guidelines simply define a "compliance and ethics program" as a "program designed to prevent and detect criminal conduct".[76] The Advisory Report notes that "At a minimum, such cultures will promote compliance with the law. To the extent that they encourage further ethical conduct, the organization and the community will benefit in additional ways."[77] The Advisory Report also states:

It is important to note, however, that this recommendation will not impose upon organizations anything more than the law requires, nor will it conflict with industry-specific regulatory requirements. It is also intended to avoid requiring prosecutors to litigate and judges to determine whether an organization has a good 'set of values' or appropriate 'ethical standards,' subjects which are very difficult, if not impossible, to evaluate in an objective, consistent manner.[78]

Despite these seemingly conflicting statements, it does appear that the Guidelines encourage judges and prosecutors to look for evidence of an ethical corporate culture, and not simply look for an effective compliance program. The Guidelines and Advisory Report clearly specify that an effective compliance program requires a firm to both "exercise due diligence to prevent and detect criminal conduct" and develop an ethical culture.[79] While the goal is compliance with the law, these are two separate but complementary means of achieving that end.

The Advisory Group recognized that the new Guidelines have "the dual objectives of reasonable prevention and positive culture".[80] Although the Advisory Report indicates that the Commission is not imposing duties on the organization beyond what the law requires, their chosen means clearly requires firms to comply with the "spirit of the law" and not just the "letter of the law". For example, the Advisory Report stated that ethical organizational cultures are "driven by values that go beyond aiming for the lowest possible standards of compliance".[81]

The minimum requirements for establishing an effective compliance program and ethical culture are based on the seven requirements of the 1991 Guidelines, but include some significant changes. The next section reviews those changes.

Amendments to the requirements for an effective program

First, the Guidelines created a new definition of compliance "standards and procedures" (Step 1), as "standards of conduct and internal control systems that are reasonably capable of reducing the likelihood of violations of the law".[82] This is consistent with changes to Step 7 that require corporations to continually assess the risk of criminal conduct occurring. Previously, organizations were only required to update their programs after a violation had occurred. Under the new guidelines, firms are responsible for updating their programs on a continuing basis to protect against the risk of violations. Together, these changes require more than merely adopting a manual that sets forth ethical guidelines for the organization. Instead, organizations must continually refine their programs to address changing circumstances and new risks. According to the Commission, "standards of conduct and internal controls are essential aspects of effective compliance programs and ... these measures should be developed, implemented, and evaluated in terms of their impact on reducing the likelihood of violations of the law."[83]

Second, the Commission sought to clarify leadership responsibilities. In the prior Guidelines, the role of leadership was only addressed by requiring that a high-level official oversee the program (Step 2).[84] Based on its investigation, the Advisory Group found that a key lesson from the corporate scandals was the lack of "specification of the roles of organizational leadership in the organizational sentencing guidelines".[85] Accordingly, the new guidelines sought to correct this problem in a few different ways. First, the new Guidelines require that the "governing authority" (i.e., the board of directors) must be "knowl-edgeable" about the compliance and ethics program (which includes information on the compliance risks facing the firm and the programs installed to combat those risks) and be "proactive" in evaluating, monitoring, and managing this program.[86] Second, the Guidelines require that "high-level personnel" must "ensure" that the organization has an effective compliance plan.[87] This includes a "Chief Ethics Officer". In short, the Chief Ethics Officer must be "within the high-level personnel of the organization", have the ability to monitor the organization, and have the access to report violations of the law to the appropriate governing body.[88] Third, those individuals with "day-to-day operational responsibility" must "be given adequate resources, appropriate authority, and direct access to the governing authority or appropriate subgroup of the governing authority". Together, these provisions reflect the philosophy that a positive organizational culture is established by requiring all levels of the organization – the top, middle, and bottom – to be active in promoting the appropriate "orga-nizational tone".[89]

Third, the Commission made it clear that ethics and compliance training (Step 4) was mandatory (that is, simply disseminating infor-mation on the program is not sufficient) and that all employees, includ-ing the board of directors and high-level employees, must receive training.[90] In addition, the Advisory Report indicated that educating employees about compliance requirements was not enough, and that organizations must also motivate all employees to comply.[91] This is consistent with changes to Step 6, which provides that organizations should not only punish those that violate the ethics and compliance program, but they should also provide positive incentives for indivi-duals to comply. This is a continuation of the Commission's philoso-phy on using a "carrot and stick" to compel changes in an organization.

Fourth, the Guidelines require the program to include a system that allows employees to report misconduct and seek guidance without fear of retaliation (Step 5). The prior version was worded such that these systems were not mandatory.[92] Based on the testimony and evidence provided to the Advisory Group, there were two common problems plaguing companies who were ultimately convicted of a crime. The first problem was that employees or management knew or suspected that illegal conduct was occurring within the organization, but did not report it because they feared "some sort of retribution" or that their jobs would be in jeopardy.[93] As a result, employees remained silent, thereby allowing the illegal conduct to continue. The second problem was that most organizations lacked any mechanism to allow employees to report wrongful conduct confidentially.[94] The lack of confidentiality and fear of retaliation were the major road blocks to allowing employees to report an organization's criminal conduct. Based on the Advisory Group's investigation, it found that 44 percent of all non-management employees do not report the misconduct they observe.[95] Of those individuals, 57 percent failed to report because they felt that such a report would not be kept confidential, 41 percent feared retaliation from their manager, and 30 percent believed that co-workers would retaliate for any report of wrongdoing.[96] The purpose of this provision is to foster an organizational culture that promotes, not penalizes employees who report violations of the law.

Overall, the new guidelines require firms to be more proactive in designing and updating their programs. Organizations are also encouraged to consider not only the risk of illegal activities by employees, but also ethical lapses.[97]

An assessment of the amendments

The most important question, of course, is whether the Guidelines will make a difference in improving the behavior of organizations. Will the guidelines continue as simply being "insurance" against prosecution, or will they actually prevent misconduct? From the prosecutor's perspective, the Guidelines may not have changed much, as the prosecutors likely considered many of the same factors for an effective program now formalized into law when deciding whether or not to prosecute a firm.[98] From the organization's side, however, there will likely be a significant impact, as firms will be encouraged by in-house counsel and consultants to update their programs. Furthermore, due to the shift to a more punitive approach to corporate crime in other areas, the Guidelines will be even more important. The impact of these changes will also be amplified by directors' duties under the *Caremark* case.[99] Under *Caremark*, a director may be in breach of their fiduciary duties if they do not consider the opportunities for a reduced sentence under the Guidelines.

The changes to the Guidelines to achieve the Commission's goal – to encourage firms to adopt programs that actually work – are supported by research from management scholars.[100] Although most compliance programs have characteristics of both compliance-based and integrity-based programs (described above), the most successful programs are those where the characteristics of an integrity-based approach dominate.One of the most important factors is that of management commitment. When management demonstrates a commitment to ethics, then all members of the organization are more likely to view ethics as a key organizational value and take legal compliance initiatives more seriously.[101] The new Guidelines expand the roles of top management, requiring them to participate in training and creating a duty to ensure the effectiveness of the program.

Commitment means more than just enforcing a program, however. As with the 1991 Guidelines, employees may still view compliance programs as attempts to protect management. Management commitment includes actions beyond the establishment of the program. For example, researchers have also identified the following factors as important for a successful, integrity-based program: fair treatment of employees, open discussions of ethics in the organization, and rewarding ethical behavior (such as an employee reporting the unethical behavior of a co-worker) and not just self-interest.[102]

Requiring organizations to treat their employees "fairly" is likely beyond the ability of the law to monitor and enforce consistently. However, the Guidelines do take steps towards creating an environment for an open discussion of ethics by requiring ongoing training and the involvement of top management in training. In addition, the Guidelines specifically require organizations to provide positive incentives for ethical behavior – another component of an effective integrity-based compliance program. With the use of reward systems, the organization is more likely to involve its Human Resources department, which brings a different perspective to the compliance program than the Legal department. According to Trevino and Weaver, the involvement of a Human Resources department goes a long way towards developing an integrity-based program.[103]

There are, of course, limits to what the law can accomplish. For example, if the goal is to develop an integrity-based program (where employees willingly adopt the values of legal compliance and ethics, and participate in developing the rules/norms of the organization), then do the Guidelines actually work against that goal by developing even more stringent guidelines? Can these external inducements "force" a company to create an ethical organizational culture? Likewise, how should the law balance between giving firms the flexibility to develop integrity-based programs and mandating best-practices, which can stifle experimentation on what works best for the firm's particular situation?

What does this mean for making corporations into real entities that balance economizing, ecologizing, and power-aggrandizing? What is the significance of the Guidelines to Peace Through Commerce? While I will conclude this chapter with additional thoughts along these lines, I would like to briefly mention four points at this juncture.

First, the Guidelines have made a difference to corporate structure and governance. They have inspired firms across the board to develop reasonably systematic compliance programs. This is a simple point: legal action is an important tool to foster corporate attention to societal concerns.

Second, these programs attempt to make corporations into their own institutes of justice. Rather than complying with a specific regulation, the Guidelines – and the programs to comply with them – try to institute a *system* of relative compliance. This is exactly what one would expect from a real entity approach.

Third, to be effective, the government has recognized that to create these real entities requires more than compliance. It requires attention to other elements. In other words, more than laws (a form of power-aggrandizing) is needed. It also requires attention to economizing and ecologizing. To be sure, corporations are primarily about economics. But to be institutions of justice, corporations have to do more than attend to the law and economics *simply to be effectively compliant.*

Fourth, this suggests that if Peace Through Commerce is dependent on corporations addressing a wider range of concerns, corporations may contribute to Peace Through Commerce, particularly insofar as the goal of peace may energize an additional reason to pay attention to ethics.

Beyond reflexivity

The controversial Sarbanes-Oxley (SOX) legislation, based on this history, can be seen as an extension of a reflexive approach. One may expect that, with the knowledge provided from the experience of the Guidelines, compliance with SOX will require more than a paper program. Like the Guidelines, the technicalities of the law can be mind-boggling. Congress rather strongly reacted to the turn-of-the-century scandals. One can argue whether or not SOX was well-crafted, but the bigger issue is the reality that legislators will act to attempt to restore public confidence in business: Hard Trust.[104]

Of course there are a myriad of other regulatory provisions that have a direct impact on the potential criminal liability of managers ranging from the failure to register non-exempt securities, to insider trading violations, to securities fraud, to intellectual property rights infringements, to violation of Organization of Safety and Health Administration (OSHA) standards, to violations of the Employee Retirement Income Security Act, to price-fixing, and to mail and wire fraud. Obviously, many other laws apply as well.

Laws may be flawed, but they are a legitimate mechanism to rein in corporate misbehavior. The laws may be an enforcement of basic duties, they may be new regulations specific to a particular industry, and now through reflexive statutes, the laws may ask companies to be real entities with attributes of just corporate cultures. The following chapters will argue that Hard Trust is not sufficient to develop these corporate cultures, but the reality is that without the whip of the law, it is questionable how many companies would bother to consider institutionalizing culture-building practices in the first place.

An old folk tale is that law typically lags behind social development. The law *is* slow in catching up with innovation and movements. The law does tend to be deliberative and time-consuming. But the law can also lead social change. Congressional pressures, including the work of senators such as Chapter 4's Everett Dirksen, pushed civil rights ahead of where a huge portion of American society was ready to be. In a different way, legislation pushing corporations to develop ethical cultures has accelerated consideration of codes of conduct, training programs, and other mechanisms. The law, in short, is an essential dimension to ensuring public trust in business.

Peace Through Commerce via Hard Trust

Peace Through Commerce

Hard Trust is essential for Peace Through Commerce. Without the coercive pressure of the law, there is little reason to believe that businesses will be self-regulating. Even when the self-regulation is an aim of government, it prescribes the kind of procedures necessary for the public to have trust in business. Markets flourish when investors and consumers believe they are protected when contracting with the company. Indeed, when Hard Trust is most thoughtfully developed, companies have the most leeway to pursue shareholder profitability because the (reasonable) assumption is that stakeholders are adequately protected. While developed countries have flawed legal regimes, they are comparatively well-developed. Those who argue for a shareholder-only approach have a point that it is likely to be relatively more successful (that is, profit along with benefit to stakeholders) in such environments. But of course, where the law is not as comprehensive, this status of law may not exist. And so, in emerging markets and in situations where globalization makes control of sovereign borders difficult, governmental law has more challenges to create the trust necessary to assure the public that it will be treated fairly by businesses. Further, even where laws are comprehensive, the goal of complying with laws will not be enough to create the desired cultures of ethics and compliance. Chapter 6 makes that argument in greater detail.

Hard Trust comes from our natural heritage of power-seeking behavior. In this case, Hard Trust assures public confidence by checking power. At its best, these rules prevent accumulation of power and provide a check against the power that can be used to abuse others. The most obvious way this happens is through powerful governments checking powerful corporate interests. Hard Trust also occurs within the corporation as well insofar as corporations develop policies that notify anyone working (or investing) in the company of the rules of the game for that particular company.

Hard Trust connects with Peace Through Commerce insofar as the power of business is checked, particularly with respect to not allowing for corruption, protecting property and contract rights, and providing ways to resolve disputes. Certain kinds of governments seem to be able to negotiate differences and resolve disputes. Those countries have rule of law societies that do not allow powerful individuals or groups to simply impose their will, but require them to work through the power-aggrandizing desire through public, political processes. Those processes themselves offer protection against hierarchical abuses of power and more closely correlate with attributes of relatively non-violent societies.

Reflexive regimes merely create incentives and procedures to encourage corporations to do this on their own and to do so more efficiently than through regulation. They embody a real entity approach to the theory of the firm, asking businesses to possess a higher level of moral maturity. They ask companies to be Honest Brokers in steering away from corruption, treating stakeholders fairly, and seeking a common good. That they try to do this is one thing. Whether they successfully accomplish the goal is another. The other elements necessary to accomplish Hard Trust's reflexive strategies are embodied in Real Trust and Good Trust.

Conclusion: segue to Real Trust

This sampling of relevant constraints on behaviors within corporations illustrates the enormity of the task managers face simply in keeping corporations from violating legal rules. That the rules exist suggests the kind of activity that not only may, but has occurred, resulting in social ills. At the same time, it is highly doubtful that any manager could possibly know of all the applicable regulations relevant for their work. This is not to suggest that the number of laws be reduced. Indeed, the activity of business interests has been such that such legal checks are necessary. In a complex society, laws are necessary to check misconduct, but given their distance from the actual knowledge and lived experience of those affected by them, other dimensions of ethical behavior are necessary even just to meet the legal standard of having effective compliance systems. If the range of laws is so vast that no one can really digest them, then simply notifying individuals of those laws is not likely to modify their behavior so that the behavior avoids law-breaking. This gap calls for additional dimensions of trust that I am characterizing as Real Trust and Good Trust.

Moreover, non-legal enforcement mechanisms stand as something of an "in-between" ground of Hard Trust and Real Trust. Real Trust responds to market pressures as well as legal ones. The law is a pressure, but there are other, quite real non-legal forces at work on business as well. They are forces of technology and public opinion.

Several years ago, for instance, I was visiting my father-in-law who then lived in New Mexico. In wandering through a farm and ranch museum, I came across a magazine article and display on the history of barbed wire. When the US West was being settled, farmers needed to protect their property from grazing cattle (as well as thieves), but law enforcement was in short supply. There was too much land, too many cattle, and too few sheriffs to patrol each farm. So technology solved the problem. Barbed wire prevented cattle from trespassing in an inexpensive way that warded them off.

The same happens today. One way to foster trust that a problematic behavior will not occur is simply to make it impossible. For instance, companies rightly fear the kinds of lawsuits that could result if employees could access pornographic websites on their office computers. And so, many companies make it impossible to access such sites. It simply cannot be done. It is a barbed wire approach. The "hardness" to this is not so much coercion as it is with the law, but impossibility. This is a notion of Hard Trust because there is a hard enforcement or prevention of an act, but it does not proceed from legal processes *per se*. Yet, neither is it about issues of social capital or aligning of incentives, which are key aspects of Real Trust. The technology component of Hard Trust stands as something of a segue between Hard Trust and Real Trust.

Similarly, even more along the lines of Real Trust is the issue of public opinion. For instance, Shell Oil company was harshly criticized for working with a corrupt government in Nigeria and being complicit in the oppression of the native Ogoni people of Nigeria, as well as in the assassination of Ken Saro-Wiwa. In response to that and other environmental criticisms, Shell performed a turnaround in its attention to issues of corporate citizenship. One can argue how well Shell has done, but it is hard to dispute that its public face was dramatically changed. Perhaps this is an effort to head off more onerous regulation and oversight, but it is a reaction to public opinion. That attention to social values of reputation and goodwill serves as a segue to the next chapter's coverage of Real Trust.

Thus, the first level of trust is Hard Trust and it is about designing the rules for an organization and enforcing those rules through punishment. The key virtue of Hard Trust is accountability. Hard Trust makes people accountable for the rules of the organization and forces them to live up to those rules.

Notes

1. See Eric Orts, *Shirking and Sharking: A Legal Theory of the Firm*, 16 YALE LAW AND POLICY REVIEW 265 (1998).
2. See e.g. Vermont Microsystems, Inc. vs. Autodesk, Inc., 88 F.3d 142, 147 (2d Cir. 1996).

3. CEO General Robert Wood Johnson believed that by putting the customer first, the business would be well served. See www.jnj.com/our_company/our_credo_history/index.htm;jsessionid=KROC5GA1 N2HIACQPCCEGU3AKB2IIWTT1.

4. Timberland and the establishment of its corporate approach when it went public.

5. F. H. EASTERBROOK AND D. R. FISCHEL, THE ECONOMIC STRUCTURE OF CORPORATE LAW (1991).

6. Dodge vs. Ford Motor Company, 170 N.W. 668 (Mich. 1919).

7. 170 N.W. 668, 684 (Mich. 1919).

8. Shlensky vs. Wrigley, 237 N.E.2d 776 (Ill. App. Ct. 1968).

9. 237 N.E.2d 776, XXX (Ill. App. Ct. 1968).

10. Milton Friedman, *The Social Responsibility of Business Is to Increase Its Profits*, NEW YORK TIMES MAGAZINE (September 13, 1970, reprint).

11. This section previously appeared in part in the FORDHAM JOURNAL OF CORPORATE AND FINANCIAL LAW as *The 2004 Amendments to the Federal Sentencing Guidelines and Their Implicit Call for a Symbiotic Integration of Business Ethics*. I am grateful to my co-authors David Hess and Robert S. McWhorter for their permission in allowing me to use this. This is particularly the case because they are responsible for nearly every one of the good points of this section. I am also grateful to Fordham for its permission in reprinting this section of the article.

12. See e.g., United States vs. Jorgensen, 144 F.3d 550 (8th Cir. 1998); Mylan Laboratories, Inc. vs. Akzo, N.V., 2 F.3d 56, 63 (4th Cir. 1993); United States vs. One Parcel of Land, 965 F.2d 311, 316 (7th Cir. 1992); United States vs. Automated Medical Laboratories, Inc., 770 F.2d 399, 406 (4th Cir. 1985); United States vs. Bi-Co Pavers, Inc., 741 F.2d 730, 737 (5th Cir.1984); United States vs. Basic Constr. Co., 711 F.2d 570, 573 (4th Cir. 1983); United States vs. Cincotta, 689 F.2d 238, 242 (1st Cir. 1982); United States vs. Hilton Hotels Corp., 467 F.2d 1000, 1007 (9th Cir. 1972).

13. Joel M. Androphy, *General Corporate Liability*, 60 TEX. BUS. J. 121, 122, "A corporation would be criminally liable for conduct engaged in by the employee if a third party reasonably believes that the employee was expressly authorized to take the action resulting in the criminal action."

14. Spencer R. Fisher, *Corporate Criminal Liability*, 41 AMERICAN CIVIL L. REV. 367, 371 (Spring 2004).

15. *Id.* at 373.

16. Paul J. Desio, *Introduction to Organizational Sentencing and the US Sentencing Commission*, 39 WAKE FOREST L. REV. 559, 560 (Fall 2004); see also United States vs. Portac, Inc., 869 F.2d 1288, 1293 (9th Cir.

1989), a corporation held criminally liable even though the agent was expressly advised that the company did not permit violations of the law. United States vs. Basic Construction, 711 F.2d 570 (4th Cir. 1983); see also United States vs. Beusch, 596 F.2d 871, 878 (9th Cir. 1979), "[A] corporation may be liable for acts of its employees done contrary to express instructions and policies, but ... the existence of such instructions and policies may be considered in determining whether the employee in fact acted to benefit the corporation."

17. Desio, *supra* note 16, at 559.

18. Sen. Rep. No. 97–307, 956 (1981). It is interesting to note that the new Sentencing Guidelines give judges even more discretion in sentencing by permitting the judge to assess the compliance and ethics program, which permits the court to use some subjectivity in conducting this assessment.

19. 28 USC § 991; see also Justice Anthony M. Kennedy, *Our Resources Are Misspent, Our Punishments Too Severe, Our Sentences Too Long*, 51 THE FEDERAL LAWYER 4, 31 (May 2004).

20. 18 USC § 18.

21. Elkan Abramowitz and Barry A. Bohrer, *A Decade with the Organizational Sentencing Guidelines*, 227 N. Y. L. J. 3, 3 (May 7, 2002); Paul Fiorelli, *Will US Sentencing Commission Amendments Encourage a New Ethical Culture Within Organizations?*, 39 WAKE FOREST L. REV. 565, 567 (Fall 2004).

22. USSC § 8A1.2, App. Note 3(k).

23. *Id.*

24. USSC § 8A1.2, App. Note 3(k)(1) – (7).

25. United States Sentencing Commission, *Sentencing Commission Convenes Organizational Guidelines Ad Hoc Advisory Group*, News Release, p. 1 (February 21, 2002).

26. Paul Fiorelli, *supra* note 21, at 567.

27. *Id.*

28. US SENTENCING COMMISSION, REPORT OF THE AD HOC ADVISORY GROUP ON ORGANIZATIONAL SENTENCING GUIDELINES, p. 26 (October 7, 2003), hereafter referred to as the "Advisory Report".

29. F. Joseph Warin and Michael D. Billok, *Navigating the Legal Requirements of Internal Compliance Programs*, THE CORPORATE GOVERNANCE ADVISOR 13–14 (November/December 2004).

30. Advisory Report, *supra* note 28, at 26; see *infra* notes and accompanying text (discussing the Thompson Memorandum).

31. Janet S. Adams, Armen Tashchian, and Ted H. Stone, *Codes of Ethics as Signals of Ethical Behavior*, 29 J. OF BUS. ETHICS 199, 199 (2001).

32. See The Ethics Officers Association webpage at www.eoa.org.

33. Jeffrey M. Kaplan, Joseph E. Murphy and Winthrop M. Swenson, COMPLIANCE PROGRAMS AND THE CORPORATE SENTENCING GUIDELINES, PREVENTING CRIMINAL AND CIVIL LIABILITY § 7:14, p. 7–30 (West. Pub. 2003).

34. *Id.*

35. Fiorelli, *supra* note 21, at 567.

36. William S. Laufer, *Corporate Liability, Risk Shifting, and the Paradox of Compliance*, 54 VANDERBILT L. REV. 1343, 1405–7 (1999).

37. William S. Laufer, *Corporate Prosecution, Cooperation, and the Trading of Favors*, 87 IOWA L. REV. 643, 648–9, 657–63 (2002).

38. Lynn Sharp Paine, *Managing for Organizational Integrity*, HARVARD BUS. REV. 106 (March/April 1994).

39. Kimberly D. Krawiec, *Cosmetic Compliance and the Failure of Negotiated Governance*, 81 WASH. U. L. Q. 487, 489 (2003); see also Donald C. Langevoort, *Monitoring: The Behavioral Economics of Corporate Compliance with the Law*, 2002 COLUMBIA BUS. L. REV. 71 (2002). "Monitoring-based systems have unexpectedly serious (and probably immeasurable) costs, which society should not impose without strong reason."

40. Krawiec, *supra* note 39, at 492–3.

41. Paine, *supra* note 38, at 111.

42. *Id.* at 111; G.R. Weaver and L.K. Trevino, *Compliance and Values Oriented Ethics Programs: Influences on Employees' Attitudes and Behavior*, 9 BUS. ETHICS Q. 315 (1999).

43. Paine, *supra* note 38, at 111.

44. For a complete, book-length description of Enron's culture from an insider, see Mimi Schwartz and Sherron Watkins, POWER FAILURE: THE INSIDE STORY OF THE COLLAPSE OF ENRON (2003). For an insider story on the role of corporate culture in the ethical failures that brought down another highly-esteemed company, see Barbara Ley Toffler, FINAL ACCOUNTING: AMBITION, GREED, AND THE FALL OF ARTHUR ANDERSEN (2003).

45. Chartwell Inc., *Top-to-Bottom Training, Employee Ethics Help Line Are Key to Corporate Culture of Ethics*, CHARTWELL'S BEST PRACTICES FOR UTILITIES AND ENERGY COMPANIES 141 (Newsletter, September 2002).

46. Fiorelli, *supra* note 21, at 567.

47. Raphael S. Grunfeld, *Enforcing a Written Code of Ethics, Well-Ingrained Guidelines Given Higher Priority, Encourage Executives to Do the Right Thing*, 228 N. Y. L. J. S3 (November 18, 2002).

48. Greg Farrell, *Enron Law Firm Called Accounting Practices 'Creative'*, USA TODAY, Jan. 15, 2002, at D1.

49. Fiorelli, *supra* note 21, at 578.

50. Lynne L. Dallas, *A Preliminary Inquiry into the Responsibility of Corporations and Their Officers and Directors for Corporate Climate: The Psychology of Enron's Demise*, 35 RUTGERS L. J. 1, 45–6 (2003).

51. *Id.* Testimony of Frank Partnoy – Professor of Law, University of San Diego School of Law, "Thoughts on Enron: What Happened, Why, and How It Can Be Avoided Again", Hearings before the United States Senate Committee on Governmental Affairs, p. 2 (January 24, 2002).

52. Anita Raghavan, Kathryn Kranhold, and Alexei Barrionuevo, *How Enron Bosses Created a Culture of Pushing Limits*, WALL ST. J. A1 (August 26, 2002).

53. *Id.*

54. Dallas, *supra* note 50, at 51.

55. John A. Byrne, *The Environment Was Ripe for Abuse*, BUSINESS WEEK 118 (February 25, 2002).

56. Byrne, *supra* note 55, at 118; Dallas, *supra* note 50, at 50.

57. Byrne, *supra* note 55, at 118; Dallas, *supra* note 50, at 49–50.

58. Byrne, *supra* note 55, at 118.

59. *Id.*

60. *Id.*

61. Fiorelli, *supra* note 21, at 565.

62. See *supra* note 22 and accompanying text.

63. Memorandum to Heads of Departments Components United States Attorneys from Larry D. Thompson, Deputy Attorney General Regarding Principles of Federal Prosecution of Business Organizations, p. 7 (January 20, 2003) (www.usdoj.gov./dag/cftf/corporate_guidelines.htm, hereinafter Thompson Memo).

64. *Id.*

65. US Sentencing Commission, *Sentencing Commission Convenes Organizational Guidelines Ad Hoc Advisory Group*, News Release, p. 1 (February 21, 2002).

66. US Sentencing Commission, TRANSCRIPT OF PUBLIC HEARING, pp. 24–6 (March 17, 2004).

67. Legal Research Network, *How Does the Low-Key Independent Government Agency Set Sentencing Guidelines for Individuals and Corporations? LRN CEO Testifies Criteria Should Include Ethics*, p. 1 (March 17, 2004), available at www.prnnewswire.com/cgi-bin/stories, last visited March 1, 2005.

68. TRANSCRIPT OF PUBLIC HEARING HELD BY THE AD HOC ADVISORY GROUP ON ORGANIZATIONAL SENTENCING GUIDELINES, FEDERAL JUDICIAL CENTER TRAINING ROOMS, Washington D.C., Plenary Session II, pp. 40–1 (November 12, 2002) Bill Lytton.

69. Dr. Stuart Gillman's Testimony to the Advisory Group on Federal Sentencing Guidelines for Organizations, p. 10 (November 14, 2002).
70. Advisory Report, *supra* note 28, at 51.
71. USSC § 8B2.1.
72. USSC § 8B2.1.
73. Advisory Report, *supra* note 28, at 52.
74. *Id.* at 51–2.
75. *Id.* at 52.
76. USSC § 8B2.1, App. Note 1.
77. Advisory Report, *supra* note 28, at 52–3.
78. *Id.* at 53.
79. *Id.* at 55.
80. *Id.* 55.
81. *Id.* at 54.
82. USSC § 8B.2.1, Application Note 1.
83. Advisory Report, *supra* note 28, at 56.
84. See e.g., USSC § 8A1.2, Application Note 3(k)(2)–(3) (pre-November 1, 2004 amendment).
85. Advisory Report, *supra* note 28, at 57.
86. *Id.* at 60–1.
87. *Id.* It is important to note that the Advisory Report breaks down "organizational leadership" into these categories when interpreting USSC § 8B2.1(b)(2).
88. An interesting issue that is not addressed or discussed in any materials relating to the adoption of the Amendments to the Sentencing Guidelines is the potential liability associated with serving as the Chief Ethics Officer. It is possible that a shareholder, member, or creditor of the organization could, in certain circumstances, bring an action against a Chief Ethics Officer for acting negligently in determining whether the organization is acting illegally. Of course, this potential exposure may provide an incentive to the Chief Ethics Officer to vigorously audit and enforce compliance with the Sentencing Guidelines.
89. Fiorelli, *supra* note 21, at 583.
90. *Id.*
91. Advisory Report, *supra* note 28, at 71.
92. *Id.* at 72.
93. TRANSCRIPT OF PUBLIC HEARING HELD BY THE AD HOC ADVISORY GROUP ON ORGANIZATIONAL SENTENCING GUIDELINES, PLENARY SESSION II, p. 14 (November 12, 2002) D. Yang.
94. *Id.*
95. Advisory Report, *supra* note 28, at 78, citing the 2003 National Business Ethics Survey conducted by the Ethics Resource Center.

96. *Id.*
97. Jeffrey M. Kaplan, *Compliance Programs 2.0: The Next Generation in Compliance Programs*, THE CORPORATE GOVERNANCE ADVISOR 10, 11 (November/December 2004).
98. Thompson Memo and Frank O. Bowman, III, *Drifting Down the Dnieper with Prince Potemkin: Some Skeptical Reflections About the Place of Compliance Programs in Federal Criminal Sentencing*, 39 WAKE FOREST L. REV. 671 (2004).
99. In re: Caremark, 698 A.2d 959 (Del. Ct. Chan. 1996).
100. For a general review of the research in this area, see Linda Klebe Trevino and Gary R. Weaver, MANAGING ETHICS IN BUSINESS ORGANIZATIONS: SOCIAL SCIENTIFIC PERSPECTIVES (2003).
101. Linda Klebe Trevino, Gary R. Weaver, David G. Gibson, and Barbara Ley Toffler, *Managing Ethics and Legal Compliance: What Works and What Hurts*, 41 CALIF. MANAGEMENT REV. 131 (1999).
102. L. K. Trevino, K. Butterfield, and D. McCabe, *The Ethical Context in Organizations: Influences on Employee Attitudes and Behaviors*, 8 BUSINESS ETHICS QUARTERLY 447 (1998); Linda Klebe Trevino, Gary R. Weaver, David G. Gibson, and Barbara Ley Toffler, *Managing Ethics and Legal Compliance: What Works and What Hurts*, 41 CALIFORNIA MANAGEMENT REVIEW, 131 (1999).
103. Trevino and Weaver, *supra* note 100, at 97.
104. Sarbanes-Oxley Act of 2002, Section 203 (15 U.S.C. 78j-l).

6 | *Real Trust*

EAL Trust is probably what most people think of when they hear the term trust, at least in business.[1] Real Trust is about people living up to the promises they made, being honest, producing products and services that are of high enough quality to satisfy customers, and rewarding people for doing the things the company says are important.[2] Real Trust is "real" because there is an inherent efficacy about it. Real Trust "pays" because there is an alignment of rhetoric and reward. Real Trust is about how good ethics is good business, usually with a long-term perspective. This suggests a combination of normative and descriptive. LaRue Hosmer once wrote that trust was the connecting link between organizational theory and normative business ethics.[3] There are moral understandings of what business should do and there is some empirical assessment of exactly how it has economic benefit. Real Trust is positioned between Hard Trust and Good Trust. An important way to generate Real Trust is for a company to implement a compliance program that is fair, consistent, and with buy-in. Thus, Real Trust can build on Hard Trust. On the other end of the spectrum, Good Trust is about engaging the passions and the human desire to do good. One way for a company to generate Real Trust is to engage those passions. And so, there is overlap between the three kinds of trust. For the purposes of the division I am proposing, Real Trust is about how moral values make business sense, assuming there is a social interest in business acting properly (Hard Trust) and assuming that people have the motivation to care about doing good (Good Trust).

Why the law needs more

One reason people have tended to be skeptical about relying only on the law is that the law is not always perceived to be fair. The positive law theorists have always been clear that law is what the sovereign says it is.[4] That doesn't make the law fair, it simply makes it enforced. This may be true, but it is not terribly satisfying from a moral standpoint. And so, the natural law position has been that a law is entitled to respect and obedience insofar as it comports with universal principles of justice. In some ways, any argument saying that a law is unfair brings with it a natural law ring.

There are, of course, different versions of natural law, some sacred and some secular. All attend to some idea of universal norms of behavior that rational human beings are aware of. These natural law arguments also have appeal and because we do intuitively assess the fairness of law, natural law provides an analysis of when and how Hard Trust might obtain moral and efficacious Real Trust support. Moreover, there is another kind of natural law that while quite different from the traditionally used sense of natural law, further connects Hard Trust and Real Trust in an efficacious way. This section spells out these two critiques of law and connects them to notions of social capital as a foundation for understanding the normative and descriptive scholarship provided by management scholars.

The following two sections will set out the contemporary approaches to business ethics found in schools of management today. These approaches are normative and descriptive. But prior to detailing those approaches, I think it is important to understand two reasons, within the study of law itself, as to why the law is not enough. These two approaches both carry the name of natural law, but they offer very different perspectives on the efficacy of natural law. More traditional natural law offers a philosophical criteria of just law. What I call "spontaneous natural law" is more akin to sentiments addressed in psychological and managerial analysis.

Good old natural law[5]

There is, of course, no "one" natural law position. One article recently distinguished among four natural law traditions just within the United States.[6] This includes a traditionalist approach, which contends for specific goods and virtues that differ, to some extent, from those proposed by Aquinas.[7] Actions are wrong if they destroy other goods even in pursuit of a basic good itself.[8] John Finnis is an influential spokesperson for this approach and the seven goods he identifies are life, knowledge, play/work, aesthetic experience, sociability, practical reasonableness, and religion.[9] An example of the application of this approach would be a condemnation of the tobacco industry. Regardless of the goods promoted by a legal business – in terms of profit and work for instance – there is a violation of a basic good of life (through undermining human health).[10]

A second approach is that of proportion with its distinguishing moral calculus called the principle of double-effect.[11] In particular, an assessment about the proportion of the good and evil involved in the action gives rise to the "proportionist" label this tradition carries.[12] An example of this approach would be affirmative action where providing a job to a minority applicant is not evil, but it does have a bad effect of "reverse discrimination".[13] One can then argue about the proportionate good of bringing about a more just society outweighing the current evil effect.[14]

A third natural law approach is that of "right reason".[15] This approach places heavy emphasis upon human ability to determine the foundations of natural law with or without theology.[16] Business ethicists who follow this approach have linked natural law to contemporary philosophical categories of utility, rights, and justice.[17]

Finally, the historicist approach to natural law emphasizes the adaptability of natural law; that is, that the Church changed its views, through natural law categories, on issues such as usury, divorce, slavery, abortion, and religious toleration.[18] An example of this would be bribery, which may not be absolutely immoral depending upon the conditions of the time and culture in which it takes place.[19] One can also justifiably view the founding of the United States and the creation of the Constitution as a part of a long tradition of natural law dialogue so that American notions of government structure and legal principles are rooted in natural law.[20] In natural law thinking one hopes to have a community governed by natural law principles in which individuals will flourish. Thus, "[i]t asserts that there are principles of sound social architecture, objectively given, and that these principles, like those of physical architecture, do not change with every shift in the details of the design toward which they are directed".[21] Natural law has had a problematic history because an interpretation of substantive universal principles is substituted for the universal principles themselves. Rather than repeating that history, I would like, instead, to argue for a natural law approach that focuses more on themes and structures rather than on substantive rules. The approach is an architecture; it has room within it for many different substantive arrangements.

To create an architectural design of reason requires the existence of a coherent plan. But how does one claim such a *telos* for human nature when an Enlightenment reason for rejecting Aristotle was that science largely decimated the *telos* accepted by Aristotle, not to mention Aquinas?[22] In revitalizing Aristotle's relationship to biology and ethics, Masters argued that "Aristotle's teleological conception of nature was based primarily on his biology rather than his physics."[23] Biologically, one may be able to find an organism's *telos*. To "pursue these goods in the right order, to the right degree, at the right time to avoid contradiction requires good habits of choice – the moral and intellectual virtues that Aristotle examines in the *Ethics*".[24] Thus, if human beings are social, there may be ways in which living together is a *telos*. A natural law approach is one that would take into account the variety of goods that human beings, in corporations or elsewhere, view as important. It would seem that sustainable peace could be a *telos* allowing individuals to survive the twenty-first century. The question thus becomes what specific structures natural law suggests to help us live together and to do so in order to create order that is also open to change and to multiple goods within the corporate community. I would like to identify five central, appropriately general yet substantive elements, each of which is, in essence, a normative principle manifesting a system of checks and balances. In other words, these elements provide a way to integrate the naturalistic values I have already sketched. In doing so, I believe that the elements suggest the creation of ethical business behavior and business cultures rather than repeating the usual natural law mistake of attempting to identify specific rules.

The first element is impartiality. Much of the legal system of the developed world is, in fact, an attempt to build in principles of impartiality in terms of due process and of holding all persons responsible under the same law. This is not to argue that developed countries implement it perfectly, but it is to provide an example of the extant application of the principle itself.

The second element is the criteria of the common good. Aquinas argues that "nothing stands firm with regard to the practical reason, unless it be directed to the last end which is the common good; and whatever stands to reason in this sense, has the nature of a law".[25] No system of laws is just unless it promotes the common good of the community. Those who have power direct the danger toward the criteria of justice. It points the person with authority to the restraints on his or her exercise of power. In fact, Finnis takes this point to the extent that he denies any reason for a person to obey authority unless that authority is, in fact, exercised for the common good (an action which all too often can mean the good of the rulers, but which should mean the good of all).[26]

A third principle is that of communication. In an important sense, communication is simply a practical safeguard to ensure that rulers are acting for the common good and to provide a method of articulating why a person is acting in an impartial manner. Yet its self-standing importance has been made preeminent by Lon Fuller, who states that the central natural law injunction is "Open up, maintain, and preserve the integrity of the channels of communication by which men convey to one another what they perceive, feel, and desire."[27]

These three principles reinforce the general notion of subsidiarity. Participating in the decisions and activities affecting them and locating problems on the level appropriate for their resolution develops the moral character of individuals so that they may live a flourishing life. It is the dialectical interaction of order and freedom through which one learns the lessons appropriate for one's life while preserving a freedom to be creative.

Subsidiarity also acts as its own (fourth) check against abusive power in the form of mediating institutions. If individuals have their own decision-making authority, then leaders are less likely to abuse power because they have other power with which they must contend. Subsidiarity also promotes communication, so that those with power (through subsidiarity) understand the reasons provided for the exercise of power over them. That process guarantees the impartiality of the norms that are being implemented. Moreover, in an age where individuals may be members of multiple communities, subsidiarity provides a meaningful way for individuals with exposure to other mediating institutions to build in an internal adaptability to the outside world.

The fifth principle is the establishment of property rights. Historian Richard Pipes has argued that property rights are natural institutions.[28] Whether found in animals, children, hunter-gatherers, or urbanites, animal life entails property ownership.[29] Rejecting a romantic notion of noble savages practicing socialism, Pipes points out that collective land systems among "primitive" peoples were nearly always family ownership systems.[30] Moreover, individuals claimed private ownership to incorporeal rights to songs, legends, designs, and magic incantations which were fiercely defended.[31] Similarly, anthropologists have found that hunter-gatherer bands sometimes stake out land territories[32] and more often to particular objects such as trees.[33] When agriculture and later industrial economics appeared, the importance of land ownership became critical.[34] The philosophical notion of the value of owning private property, according to Pipes, traces to Aristotle, who in opposition to Plato argued that property is an attribute of a household not of the state.[35] Moreover, Aristotle argued that property was better cared for in the hands of private owners.[36] This notion was built upon by Aquinas and even more enthusiastically by the Protestant Reformers,[37] and philosophically by Locke.[38] A central attribute of private property ownership undermines feudal ownership of wealth, where land always reverts to the lord and is only derivatively held by vassals.[39] This counterweight to centralized power, according to Pipes, also gave rise to democratic politics in England and the securing of basic human rights and freedoms.[40]

Thus, one can conclude that one of the most effective checks on royal power has always been property rights. This is corroborated by biologist Matt Ridley, who argues that the most effective protection of a commons is not socialized ownership, but private property.[41] Moreover, legal historian Stephen Presser contends that the "theory was that ownership of property conferred a stake in the community, and led one better to act in the interests of all".[42]

The result of the implementation of the substantive content of the law must be tested against the moral principles themselves. Reciprocity is an element that is readily seen; all the substantive principles described are implementations of reciprocity. But does their implementation lead to a flourishing life? Finnis responds that:

This sense of "(basic) reason for action" holds for all the other basic human goods: *knowledge* of reality (including aesthetic appreciation of it); *excellence in work and play* whereby one transforms natural realities to express meanings and serve purposes; *harmony between individuals and groups* of persons (peace, neighborliness, and friendship); *harmony between one's feelings and one's judgments and choices* (inner peace); *harmony between one's choices and judgments and one's behavior* (peace of conscience and authenticity in the sense of consistency between one's self and its expression); and *harmony between oneself and the wider reaches of reality* including the reality constituted by the world's dependence on *a more-than-human source of meaning and value*.[43]

We can therefore say that natural law emphasizes the importance of checks and balances and that five pillars – commitments to impartiality and the common good of all, communication through the institution, vibrant mediating institutions, and invigorated property rights of those who are members of the institution – can support the creation of a corporation that is open to a variety of human goods and which creates order while remaining open to change. It also aims for a sense of harmony within oneself and harmony among neighbors. Applying these attributes to an entity conception of corporations, one would expect that they apply rules impartially. That is, they make high-level officials subject to the same rules as low-ranking workers. They would emphasize a common good of the corporate community. That is, there would not be a commitment to individual interests of a particular group but to the collective identity of the corporate community. There would be vibrant communication. This would entail communication in multiple directions and also in terms of training programs. There would be empowered individuals addressing moral and other issues in their own work groups. This exercise of the principle of subsidiarity or mediating institutions makes individuals into moral agents within the company to fix moral problems and to call out miscreants. Finally, it would create a "stake" in the corporation of those who work there. That stake may be financial, but it could also have an incorporeal dimension to it as well.[44] Interestingly, these attributes are very much what have been consistently recommended by management scholars on how to create what I call Real Trust.

A different kind of natural law and a step toward Real Trust

Two stories illustrate important aspects of natural law. Both are about how rules need to make sense to those affected by them. Ancient Hawaii provides an example here as does laws against bribery; that is the first story. A Frenchman's description of the evolution of society provides the second.

In its most basic form, bribery is a conflict of interest. Philip Nichols concisely summarizes government corruption by stating that it is a "transaction in which an official misuses his or her office as a result of considerations of personal gain, which need not be monetary".[45] Thomas Dunfee has argued the same abuse is possible in private business as well, where a person uses a corporate position for personal

172 Business, Integrity, and Peace

benefit.[46] Two moral arguments essentially exist against bribery, whether governmental or private. The deontological argument is that bribery violates a moral duty, typically a fiduciary duty of some type. That is, an employee places their interests ahead of the person (corporation generally or the shareholders) employing him. The consequentialist argument is that bad things occur where bribery is present. These include inefficiency in the allocation of resources and creating corrosive social effects on governments and other institutions.[47] Extending that argument, remember the earlier study showing a direct, linear statistical correlation between corruption and the likelihood of violence?[48] Regardless of whether one focuses on deontological or consequentialist arguments against bribery, the result typically is the same: rules that restrict the practice. Laws prevent bribery either because there is something inherently unethical about the practice itself or because there are sufficient, deleterious consequences so as to require the outlawing of the practice. These results represent efforts to create Hard Trust; that is, clear legal rules prohibiting certain kinds of behavior and punishments if those rules are violated. An anthropological foray to historical Hawaii, however, demonstrates the danger of relying solely on that approach and in doing so, it will show why only relying on Hard Trust to foster ethical business behavior will be problematic.[49]

Alasdair MacIntyre reports that when Captain James Cook made his third voyage to the Polynesian islands in 1778, his crew was surprised that while sexual mores were very lax, there were strict prohibitions on women eating with men.[50] When asked why, the Polynesian islanders simply told the sailors that the practice was *kapu* (sometimes translated as *taboo*).[51] In actuality, the notion of *kapu* prohibiting women and men from eating together was based on the creation myth Hawaiians called the *Kumulipo*, a myth taken with great seriousness in pre-westernized Hawaii. The *kapus*, derived from the proper construction of relationships within the *Kumulipo*, were checks that kept powerful forces of the universe in balance. They restricted Hawaiians, commoners in particular, from doing certain things and deferring significantly to the welfare of the ruling class, but it was within the understanding that the ruling class had reciprocal duties to commoners; if those were not upheld, cosmological disaster would result. When an outsider (Cook) disrupted the system – by allowing inclusive eating – and when no cosmological disasters afflicted Cook's men, the cultural underpinnings of the *kapu* began to break. In other words, the social context of Hawaiian society was disrupted, so that *kapu* rules were no longer connected to a coherent system, but instead were increasingly detached from social reality.

Even more problematically, the ruling class, the *Ali'i Nui* (the nobles) and the *Moi'i* (the king), used *kapu* as a way to prevent commoners from obtaining access to western luxuries and further believed themselves no longer vulnerable to cosmological retribution for not taking care of commoners. They accepted bribes, thereby further disconnecting their own good from the common good of the *maka'aina* and making *kapu* itself unintelligible by precluding the communication of its rationale in a way that would gain cultural assent. In short, the coercive authority of rules were maintained without the reciprocal obligations borne by the elites. Between 1795 and 1819, King Kamehameha also used *kapu* rules to regulate trade with European countries, thus changing *kapu* rules from ritual practice to practical economization. As anthropologist Marshall Sahlins indicates, the *kapu* became a proprietary right equivalent to a "no trespassing" sign.[52] No intelligible rationale for it existed other than to know that it was prohibited. What once was a behavioral system connecting individuals with cosmic identity linked through a commitment of all to a common good was undermined when the rules of behavior no longer made any sense to the governed.[53]

To place this in contemporary corporate terms, rules need to make sense if they are to be trusted. That does not happen when the only reason people have to follow a rule is that a powerful person or institution will impose punishment for breaking them. Rules against bribery are examples of this. Bribery contributes to a great many social and economic dysfunctions.[54] But it is tempting to overlook explaining what these dysfunctions are in favor of a simple, clear rule of "don't bribe". Frankly, however, if the only reason for not bribing is that people will be punished if they do it, the pursuit of individual self-interest still encourages people to simply find ways not to get caught.[55] What makes a rule against bribery compelling is if people understand that it is part of a larger system that will benefit all members of society and that will require those in authority to reciprocally benefit – or at least not take advantage of – those in subordinate positions. Real Trust results when individuals do understand the laws that govern them. This may occur through training or by employees having the opportunity to participate in the creation of rules that govern them. Simply put, the imposition of rules is not necessarily very effective.

Hard Trust has *kapu*-like dangers. Hard Trust rules can specify what obligations people in a corporation have, but if the rules are so abstracted from what employees understand to make sense, Hard Trust can simply seem to be arbitrary. A second example paints a similar picture, but with a much broader brush.

Over forty years ago, Jacques Ellul pointed out why rules are such a problem for societies.[56] Ellul, a lawyer and lay theologian, argued that, historically speaking, law developed in four stages.[57] In the first stage, law and religion are the same thing. There is no separation between political and spiritual authority. The person who is the ruler of a tribe is also its spiritual leader as well.[58] In the second stage, there is a separation between political and religious authority so that there are specialized rulers as well as spiritual shamans.[59] The people of the community, however, all remain of one religious orientation. Through custom, they spontaneously "know" what the law is even though religion and government separate.

In stage three, more specialists appear. These are scholars, particularly "lawyers", who attempt to formalize the behaviors by which the community operates. They do so as a way to systematize behaviors for a growing population and also to clarify acceptable behavior in a community growing more diverse.[60] Thus, these scholars attempt to formalize the history of the community's rules in a specific formula. This leads to stage four which occurs when, inevitably according to Ellul, those with great resources pay those with outstanding legal talent to interpret the meaning of the rules or to draft rules that are in the best interests of those in power. At this stage, Ellul argues that there is little hope for there to be any connection between what the majority of people in society feel is fair and what the rules actually are. Instead, the rules are simply a legalistic game played by the wealthy and powerful in an effort to pursue their own self-interest. Ellul justifies his argument through specific historical examples which need not detain us presently.[61] For purposes of corporate governance, however, two insights are particularly important.

First, there is an intuitive logic in Ellul's schema. One need only look to Washington lobbyists to see how wealthy interests seek to have laws enacted to benefit their narrow interests. One need only look within the general counsel's office to find the clever talent corporations utilize to find legal loopholes, to use the law as a competitive advantage or to tweak rules for litigation advantage. Or, as J. Pierpoint Morgan once said, "Well I don't know as I want a lawyer to tell me what I cannot do. I hire him to tell me how to do what I want to do."[62] This is not to condemn such efforts; they are part of the way contemporary society is constructed. Yet, it is part of a system described by Ellul in which the law is not equated with the administration of justice as much as it is a constraint placed on behavior. As a constraint, it is a rule to be probed much like a toddler would with a parental edict. One presses to see when a rule will be enforced, what one can get away with (often through artful explanation), and whether there are rules at all. With respect to rules of behavior mandated within a corporation, some companies spend little time educating employees as to why a corporate code of conduct is part of an overall system of fairness for the organization. In other words, companies may rely on Hard Trust to the exclusion of Real Trust and thereby create a system that does little to encourage ethical business behavior.

The second interesting point is the natural law stage. In the previous section, I used natural law as a way to describe legal systems that tried to meet moral standards of fairness. These natural law structures are a good start for an organizational system perceived to be fair because the standards tend to be universal. However, Ellul uses another sense of natural law that resonates more with the perception of fairness within the system. Organizational scholars today refer to this as organizational justice.

Ellul argues that the best a society can hope for occurs in stage two where there is a spontaneous understanding of what the laws of society are. When people are so engrained with custom and rules so matched with individual understandings of fairness, people "naturally" understand what appropriate behavior is. At this stage, there is less need for formalized legal systems. With less need for such systems, then there is less opportunity for specialists to twist language, which Ellul fears in stages three and four. When rules become abstracted from lived lives, then rules become ineffective. The time when organizations enmesh rules and behaviors is when there is a culture of ethical business behavior. In other words ethical norms are best approaches when companies pay attention to Real Trust.

This is, in fact, much of the argument made by contemporary ethics scholars such as Lynn Paine as well as the research conducted by Linda

Trevino, Gary Weaver, *et al.* Paine notes that rules-based systems are not as effective as "integrity" systems which have a more aspirational character. Integrity-based systems integrate an overall sense of fairness rather than simply avoiding coercive punishment.[63] Trevino's studies show that compliance-based systems have trouble being effective if not partnered with more comprehensive, culture-building efforts. Worse, paper programs, where corporations rhetorically mouth Hard Trust and Real Trust approaches, are ineffective.[64] Rules are not unimportant; in fact, in a diverse society without the kind of long-term, engrained social enculturation Ellul relies upon, rules are necessary so that diverse people (as well as confused employees or even troublemakers) know what behaviors are acceptable and what are not. Yet, Ellul is right that for laws to be effective, they must resonate with a person's sense of fairness.[65] Ellul probably overstates his case, but there is also a truth to his typology. It holds in business as well. Law, Hard Trust, is important. We do not live in the kinds of homogenous societies Ellul focused his natural law. We live in a diverse, globalized economy with a highly mobile workforce. Law is important to make clear to everyone what the rules are. At the same time, more than law is needed in order to give those governed by it an understanding as to why the law makes sense. Linking incentives and rewards to individual self-interest is largely the work of Real Trust.

Real Trust also connects with notions of social capital increasingly developed in schools management. Social capital derives from the work of scholars such as James Coleman, Mark Granovetter, and Robert Putnam. Drawing on metaphors of financial capital and human capital, these scholars look at the network of relationships that occur in certain kinds of communities that allow individuals to flourish in economic systems.[66] Such networks thrive on a developed sense of reciprocity, particularly in long-term forms. Speaking more naturalistically, they build on Robert Axelrod's notions that, in the long term, advantageous survival strategies call for reciprocal tit-for-tat.[67] That is, it is not in an individual's self-interest to take advantage of others in the society, although that is always a temptation if one can do so without getting caught,[68] but instead to act in ways that contribute to a network of relationships where certain virtues become the expected norm of behavior and, in the long run, pay off. Or, to push the naturalistic evidence further, the notion of "generous tit-for-tat" argues that not only should one mirror the actions of others, as Axelrod suggests, but in order to avoid a degenerative spiral of feud-like behavior (which could be a negative tit-for-tat) that erodes trust, a point of forgiveness for past actions can reverse the spiral.[69]

Coleman argues that individuals achieve more in communities with high levels of social capital, because individuals leverage their capabilities with networks providing support for flourishing behavior.[70] Granovetter emphasizes that within communities are embedded relationships that are not easily categorized, but are hard, concrete realities in which relationships give rise to a trust that permeates an economic community.[71] Putnam concentrates on how associational networks, such as mediating institutions, foster the kinds of expected trust in certain kinds of behavior that people intuitively understand as expected norms of behavior. It is not a far reach to connect all of these to the kind of "natural law" Jacques Ellul spoke of as being an essential ingredient of a functioning society.

What connects Real Trust and social capital are notions of integrity and trust.[72] At its root, integrity is a concept of wholeness. To integrate is to bring things together. An integer is a whole number. Integrity is a holistic practice of a set of virtues that makes a whole person. So promise-keeping, truth-telling, honesty, and quality are all associated with integrity.[73]

Today, schools of management actively address corporate responsibility with an eye toward examining how much integrity is practiced toward multiple stakeholders. Of course, some attention to the topic has always been present, but the last twenty to thirty years have seen an explosion of activity. Two main approaches exist. The first is a descriptive approach reaching back to the early work in the field by scholars such as Raymond Baumhart.[74] This approach attempts to see what, in fact, are the relationships between considerations of corporate responsibility and profitability. Baumhart asked what business people think about ethics. In the following twenty-five years normative approaches dominated the field – what *should* corporations do. This literature is the topic of the next section. Today, the major focus seems to return to a descriptive approach: whether corporate social performance and corporate financial performance are related as well as considerations about how to make ethics programs effective and how corporations can be agents of social change. This is the topic of the following section.

Normative dimensions

Traditional natural law is about fairness. Are actions and rules just? Natural law is, of course, not the only philosophical approach to justice. Indeed today, one could argue that natural law is very much a minority approach. The emphasis on evaluating rules and justice according to *some* notion of justice or fairness, however, is continuous. The normative school of business ethics in schools of management can be seen as an attempt to provide this kind of evaluation. Again, the natural law approach is very much a normative position within the school of business ethics itself, but the approaches taken follow directly from the sentiments characteristic of natural law itself. And so, normative business ethics makes moral evaluations of business affairs.

The Philosopher's Formula is borrowed from William Frederick. Written wryly, this formula does a fairly good job of summarizing the various kinds of philosophical principles at stake in the development of stakeholder theory. Frederick describes this formula as follows:

$$EBB = f(R_k + J_r + U)^{75}$$

In this framework, EBB stands for Ethical Business Behavior. R_k stands for Kantian-based Rights. J_r stands for Rawlsian Justice. U stands for Utilitarianism. In applying this formula, one should remember it is more a summary of philosophical attempts to specify duties under stakeholder theory, rather than a formula advocated by any particular scholar. The formula is a summary of the large majority of normative scholarship within schools of business.

Patricia Werhane has developed a refined framework in which she requires first, that the rights are identified by categories according to whether they affect basic or secondary rights of the affected stakeholders. A basic right is something without which life would be intolerable. These would include, for instance, life itself, basic food, water, and shelter, freedom from torture, and the right to equal consideration. If there is a conflict between a basic right and a non-basic (or secondary) right, then basic rights "trump" non-basic rights. If there are conflicts between rights of equal stature (basic vs. basic or secondary vs. secondary), then one should attempt to find a compromise that honors both rights. If this is not possible, then one should take a corporate action that minimizes harm to the greatest extent possible and finally, if after

Table 6.1. Real Trust

Rights	Things Without Which Life Would Be Intolerable	Corporate Should Not Negatively Impact Life, Food, Water, Shelter, Basic Health, Freedom from Torture
Justice	Equality Adjusted for Context	Equal Treatment for Those in Similar Situations – e.g. Equivalent Pay for Men and Women In Unequal Situations, Protect Those Who Are Most Vulnerable Allow for Cultural Differences on What Constitutes Vulnerability, but Not So As To Violate Clear Moral Norms
Utilitarianism	Greatest Good for Greatest Number: Managerial Win-Wins by Aligning Moral Values With Managerial Incentives	Citizenship Factors Such as Job Satisfaction, Good Leadership, Perceived Organizational Justice Establishment of Ethical Culture Through Values Statements, Training Programs, Award Incentives, Mentors, Rituals

going through these steps no resolution is obvious, then one should do a cost-benefit analysis to determine corporate action. Werhane's concern is that mangers are well-trained to perform cost-benefit analysis, but in doing so, they may not take into account what is at stake for some constituents. Thus, one must make sure rights are protected.[76]

How might this be applied? In my classes, I teach a case about the food company, Green Giant, closing its agricultural plants in California and moving them to Mexico. The climate is more conducive to growing vegetables year-round there and, of course, the cost of labor is much lower. In order to grow the vegetables, Green Giant had to irrigate extensively. Perhaps coincidental to the pumping of 500,000 gallons of water a day, the water table dropped so that where previously families could drill 60 feet to obtain water, after the plan was in operation, families had to drill 450 feet. Most families couldn't afford to do so and so had to give their children polluted water to drink. In this case, a basic right of clean water was violated and so if the company were to proceed, it would (and apparently did) bring in clean drinking water. That solution may not have addressed the environmental consequences of a lowered water table, but it would ease the threat of giving children sewage water to drink.

In other words, the company could only proceed to concerns about profitability – a secondary right – after it had made sure that no basic rights (clean water) were denied. One could make this dilemma harder. What if, without the jobs Green Giant offered through the expansion of its plant, people would have starved? This would require some empirical proof, but if this was the case, then there could be a basic right of food (accompanying the job) versus the lack of clean water. There would be a context between rights of equal stature. In such cases, compromise becomes the answer. Trucking in clean water again might end up being the remedy. (This "answer" however, would not address the impact on those in the community who did not get a job with Green Giant or a company started to serve Green Giant. This analysis simply illustrates an application of rights theory. There are other aspects of the case too, including how the company handled the closing of the California facility and other environmental issues.)

The second framework is based in terms of justice, particularly as elaborated by Harvard philosopher John Rawls[77] and as refined by business ethicists Tom Donaldson[78] and Tom Dunfee.[79] This also is known as a social contract approach in that in order to create a set of rules that are perceived to be "fair", one should imagine a hypothetical negotiating session among individuals who do not know what attributes they will have when they are born. One doesn't know if they will be rich or poor, smart or dumb, tall or short, or any other unique characteristics that mark us. In such an "original position", Rawls argues that, because one does not know if one will be born to an advantageous or disadvantageous situation, several rules would be agreed to. One that is particularly important is that of the protection of the vulnerable because, in fact, one could be born into a precarious situation. In addition to this principle of protecting the vulnerable, justice carries with it a principle of treating people equally. Those making similar contributions, therefore, should be rewarded, similarly acknowledging, however, that the people are not born into positions that are equal, thereby necessitating attentiveness to vulnerability.[80]

A final dimension of social contract justice is that of Integrative Social Contracts Theory advocated by Donaldson and Dunfee.[81] In this approach, one adds to philosophical notions of contractual justice the dimension of extant social contracts or, in other words, what societies have already agreed to as rules of behavior. A motivating purpose for this framework is to recognize that societies do have rules of conduct and there should be "moral free space" for different cultures to prescribe rules of behavior appropriate for their community. Thus, one society may reward giving jobs on the basis of merit and others according to relationship. There are social reasons that can justify either approach. Nevertheless, these extant social contracts are still subject to overarching "hypernorms" that should not be violated. An example of this, according to Donaldson and Dunfee, is bribery because although societies may have bribery in their culture, it is universally condemned and skews resources inefficiently so that neither equal contributions are rewarded nor are the vulnerable made better off.[82]

The third element of the Philosopher's Formula is utilitarianism: the greatest good for the greatest number.[83] In a sense, stakeholder theory can be thought of as a utilitarian approach but that the greatest number for whom a greater good is being sought is not only the shareholders, but all the stakeholders. This framework still requires some sort of "counting" in order to determine what preferences (also known as "utiles") stakeholders have, but as a matter of fact, we make decisions on utilitarian calculations all the time. The fact that the United States suffers over 40,000 deaths a year from automobile accidents is a cost outweighed, we collectively believe, by the benefits of being able to drive cars. We may have more broken bones, but fewer deaths, if we returned to riding horses. But we have made a collective judgment as to what produces the most happiness for us. Similarly, even in a stake-holder management of the firm, one takes into account what will provide benefits for all the stakeholders.[84]

These normative approaches, along with a virtue approach I will speak of later, have dominated the field of business ethics for a couple of decades. The approaches require companies to take into account stakeholders in their actions. From a moral perspective, a stakeholder is a human being who is an "end" not a "means" and so we should treat all stakeholders with basic respect and dignity. These are moral duties inherent in all human life, business or non-business. There is a consensus among normative scholars that companies should treat stakeholders with respect. Companies should not simply maximize profit, they should do so within a framework that also provides a level of concern for vulnerable stakeholders. *How* one goes about that and what weights one is to give to various stakeholders is the subject of energetic debate. But the general normative consensus is that businesses are institutions with obligations to the wider world, particularly insofar as they impact vulnerable stakeholders.

Of course, to integrate them into business life, these moral precepts tend to seek justification for why they are good business too. Even if they are not good business, moral philosophers would generally agree that they should be followed. But of course, everyone would be much happier if good ethics *is* good business. (Finding such evidence also makes the life of an ethicist in a business school much more pleasant.) These twin notions are the dialectic of Real Trust.

Creating conditions that foster Real Trust thus stress acting fairly and, by doing so, creating social capital so that integrity is rewarded and becomes a habit. This requires rewarding people for doing the right thing as a management function. Several years ago, LaRue Hosmer developed a small vignette about a recent MBA graduate who worked for a department store in the gourmet food section. In this real case, the store sold individually wrapped, sealed specialty cookies. Unfortunately, some customers found that bugs were crawling around on the cookies when they opened them. The graduate's manager instructed her to "dump" the cookies, but the graduate discovered that this did not mean to throw the cookies in the trash. Instead, the manager said that she knew of a convenience store in the inner city where they could sell the infested cookies at a discount and get some of their money back.[85]

There are many things wrong with this solution, but from a twisted perspective, the supervisor's directive made sense. It made sense because the manager's annual bonus was based on profitability per square foot. So was her future allocation of square footage in the store.[86] In short, the company rewarded her to maximize her profitability in whatever way she could. The manager simply followed the logic of the financial incentives.

One could argue that the manager still should not have sold the cookies. That refusal would, in fact, be consistent with the normative theories. But the point is that if an organization wants to be an ethical one, it cannot rely on individual people to fall on their swords regularly to make it happen. Incentives need to be developed for rewarding people for not selling infested cookies and punishing them if they did. This means that ethics is not as much hiring people with personal integrity only; it means that ethics is also about organizational structures that reward the right things. In other words, to foster integrity, one needs to address utilitarian considerations in which just treatment of stakeholders is rewarded so that a greatest good is achieved. Or, to put it in more conventional business terms, it is important to create win-win environments for multiple stakeholders. That is the second part of the Real Trust dialectic.

Descriptive dimensions

In Chapter 4, I described how the three approaches to business ethics – legal, managerial, and asthetic/spiritual – connect with the value clusters of power-aggrandizing, economizing, and ecologizing. While I am taking liberty with Frederick's analysis, I believe the legal is derived from power relationships because of the coercive checks the legal provides for corporate behavior. In a realist sense, law checks the increase of corporate power in society. At its best, of course, law also has a moral (ecologizing) dimension as well and can also have efficiency considerations (particularly given the influence of law-and-economics scholarship for whom efficiency is a cardinal legal virtue). The managerial flows from our economizing values. Here again, the just-described normative approach to business ethics informs business of moral concerns just as natural law does for the legal. Yet the reality is that to gain currency within schools of management and within the board room, business ethics, even if normatively driven, have had to make the "business case" for ethics. In doing so, managerial approaches, even normative ones, take on even stronger economizing dimensions. Little ambiguity exists, however, on the descriptive side. There, efficacy is a central value. The connection between good ethics and good business and how to most effectively tie the two becomes a central aim of descriptive scholarship. So too does the alignment of psychology, custom, culture and policies become

important in descriptive business ethics just as it did in Ellul's spontaneous natural law.

Since the mid-1990s, management scholarship has seen a revival of
empirical study of corporate responsibility. Although the field is
diverse and wide-ranging, two main strands can be identified. The
first strand attends to the processes that make corporate compliance
programs efficacious. The second strand examines whether there is a
linkage between corporate responsibility and profitability.

Efficacious ethics

The previous chapter showed how government today asks corporations to institute programs that assure compliance with the law. These
ethics programs, perhaps itself a misnomer, have been around since
1991. Do they work? Since they have been around for a while, studies
have demonstrated what works and what doesn't work. In a series of
path-breaking articles, a research team led by Linda Trevino and Gary
Weaver report findings of what actually works in instituting compliance programs. Their research to my mind reports three important
things. First, of course, paper programs don't work well. That is, if a
company puts together a set of rules to show a prosecuting attorney
that it had a program, but employees thereafter had no exposure to it,
the program will simply linger in desk drawers around the office.
Second, the specific content of the program is not as important as
following through with whatever program has been put into place.
To comply with the Sentencing Guidelines or Sarbanes-Oxley, for
instance, a company must follow several criteria. These, as we have
seen, will include a code of conduct itself, high-ranking oversight, and
an opportunity for employees to voice concerns. How those kinds of
components are enacted, however, can vary. But as long as there is
follow-through on what was promised – the notion of procedural
justice – employees have respect for the program. If that doesn't happen, then cynicism will set in and the program will not be effective.[87]

Note again that the test is effectiveness rather than a normative duty
or aspiration. This research moves away from normative both in terms
of looking at what works and also with a conclusion that procedural
justice is more important than substantive justice. The third component
continues along the same track. Its conclusion is that if there is a
perception that rules and codes of conduct only apply to rank and file

employees, but not to high-ranking officials, then the program is doomed to cynical ineffectiveness.[88] While not cited by the researchers, two examples demonstrate this important point.

First, as noted in the previous chapter, Enron had a well-designed corporate compliance program. One aspect of that program was a conflict of interest policy that did not allow high-ranking officials to have ownership interest in a related entity. Yet when Andrew Fastow designed the special purpose entities (SPE), which allowed Enron to get debt off its books and which also enriched the 3 percent controlling owner of the SPE, it formally suspended its code of conduct to allow Fastow to take such an interest. The Board did this, not once, but three times![89] What kind of message do you think that sends?

Or let me give another, more personal example. When I first began teaching Executive Education classes, I early on taught a class on ethics to a group of about thirty mid-level managers from the (then) Big Three auto companies. We were discussing how to make ethics a part of everyday decisions rather than as something to be discussed only in a crisis. One fellow became very animated and screamed "I wanna know how my people will know that I mean business! And if they screw up, I'm gonna bust their ass and get 'em outta here!" The veins on his neck bulged, he yelled, and he pounded his fist on the table. It was quite a scene.

I suggested that the one thing he could do would be to be sure that everyone knew that the rules applied to him too. He got up and left the room in disgust.

This seems to be exactly what Trevino and Weaver are saying. What makes programs real is execution and making sure that the rules apply to everyone without exempting top management.

Remember that laws require "effective" programs. With empirical evidence now of what constitutes effective programs, it is simply negligence for a company to run a paper program. And so, one important aspect of Real Trust is to execute effective programs. More than overlaing the law is necessary for that to happen.

Corporate financial performance and corporate social performance

Of all the themes used to advocate ethical business behavior, the claim that good ethics is good business surely must be used the most. Particularly when qualified that in the long run, ethical business behavior pays, the business case for ethics is an old one. Sometimes this is stated flippantly; sometimes even involving theological principles such as karma or divine justice. Other times, it is argued on financial terms. Management scholars now try to more specifically determine whether there is a connection or not. In doing so, they often use the term corporate social responsibility (CSR) rather than business ethics. Business ethics and CSR, depending on how they are defined, can be a subset of each other; some even can make them wholly distinct. While there is intellectual traction to be gained by such separations and definitions, I think the distinctions tend to draw too fine a line. CSR certainly looks at broader issues than compliance (where ethics is often grouped with the law), but as we have just seen, ethics programs may wish to aim for more than compliance to simply get to compliance. Further, normative theories do not limit themselves to narrow compliance notions. So while a distinction can be maintained, the division between corporate social responsibility and business ethics is highly arbitrary. When management scholars look at issues of corporate social responsibility, business ethics, corporate social performance, and corporate citizenship, they are roughly looking at the same thing.

Studies of efficacious ethics take as their starting point the assumption that there is some need for a compliance and/or ethics program. That may be driven by the aspirations of the business or it may be the result of legal concerns. The aim of these scholars, however, is simply to determine what is effective. The aim of the studies tying corporate financial performance (CFP) and corporate social performance is whether responsibility pays.

The results of these studies are mixed. Some show positive correlations between corporate social performance and corporate financial performance. Others do not. In three meta-studies, the conclusion was that corporate social performance is (a) neutral, (b) slightly correlated with corporate financial performance, or (c) that, at least, it doesn't hurt.

Abagail McWilliams and Donald Siegel, for instance, argue that the relationship between CSR and CFP is neutral.[90] They note that various studies have shown different results that conclude little. This ambiguity leaves managers up in the air as to what they should do. In analyzing publicly traded firms, they say that two major demands for CSR come from consumers and employees. Consumers may prefer to buy from CSR companies. To respond to this, companies need to differentiate products, which in turn makes R&D a priority for CSR. To reach these consumers, advertising and firm reputation make a difference. Affluent consumers also tend to be less price-sensitive and therefore more evaluative of CSR activities. With respect to employees – the second demand driver – McWilliams and Siegel predict positive correlations between unionization and a shortage of skilled labor. That is, in those instances where labor pressures management, the interests of employees can cause corporate aims to include a CSR strategy. The same holds true for companies with government contracts. In those instances, wider stakeholder interests of concern to the government are more frequently built into contracts. These might include ecological concerns or hiring preferences. Finally, large firms share lower average costs and therefore are able to differentiate their products more easily. While a small firm may have a niche product, large firms can respond more easily to these other demands. Thus Siegel and McWilliams show that while studies are neutral in showing a connection between corporate financial performance and corporate social performance, companies marketing to affluent consumers, with strong employee voice, working with government, and which are large, are more likely to find rewards in pursuing a CSR strategy. Pursuing a CSR strategy may not be a financially mandated way of doing business, but neither is it a financial dead end. From the results of these studies, one could not say that good ethics is always good business. Sometimes it may be and sometimes it may not be. It is a viable strategy, however, that companies *can choose* to pursue. This is worth bearing in mind when thinking about Peace Through Commerce. Making peace an aim does not guarantee financial success, but it may be a strategy a company *could pursue* with realistic financial results. Perhaps a slightly different example may help to illustrate this point.

In one of my classes, students once engaged in a spirited discussion about using sexy images to market products. While most students had objections to a gratuitous portrayal of a product – such as when one opens a can of beer, one is immediately surrounded by beautiful, young, scantily clad women – companies do this because, many students said, sex sells. "Everybody does it", several said, to bolster the point. The success of Hooters Restaurants proves the point: sex sells.

But this proves the opposite point, I said. Hooters may be successful, but the overwhelming majority of restaurants do not have waitresses in barely nothing. Companies make choices. They can pursue strategies that differ from others even within an industry. BP looks different than

Exxon; Pfizer looks different than Johnson & Johnson. Hooters looks different than Applebys. Choosing to pursue good ethics does not guarantee success any more than ignoring ethics does. Both can be viable business strategies. The question is what strategic choices people *want* to make. That is the essence of what these studies show. Financially and empirically speaking, one does not *have* to pursue corporate responsibility, but doing so is a financially viable choice a business can make.

Joshua Margolis and James Walsh[91] also conducted a meta-study that is now frequently cited. In looking at dozens of previous studies, they concluded that there was a slightly positive correlation between CFP and CSR and little evidence of negative association. Similarly, Marc Orlitzky, Frank Schmidt, and Sara Rynes[92] provide a meta-study of CSR and CFP. They argue that CSP is likely to pay off although varieties of CSP are more highly correlated with accounting-based measures than market-based. They too conclude that there is no penalty to engage in CSR. Thus, pursuing a strategy of corporate responsibility may not be a mandated way of doing business, but neither is it "running a charity", a sarcastic excuse sometimes given by managers who eschew responsibility considerations.

A final study providing a valuable caveat to these explanations of the relationship between corporate social performance and corporate financial performance comes from Jennifer Griffin and John Mahon.[93] They note that researchers have used eighty different financial measures and fifty-seven of them have been used by only one researcher one time. Instead, Griffin and Mahon focused on just one industry – the chemical industry – in doing their study. They believe that it is important to conduct studies in a particular industry. Otherwise, there are too many variables to control in trying to determine the relationship between corporate financial performance and corporate social performance. In some industries, the correlation could be very close; in others, corporate social performance may make little difference to corporate financial performance. Because of this complexity, they call for (1) the use of multiple measures of social performance, (2) consistent use of financial performance, and (3) a focus on a single industry over time.

Symbiotic integrations

These two strands of descriptive ethics beg for integration. In making the integration, management scholars begin to slide back into normative arguments. Should corporations act as agents of social change? In a follow-up work to their book *Profits and People*, Margolis and Walsh suggest that while CFP and CSR are connected, an unanswered question is whether corporations really impact society constructively in taking on these initiatives and further, why managers do it.[94] It may well be that they don't do it for financial reasons. Margolis and Walsh quote Tetlock[95] that:

disagreements rooted in values should be profoundly resistant to change . . . libertarian conservatives might oppose the (confiscatory) stakeholder model even when confronted by evidence that concessions in this direction have no adverse effects on profitability of shareholders. Expropriation is expropriation, no matter how prettified. And some egalitarians might well endorse the stakeholder model even if shown compelling evidence that it does enhance profits. Academics who only rely on evidence-based appeals to change minds when disagreements are rooted in values may be wasting everyone's time.[96]

The previous analysis may show that the financial performance–social performance door is wide enough to walk through, but we may simply be looking at two entirely opposed ideological perceptions about the role of the corporation in society. This is enough of a connection, though, to merit a 2007 special issue of the *Academy of Management Review*. The contributions to this special issue ranged from looking at non-legal certification standards as a way to provide guidelines to corporate responsibility,[97] to offering more refined financial performance–social performance studies,[98] to studies differentiating the embrace of social change on the basis of firm levels of individual, organizational, national, and transnational.[99] These are a sample of the articles in this special issue and they pick up on an energetic theme of how corporations can contribute to social goods, perhaps most prominently championed in what corporations can do to lift the plight of the poor in the work of C. K. Pralahad[100] and Stuart Hart.[101] These approaches assume at least a financial neutral in pursuing social goods.

So, do corporations positively impact social issues? It is an important question, but I don't know that anybody really knows the answer. The efforts corporations have made to address social concerns – particularly on broad issues of poverty and peace – haven't been around long enough to know for sure. The normative folks, like myself, may view consequentalist concerns as secondary. I suspect, though, that we will see a large amount of scholarly attention paid to this issue over the next twenty-five years. The question Margolis and Walsh pose is whether there is a utilitarian synthesis of moral goods and efficacious consequences on a social scale.

Mark Bolino and William Turnley offer a glimpse of this kind of utilitarian synthesis in their work on corporate citizenship.[102] Bolino and Turnley argue that one cannot simply hope that workers will embrace the notion of corporate citizenship.[103] They argue that workplace behavior that asks employees to go "beyond the call of duty" requires organizations to act in ways that inspire such aspirational behavior. Such a connection between organization structure and employee motivation is a critical feature of the final kind of trust, Good Trust, but given the specific ways that Bolino and Turnley suggest will inspire such attitudes, it is worth including them as part of Real Trust. That is, to inspire individuals to do more than what they are required, by duty, to do, organizations should aim to create job satisfaction for employees, to provide good leadership, and to be perceived as achieving organization justice.[104] Social capital "exists in the relations between persons ... [and] facilitates productive activity. A group within which there is extensive trustworthiness and extensive trust is able to accomplish much more than a comparable group without that trustworthiness and trust."[105] Building on the contemporary scholarship on social capital,[106] Bolino and Turnley argue that it is this social capital that engenders commitment to the organization and inspires employees to go beyond minimalist expectations of duties. Thus, those companies that engage not only an employee's desire to obtain a financial reward, but those that get to softer, yet vital meaning-making kinds of issues such as job satisfaction, promoting feelings of being treated fairly, and being inspired by their leadership, build social capital that translates into good citizenship.[107]

What makes these citizenship dimensions of utilitarianism is that they attempt to create a "greatest good" for a larger range of stakeholders than would be necessarily captured by a shareholder-only approach. Shareholder theory is also utilitarian in that it attempts to create a good – economic value – of a greatest number, defined as the shareholders. It is possible that through an "enlightened" approach to shareholder theory that one would also attempt to treat certain stakeholders well – by doing so, one could enhance shareholder value.[108] The paradox is that engaging employee citizenship is likely to be done when there is both a tie to shareholder profitability as well as a sincere valuing of stakeholder-employees as an independent, intrinsically important group.[109] Real Trust attempts to integrate the greatest goods for both shareholders and employees by creating good corporate citizens (best done when sincerely aimed at), who therefore are willing to go the "extra mile" leading to a more productive workplace. Thus the range of those "greatest numbers" for whom a "greatest good" is maximized is increased, a utilitarian result. The same approach holds true in other stakeholder examples, including doing well by the shareholders by treating customers well[110] or in the case of "green" management, where one does well by attending to ecological concerns.[111]

Building social capital builds Real Trust because stakeholders trust the organization to treat them fairly. It integrates moral notions of fairness, such as respecting rights and administering justice within the context of creating an organization that maximizes good on a number of different levels. It also comports with traditional natural law considerations of impartiality, aiming for a common good, effective communication, subsidiarity (more on that in the next chapter), and property-like "stakes" in the company. Moreover, it allows corporate rules to make sense, to develop cultures where there is a spontaneous engagement of ethics: the Ellulian version of natural law.

Conclusion

Peace Through Commerce

Real Trust works within the framework of business to make businesses into organizations in which the public can have confidence. Management scholarship demonstrates normative reasons why businesses should as well as instrumental reasons why businesses do have an inherent self-interest to do this. Real Trust is rooted in our nature and is a mechanism that can be aimed toward peace. It is part of our economizing nature and because economic development is a central way in which violence can be mitigated, it becomes a potential source for peace itself.

There is a long line of scholarship that argues that trade leads to peace. We have already seen some of that literature. Kant, Montesquieu, and Hayek all saw benefits to trade that would lead away from violence. As we have also seen, though, Germany and the Soviet Union traded with each other right up to the time of Germany's invasion. Nearly all the warring parties of World War I traded with each other. There are limits to how commerce promotes peace. But a certain kind of commerce, one founded on ethical business behavior, may contribute to peace in greater ways because business then can foster economic development while limiting abusive treatment of stakeholders that could cause resentments. Broadly construed, there are sources within schools of management and within business itself to provide this best of all worlds approach to common business ethics practices. Normatively and descriptively, these practices can go a long way to create the kind of business practices that would lead to Peace Through Commerce. Nevertheless, I am skeptical of how this can be done without the coercive pressure of law (Hard Trust) and the passionate commitment to doing good (Good Trust) that extends beyond the province of Real Trust.

Segue to Good Trust

When I was growing up in the rural Midwest, I had the good fortune of being around business people who were some of the most profoundly ethically inspiring individuals I have ever encountered. Bankers such as Howard Grigsby and Eldon Duncan, lawyers like Stephen Evans and Lyman Fort, home service contractors like Ivan Jacob and Gene Ray, and car dealers like Clarence Neff and Russ Davison (and I leave out many other worthy examples in this listing) would never have thought to focus only on the profitability of their businesses. They were profitable, but that was only one aspect of their work. I could tell stories about all of them, particularly with respect to my father and Clarence Neff whom I knew the best, but I'd like to tell a simple story about Russ Davison.

Russ inherited a Ford dealership from his father. Decades before big auto companies marketed the benefits of "no-hassle bargaining" Russ perfected it. Russ didn't negotiate. He told you what he could sell the car for and that was it. He wasn't in a position of power. In his town of only 800 people, there were two other dealerships within one hundred yards of Russ's and in a town of that size and with larger dealerships in nearby cities, there was no oligopolistic pricing power. People accepted Russ's price because they knew it was the best he could do. People trusted Russ. One reason they trusted him was that Russ was in a small community in which notions of social capital were crucial. If Russ took advantage of someone, he had to face the reality that the news would spread very quickly. The local restaurant, The Hurry-Back Grill, was only fifty yards from Russ's dealership, so if he did treat someone unfairly, that information would quickly and efficiently get circulated. In such a web of networked relationships – to use some fancy business school jargon – Russ's reputation, goodwill, and social capital concerns would operate as an effective check against misbehavior. This is Real Trust and it had to have an impact on Russ at some level. So too, today, the more companies recognize how their businesses are embedded in a global communications network where social capital, reputation, and goodwill are important, Russ's experience in a Norman Rockwell-like farm town might be replicated.

But there was another reason why people trusted Russ so much. Yes, Hard Trust would punish fraud and dirty dealing. Yes, Real Trust would make Russ aware of softer incentives and the need to live up to promises, to be fair to customers and employees, and to be a good citizen. Russ, though, also pursued Good Trust: he *wanted* to be a particular kind of person who valued and was valued by his community. He *wanted* to be trustworthy whether there were any external checks on him or not. Russ was no saint, but he tried very hard to be a good person. That affective, aspirational, and aesthetic quest for excellence and community is the final aspect of trust and that is the topic of the next chapter.

Notes

1. Michele Williams, *In Whom We Trust: Group Membership as an Affective Context for Trust*, 26 ACADEMY OF MANAGEMENT REVIEW 377–96 (Jul 2001); Frank Jeffries, *Trust and Adaptation in Relational Contracting*, 25 ACADEMY OF MANAGEMENT REVIEW 873–82 (Oct 2000); Andrew Wicks, Shawn Berman, and Thomas Jones, *The Structure of Optimal Trust: Moral and Strategic Implications*, 24 ACADEMY OF MANAGEMENT REVIEW 99–116 (Jan 1999).
2. See generally F. A. HAYEK, THE FATAL CONCEIT: THE ERRORS OF SOCIALISM (1990).
3. LaRue Tone Hosmer, *Trust; The Connecting Link Between Organizational Theory and Philosophical Ethics*, 20 ACADEMY OF MANAGEMENT REVIEW 279-4-3 (1995).
4. H. L. A. HART, THE CONCEPT OF LAW (2d edn. 1994).
5. Section 6.I A appeared in my book, ETHICS AND GOVERNANCE: BUSINESS AS MEDIATING INSTITUTION 52–61.
6. Manuel Velasquez and F. Neil Brady, *Natural Law and Business Ethics*, 7 BUS. ETHICS Q. 83 (1997).

7. *Id.* at 92.
8. *Id.* at 92.
9. *Id.* at 92.
10. *Id.* at 93–4.
11. *Id.* at 95.
12. *Id.* at 96.
13. *Id.* at 97.
14. *Id.* at 97.
15. *Id.* at 97.
16. *Id.* at 97.
17. *Id.* at 98.
18. *Id.* at 99.
19. *Id.* at 100.
20. DOUGLAS W. KMIEC AND STEPHEN B. PRESSER, THE AMERICAN CONSTITUTIONAL ORDER: HISTORY, CASES, AND PHILOSOPHY 1 (1998).
21. LON FULLER, ANATOMY OF THE LAW 181 (1968).
22. LARRY ARNHART, DARWINIAN NATURAL RIGHT: THE BIOLOGICAL ETHICS OF HUMAN NATURE 4 (1998).
23. *Id.*
24. *Id.* at 24.
25. THOMAS AQUINAS, TREATISE ON LAW 7 (from Summa Theologica Questions 90–7).
26. JOHN FINNIS, NATURAL LAW AND NATURAL RIGHTS 360 (1980).
27. LON FULLER, ANATOMY OF THE LAW 186 (1968).
28. RICHARD PIPES, PROPERTY AND FREEDOM 116 (1999).
29. *Id.* at 64–120.
30. *Id.* at 79.
31. *Id.* at 80.
32. *Id.* at 86.
33. *Id.* at 87.
34. *Id.* at 92–7.
35. *Id.* at 7–8.
36. *Id.* at 8.
37. *Id.* at 17.
38. *Id.* at 34.
39. *Id.* at 5.
40. *Id.* at 121–58.
41. MATT RIDLEY, THE ORIGINS OF VIRTUE: HUMAN INSTINCTS AND THE EVOLUTION OF COOPERATION 231–46 (1997).
42. STEPHEN B. PRESSER, RECAPTURING THE CONSTITUTION: RACE, RELIGION, AND ABORTION RECONSIDERED 62 (1994).

43. John Finnis, *Natural Law and Legal Reasoning*, in NATURAL LAW THEORY: CONTEMPORARY ESSAYS 135 (Robert P. George, ed., 1994).

44. Lee Preston and Thomas Donaldson, *Stakeholder Management and Organizational Wealth*, 24 ACADEMY OF MANAGEMENT REVIEW 619–21 (Oct 1999); Thomas Donaldson and Lee Preston, *The Stakeholder Theory of the Corporation: Concepts, Evidence and Implications*, 20 ACADEMY OF MANAGEMENT REVIEW 65–91 (Jan 1995).

45. See Philip M. Nichols, *Regulating Transnational Bribery in Times of Globalization and Fragmentation*, 24 YALE J. INT'L L. 257 (1999) at 258, citing David H. Bagley, *The Effects of Corruption in a Developing Nation*, 19 WORLD POL. QUART. 719, 720 (1966).

46. See David Hess and Thomas W. Dunfee, *Fighting Corruption: A Principled Approach The C[su'2'] Principles (Combating Corruption)*, 33 CORNELL J. INT'L L. 593 (2000).

47. See THOMAS DONALDSON AND THOMAS W. DUNFEE, TIES THAT BIND: A SOCIAL CONTRACTS APPROACH TO BUSINESS ETHICS 121 (1999).

48. Fort and Schipani, *The Role of the Corporation in Fostering Sustainable Peace*, 35 VANDERBILT JOURNAL OF TRANSNATIONAL LAW 389 (2002).

49. The following is adapted from Timothy L. Fort and James J. Noone, *Gifts, Bribes, and Exchange: Relationships in Non-Market Economies and Lessons for Pax E-Commercia*, 33 CORNELL INTERNATIONAL LAW JOURNAL 515.

50. See generally ALASDAIR MACINTYRE, AFTER VIRTUE (1981).

51. See *id. at* 18.

52. See MARSHALL SAHLINS, ISLANDS OF HISTORY 142 (1985).

53. See MACINTYRE, *supra* note 50 at 105.

54. Donaldson and Dunfee, *supra* note 47 at 228–9; Fort and Schipani, *supra* note 48.

55. This is at the essence of classic tragedy of commons kinds of stories. Garrett Hardin, *Tragedy of the Commons*, in ECONOMICS OF THE ENVIRONMENT: SELECTED READINGS (1993).

56. JACQUES ELLUL, THE THEOLOGICAL FOUNDATION OF LAW (Marguerite Wieser, trans., 1960).

57. Ellul actually characterizes it as a three-part development, but stages three and four as I describe them seem to be separate, though certainly related stages within Ellul's original stage three.

58. ELLUL, *supra* note 56, at 18.

59. ELLUL, *supra* note 56.

60. ELLUL, *supra* note 56.

61. For a discussion of Ellul's argument in the context of historical issues, see TIMOTHY L. FORT, LAW AND RELIGION (1985).

62. Quoted in ROBERT L. HEILBRONNER, THE WORLDLY PHILOSOPHERS (1953, 1999).

63. Lynn Sharp Paine, *Managing for Organizational Integrity*, HARV. BUS. REV. (Mar/Apr 1994) at 11.

64. L. K. Trevino, K. Butterfield, and D. McCabe, *The Ethical Context in Organizations: Influences on Employee Attitudes and Behaviors*, 8 BUSINESS ETHICS QUARTERLY 447 (1998); Linda Klebe Trevino, Gary R. Weaver, David G. Gibson, and Barbara Ley Toffler, *Managing Ethics and Legal Compliance: What Works and What Hurts*, 41 CALIFORNIA MANAGEMENT REVIEW 131 (1999).

65. See Timothy L. Fort and James J. Noone, SYMPOSIUM FIGHTING INTERNATIONAL CORRUPTION AND BRIBERY IN THE 21ST CENTURY: *Gifts, Bribes, and Exchange: Relationships in Non-Market Economies and Lessons for Pax E-Commercia*, 33 CORNELL INT'L L. J. 515 (2000).

66. See MAKING DEMOCRACY WORK (Robert Putnam *et al*, eds., 1993).

67. ROBERT AXELROD, THE COMPLEXITY OF COOPERATION (1997).

68. See F. A. HAYEK, THE FATAL CONCEIT 70–4 (1988), arguing for norms of reciprocity and integrity virtues such as truth-telling, promise keeping, and protection of contracts and property, while also recognizing that these virtues require coercive legal (and religious) enforcement because of the temptation to benefit from others practicing these virtues while behaving opportunistically whenever one can.

69. ROBERT M. AXELROD, THE EVOLUTION OF COOPERATION 211, 1390 (1984).

70. See JAMES COLEMAN, FOUNDATIONS OF SOCIAL THEORY (1990).

71. Mark Granovetter, *Economic Action and Social Structure: The Problem of Embeddedness*, 91 AM. J. SOC. 481, 481–2 (1985).

72. See e.g. Hosmer, *supra* note 3, at 379.

73. Hayek, *supra* note 69.

74. RAYMOND BAUMHART, WHAT BUSINESSMEN SAY ABOUT ETHICS (1968).

75. WILLIAM C. FREDERICK, VALUES, NATURE AND CULTURE IN THE AMERICAN CORPORATION 251 (1995).

76. PATRICIA WERHANE, PERSONS RIGHTS AND CORPORATIONS (1985).

77. JOHN RAWLS, A THEORY OF JUSTICE (1971).

78. THOMAS DONALDSON, CORPORATIONS AND MORALITY (1982).

79. DONALDSON AND DUNFEE, *supra* note 47.

80. *Id.* at 26, citing RAWLS, *supra* note 77, at 367.

81. DONALDSON AND DUNFEE, *supra* note 47.

82. *Id.*

83. FREDERICK, *supra* note 75, at 251.

84. William M. Evan and R. Edward Freeman, *A Stakeholder Theory of the Modern Corporation: Kantian Capitalism*, ETHICAL THEORY AND

BUSINESS 97, 101–5 (Tom L. Beauchamp and Norman E. Bowie, eds., 7th edn., 2002).

85. HOSMER, *supra* note 3.

86. *Id.*

87. LINDA KLEBE TREVINO AND GARY R. WEAVER, MANAGING ETHICS IN BUSINESS ORGANIZATIONS: SOCIAL SCIENTIFIC PERSPECTIVES (2003); see also references *supra* in note 64.

88. TREVINO AND WEAVER, *supra* note 87.

89. William Powers, *Report of the Special Investigation Committee to the Members of the Board of Directors, Enron Corporation* (February 1, 2002), at http://fl1.findlaw.com/news.findlaw.com/wp/docs/enron/spe cinv020102rpt1.pdf.

90. Abagail McWilliams, *Corporate Social Responsibility: A Theory of the Firm Perspective*, 26 ACADEMY OF MANAGEMENT REVIEW 117–27 (2001).

91. JOSHUA DANIEL MARGOLIS AND JAMES PATRICK WALSH, PEOPLE AND PROFITS (2001).

92. Marc Orlitzky, Frank L Schmidt, and Sara L Rynes, *Corporate Social and Financial Performance: A Meta-analysis*, 24 ORGANIZATION STUDIES 403–41 (2003).

93. Jennifer J. Griffin and John F. Mahon, *The Corporate Social Performance and Corporate Financial Performance Debate: Twenty-Five Years of Incomparable Research*, 36 BUSINESS & SOCIETY 5–31 (1997).

94. Joshua D. Margolis and James P. Walsh, *Misery Loves Companies: Rethinking Social Initiatives by Business*, 48 ADMINISTRATIVE SCIENCE QUARTERLY 268 (2003).

95. P. E. Tetlock, *Cognitive Biases and Organizational Correctives: Do Both Disease and Cure Depend on the Politics of the Beholder?* 45 ADMINISTRATIVE SCIENCES QUARTERLY 293–326 (2003).

96. Margolis and Walsh, *supra* note 94, at 281.

97. Ann Terlaak, *Order Without Law? The Role of Certified Management Standards in Shaping Socially Desired Firm Behaviors*, ACADEMY OF MANAGEMENT REVIEW (forthcoming, 2007).

98. Alison Mackey, Tyson B Mackey, and Jay B. Barney, *Corporate Social Responsibility and Firm Performance: Investor Preferences and Corporate Strategies*, ACADEMY OF MANAGEMENT REVIEW (forthcoming, 2007); Michael J. Barnett, *Stakeholder Influence Capacity and The Variability of Financial Returns to Corporate Social Responsibility*, ACADEMY OF MANAGEMENT REVIEW (forthcoming, 2007).

99. Ruth V. Aguilera, Deborah E. Rupp, Cynthia A. Williams, and Jyoti Ganapathi, *Putting the S Back in Corporate Social Responsibility: A Multi-level Theory of Social Change in Organizations*, ACADEMY OF MANAGEMENT REVIEW (forthcoming, 2007).

100. C. K. PRAHALAD, THE FORTUNE AT THE BOTTOM OF THE PYRAMID: ERADICATING POVERTY THROUGH PROFITS (2004).

101. STUART L. HART, CAPITALISM AT A CROSSROADS: THE UNLIMITED BUSINESS OPPORTUNITIES IN SOLVING THE WORLD'S MOST DIFFICULT PROBLEMS (2005).

102. Mark C. Bolino and William H. Turnley, *Going the Extra Mile: Cultivating and Managing Employee Citizenship Behavior*, 17 ACAD. MGMT. EXECUTIVE 60 (2003). Bolino and Turnley, of course, are not the only management scholars looking at such issues, but they do summarize corporate citizenship in a straight-forward, helpful way.

103. *Id.* at 67–8.

104. *Id.* at 60–4.

105. COLEMAN, *supra* note 70, at 382–3.

106. Some of the central figures on the development of the idea of social capital include Mark Granovetter, *Economic Action and Social Structure: The Problem of Embeddedness*, 91 AM. J. SOCIOLOGY 481 (1985); James S. Coleman, *The Creation and Destruction of Social Capital: Implications for The Law*, 3 J. LAW, ETHICS, & PUB. POL. 375 (1988); Rafael La Porta, Florencio Lopez-de-Silanes, Adrei Shleifer and Robert Vishny, *The Quality of Government*, 15 J. LAW, ECON. & ORGANIZATION 222 (1999).

107. Bolino and Turnley, *supra* note 102, at 62.

108. See Michael Jensen, *Value Maximization, Stakeholder Theory, and the Corporate Objective Function*, 12 BUSINESS ETHICS QUARTERLY 235–56.; see also, Milton Friedman, *The Social Responsibility of Business Is to Increase Its Profits*, NEW YORK TIMES MAGAZINE (September 13, 1970, reprint).

109. See e.g. LYNN SHARP PAINE, VALUE SHIFT: WHY COMPANIES MUST MERGE SOCIAL AND FINANCIAL IMPERATIVES TO ACHIEVE SUPERIOR PERFORMANCE (2003), noting how AES was questioned by the Securities Exchange Commission after stating that the company wished to treat employees well because doing so was intrinsically important in its own right.

110. See e.g. NANCY MANN AND W. EDWARDS DEMING, THE KEYS TO EXCELLENCE: THE DEMING PHILOSOPHY (1989).

111. See e.g. S. SHARMA AND J. A. ARAGON-CORREA, ENVIRONMENTAL STRATEGY AND COMPETITIVE ADVANTAGE (2005); S. Sharma and H. Vredenburg, *Proactive Corporate Environmental Strategy and the Development of Competitively Valuable Organizational Capabilities* 19 STRATEGIC MANAGEMENT JOURNAL 729–53 (1998).

7 | *Good Trust*

THERE are three reasons why a business leader would want to undertake any consideration of ethics. They are legal, economic, and moral identity. I have already sketched the legal and economic dimensions. A firm may consider ethical concerns because of legal pressures or because they see the economic benefits of pursuing them. The moral identity dimension is Good Trust. It is Good Trust because it is a place where individuals find a sense of their own well-being in the welfare of others. One could also call this "Beautiful Trust" too, because it is about the passion and beauty of people caring for others. At its core, Good Trust is about getting people to really care about ethics, not just because that is what is required by law (Hard Trust) or what is rewarded (Real Trust) but because it is something that inspires them.

The task of Good Trust is to foster or to free passion apart from its deleterious effects. Good Trust is about engaging human quests for moral excellence and spiritual identity. All of the rules of the moral theory, and all of the financial rewards for behavior will only go so far if a person simply does not want to be ethical. All the theory in the world equals zero if the motivation for implementing it is zero. So energizing a passion about behavior enervates all aspects of ethics.

At the same time, one can be passionate about very troubling things. History is replete with people and movements torturing and killing in the name of some higher principle. Inner city youth gangs and the KKK are passionate about their identities that give their members a sense of meaning. Sometimes, religion gets blamed for this, but non-theistic movements (for instance communism and fascism) have perpetrated some of the most egregious oppressions of all time, quite often in natural law terms. Energizing passion is one thing. The aim toward which that passion is pointed is another.

Moreover, one can be passionate about things that give great meaning, but are simply different kinds of experiences than the one I am talking about. That's true even on the same topic of war and peace.

In his book, *War Is a Force That Gives Us Meaning*, Chris Hedges graphically describes the horrors of war and the ways in which it acts not simply as a narcotic – numbing one from grasping the savagery actually taking place – but also as something so engaging and beyond oneself that it provides a powerful sense of meaning.[1] I have no reason to doubt this. Fighting a war for an ideal or simply to survive engages the most basic and the most inspiring of bravery and sacrifice. That is a kind of meaning that is important, but it is not quite the kind of meaning I have in mind in a book about how corporate responsibility in the twenty-first century should be pointed toward peace and stability. Yet, there is a common element in that there is a sense of value in going beyond an individual self-interest to foster a common good. That formulation – going beyond self-interest to foster a common good – is at the heart of what ethics and spirituality are about.[2] There may be dangers associated with it, but it remains a critical point of promoting ethical business behavior.

Three critical dimensions comprise Good Trust. The first is a notion of "music". That is, a sense of spiritual and aesthetic, harmonic artfulness that defines a quest for moral excellence. The second is an organizational dimension where there are communal identities formed and which dialectically interact with individuals. This is a notion of "mediating institutions", which are particular kinds of communities that foster personal meaningfulness and moral identity. The third is a bigger sense of mediating institutions – perhaps one could call it "more mediation" – that connects very concretely and specifically with a teleological goal of how corporations can contribute to sustainable peace. That is a necessary goal in order to counteract the tendencies for the first two characteristics to remain in check and not become abusive in their own right. Thus, Good Trust becomes M^3: Music, Mediating Institutions, and More Mediation.

Remember the cheesy example I used at the end of Chapter 4 about the schools' songs of the University of Michigan and the University of Notre Dame? When each band plays the other school's (great and famous) song, one hears all the rules of music obeyed (Hard Trust). One also see rewards for the band politely playing the other school's song because the fans whose band played clap and the fans whose song was just played clap too (Real Trust). But it is when the band plays its own song, with pride, passion, heart, and identity that one hears when it is put all together. There is a spiritual element in Good Trust and that can make people uneasy.

As management guru Tom Peters once sarcastically wrote:

> when talk turns to the spiritual side of leadership, I mostly want to run. It should be enough if I work like hell, respect my peers, customers and suppliers, and perform with verve, imagination, efficiency and good humor. Please don't ask me to join the Gregorian Chant Club too.[3]

Yet, the mixing of leadership theory and religious rhetoric occurs not infrequently, at least in popular renditions. Thus, James Autry describes management as a "sacred trust",[4] and quality theorist Joseph Juran refers to Jethro, the father-in-law of Moses, as the first management consultant (and one who utilizes a quality management system based on delegation of responsibility).[5] Juran also claims that adopting quality management principles is primarily "an act of faith or belief"[6] and Mary Walton summarizes the work of W. Edwards Deming as "quality must become the new religion".[7]

This rhetoric can be dismissed as just that: rhetoric. Yet the intersection of religion and work is hardly abating. One could also claim that these popular renditions of management theory are not based in scholarly research, yet Laura Nash's work on evangelical executives demonstrates that, with the important and significant exception of the treatment of women, the companies led by evangelical CEOs are very law-abiding and the people who work for them believe they are treated well and paid well.[8] This is not to argue that the intermixing of spirituality and business is a good thing; it could be a good thing, a bad thing, or even an ugly thing. Yet it is hard to leave religion and spirituality alone. Management theory that attempts to engage passions at work generally offers a secular version of long-standing theologies of work. Those theologies, whether a Calvinist/Lutheran notion of Calling and Vocation or a Catholic sense of Solidarity and Co-Creation, all provide that work is not just work; it is also a connection to an overarching sense of transcendence. Engaging workers in this kind of thinking significantly raises the stakes of the meaningfulness of work.

The spiritual sense: music

Let me begin with a cautionary note. I want to talk about a naturalistic characteristic that human beings have that causes them to desire to quest

Table 7.1. Good Trust

The Why Be Ethical Question	Legal Regulation: Punishment for Failures	Hard Trust Model
	Economic Consequences: Good Ethics is Good Business	Real Trust Model
	Moral and Identity Reasons: Moral Excellence and Spiritual Identity	Good Trust Model
Moral Excellence	Mediating Institutions	Magic Numbers and Moral Identity
Spiritual Identity	Spiritual Quests for Moral Excellence	Ethics as a Way of Life Leading to Internal and Social Peace
Literary Inspiration	Aesthetic Aims	Existential Visions of the Good
Bias Adjustments	Inherent Problems of Hindsight, Outcome, Belief, Confirmation, Conjunctive/Adjunctive, Overconfidence, Bias, External Commitment, Adjustment	Hard Trust Checklists Real Trust Integration Externalized Goods

for a sense transcendence. This is, I will argue, innate. Religion is one way this desire plays out, but it is not the only way. Non-religious spiritualities and quests for excellence that have no formally articulated identification with either religion or spirituality are obviously present. As the argument of this section proceeds, the reader will see that although "religion" is the vehicle of analysis, the idea is one of a quest for transcendence that transforms our sense of self-interest. And so, I do not want to take the time to make carefully delineated differentiations between religion, spirituality, and non-theistic quests for moral excellence. There may be times and places for those differentiations – although I must confess my own skepticism about their adequacy – but the naturalistic analysis provided here does not "draft" an atheist into being religious; it simply uses moral notions of transcendence, as particularly exemplified and analyzed via religion, as a way human beings have used teleological ideals to overcome a narrow view of self-interest.

Religion's naturalistic inevitability

The reason management scholars can't quite leave religion and spirituality alone is because it is a fundamental aspect of our human nature. We may sometimes wish that we were more rational, but evolutionary theorists now believe that spiritual belief has been part of our evolutionary, competitive advantage. It helps us to survive. Of course, just as I have argued that the twenty-first century is a time and place that no longer allows us to afford a value-maximizing notion of the corporation, so too one could argue that weapons are too dangerous now to continue to rely on religions that teach us we will enjoy eternal bliss by blowing up ourselves and others.[9] There is a point to that view, but just as corporations extrude a natural economizing value, so too does religion and spirituality extend a natural ecologizing value. We may indeed need to soften the harsher elements of each as they have been practiced, but they cannot be wished away.

Religion and spirituality are one way through which a person may seek moral excellence. Companies today find themselves in what one scholar called a "God rush".[10] Quite a few companies have supported employee efforts to develop a spiritual focus or to participate in conferences. These include Aetna Life Insurance, AT&T, Aveda, Bank of Boston, BioGenex, Boeing, Carlisle Motors, Cascade Communications, Cell Canada, Cirrus Logic, Deloitte & Touche, Digital Equipment, Elf Aquitaine, Espirit, Ford, Gillette, Goldman-Sachs, Hydro-Ontario, KPMG, Lotus Development, Lucent Technologies, Medtronic, Motorola, Nortel Networks, Odwalla, Pizza Hut, Raytheon, The Royal Bank, ServiceMaster, Shell, Southwest Airlines, Starbucks, Stonyfield Yogurt, Sun Microsystems, Taco Bell, Timberland, Wal-Mart, World Bank, and Xerox.[11] In short, interest in spirituality at work is becoming mainstream and widespread. Why such interest?

According to Thierry Pauchant, it is the result of a search for meaning because of

[n]umerous factors . . . In a broad sense, several changes have contributed to an increased sense of insecurity in the general population and to the upending of traditional paradigms that gave meaning to their world and their lives. We

can refer to problems of international security, the rise of terrorism, and dogmatism – as exemplified by the September 11 tragedy, the appearance and growth of AIDS and the ecological crisis. We can also point to the decline of traditional religion in the West ... Other observers have attributed this increased quest for meaning to the fact that a large portion of our Western population – the baby boomers – is aging and that these people are now faced with the prospect of the end of their lives. Other factors have also created upheaval in the institutional and economic worlds: increased unemployment, fiercer competition, an increased rate of change, major restructuring, and corporate scandals.[12]

One way to look at this is through the work of Loyal Rue. In a book I wrote simultaneously to this book, *Prophets, Profits, Passions, and Peace*, I spent considerable time dealing with Rue's work. Let me abbreviate that treatment a bit here. Drawing on an evolutionary perspective, Rue argues that religion serves to energize embedded emotions in the service of a common good. Religion shows to an individual believer (of Islam, Buddhism, Christianity, Hinduism, Judaism, etc.) how they can enhance their feelings of self-worth by sublimating instinctive immediate desires for materials and sensual pleasures in the goal of fostering a common good. Religions thus are very much about long-term kinds of Real Trust and bring with them coercive sanctions (ostracism or promises of eternal punishments) or Hard Trust. In this sense, "religion is not about God" (the title of Rue's book) but it is about the sophisticated construction of a cultural ethos that endures because it encourages sublimation in the service of the common good. In doing so, "we enhance our prospects for reproductive fitness".[13]

That much seems fairly straightforward. However, what opens Rue up to multiple religions is his view that religion is not about God, it is about us; or to put it more precisely:

This leaves us in the odd position of asserting that while subjective and conventional religious meanings may be about God, religion in general is not – it is, rather about influencing neural modules for the sake of personal wholeness and social coherence. An adequate general theory of religion should be able to bring substance to these claims (Part One of the book). And further, it should be able to show us how conventional religious meanings have been honed to promote personal wholeness and social coherence (Part Two).[14]

Religion – whatever religion that is – does integrate personal wholeness and social cohesion. That religion – whatever it is – does have a strong tradition of peace that features its better angels. All major religions do. But how we act, our behaviors, are not innately stitched in to our nature.

Nobody inherits behavior. What we inherit are genes that code for proteins that build the tissues of mechanisms for organizing behavior. So the evolution of behavior really comes down to a story about the evolution of *mediators* of behavior. The general thrust of the story is this: Over time, there has been a gradual process of systemic development in which behaviors have become mediating by ever more complicated mechanisms, enabling ever more complicated and variable interactions between organisms and their environments. Human nature, we may say, is embedded in the logic of these behavior mediation systems.[15]

Rue starts at the cellular level describing what he calls "lock and key biochemistry".[16] That biochemistry is what permits cells to work together and develop higher-order complexity. This he says, is true of "alga swimming after a sunbeam or an ambassador negotiating a treaty".[17] Multicellular creatures result when there is a lock-and-key system that allows for the transportation of nutrients and information throughout the body.[18] In short, lock-and-key biochemistry allows individual cells to work with other cells to better function and to enhance the likelihood of survival. In a very real way, this lock-and-key biochemistry links "self-interest" to a common good by making survival fostered by cooperation.

What is at the heart of the cellular and neurological level holds true on a larger, biological, systemic level as well.

Physiological drive systems evolved as new strategies for mediating behaviors. They are higher-order homeostatic systems featuring emergent properties of subjective experience – thirst, hunger, fatigue, stress, pain, and cravings of various qualities. When an animal is aroused to thirst, it will engage in exploratory behaviors directed toward circumstances where it can drink, whereupon it will experience pleasure. The desire is thereby satisfied and the system is restored to equilibrium.[19]

Evolutionary pressure places an emphasis on making maximum use of the traits a species possesses.[20] One way to efficiently do this is by "neural plasticity". Animals may interact with many diverse environmental features and if the brain can adapt "on the run" those creatures have an advantage. In fact, this capability is more efficient than an inherited genetic behavior because the animal can adapt to ecological challenges and opportunities. These plastic capabilities are the ability to learn and to memorize, also called an "engram" by Richard Semon. While a bacteria is doomed to behave in just one way, a wolf may adjust to several different environmental settings.[21] Animals, including humans, can learn and adapt. So then, are we free of genetic constraints?

Why not go beyond mere plasticity to create ultimate learning machines: Creatures so free and variable in their behavior, so fluid in their nature that they may be said to possess no determined nature at all, apart from their powers of self-determination? Indeed, many social scientists and existential philosophers have insisted that human beings are just such creatures. Philosophers may say what they like, of course, but no one has yet shown how a creature of indeterminate nature could possibly exist. To survive by engrams alone would require a brain the size of Chicago and a curriculum of learning that would last for centuries. And even then, such a being would spend most of its time and energy on the aimless construction of engrams that would be totally irrelevant to its survival interests. The natural world has no tolerance for such monstrosities. The so-called tabular rasa that figures into much social science and philosophy is a ridiculous fiction, not something natural selection would come up with. A far better option was to coordinate the engram strategy with genetic information.[22]

Like the arguments of Bill Frederick, these are naturalistic categories of behavior and life. Following their train allows us to see how religious belief can help us to survive.

For example, the amygdal in the limbic area of the brain controls defensive behaviors in reptiles and according to Rue, is "the heart and soul of the fear system" in rats, cats, dogs, rabbits, monkeys, and humans.[23] It may therefore be the case that "neural structures in the limbic region of the brain gradually took on new functions, leading to the development of emotional systems in mammals (and to some extent in birds)".[24] Such emotions might have been associated with the recognition of pain and pleasure: "the adaptive value of fear and disgust would be in motivating animals to avoid dangerous predators and harmful substances, while the adaptive value of desire and longing would be to generate the conjugal and maternal bonding typical of mammals".[25] Taking an additional step, an elaboration of "desire and longing might produce affection, sympathy, or gratitude".[26]

When an asteroid hit the earth sixty-five million years ago, Rue argues, reptilian domination (i.e. paradigmatically, the dinosaurs), opened up to early mammals who were able to thrive by competing via social cooperation.[27] Anthropologists have shown that notions of inclusive self-interest would be linked to the common good by fostering the survival of genes.[28] But once in our emotional makeup, sacrificial behavior and other emotions were not limited to genetic kin, but also fostered broader social cooperation.[29] At this point, Rue has the stage set for human behavior and mediators of value.

Rue argues that children, starting at about eighteen months old, start to see others as agents rather than merely objects and begin to apply the person-as-agent concept to themselves so that

As children assimilate the logic of social roles they learn to apply the standards of performance implicit in those roles. And once the standards are internalized the child will apply them reflexively in a narrative process of self-monitoring ... Consistently poor performance will contribute to a sense of negative self-esteem, while good outcomes will count as evidence favoring a sense of positive self-esteem ... Once this self-monitoring system is established, it functions as a powerful organizer of an individual's experience and activity, influencing nearly all aspects of information processing, including attention, perception, memory, concept formation, and all manner of judgments concerning which things matter. It is not an exaggeration to say that of all our behavior mediation systems, self-esteem is the most dominant.[30]

The self-esteem system (Rue's term) is very plastic in being able to respond to varying circumstances. Our need for self-esteem causes us to react to

social signals of approval or disapproval. For example, if you get praise for recycling your newspapers and scorn for not recycling, then you will eventually link your self-esteem to recycling. The power of social signaling is truly awesome. Just consider what people are motivated to do in the name of self-esteem: We risk our lives in battle for the adulation of heroism, we pierce, pain or starve our bodies to meet social standards of beauty, we endure surgery for attention-getting breasts, and we steal, deceive, and murder to acquire status symbols."[31]

One might say that our individual moral identity is deeply dependent on our relationship to our communities. These communities reward recycling of newspapers and they also form language, culture, and religion.[32] These symbolic systems began to be established two million years ago in a co-evolutionary process between language and the brain.[33] In this process, "something genuinely novel emerges in the event of symbolic communication: A new system for preserving and processing information is established outside the body."[34] Because "a private language is an oxymoron",[35] so too are other symbolic systems of ethics, culture, and religion. Cultures then devise cosmology and morality[36] and focus on personal wholeness and social coherence.[37]

Thus, our human nature is not that of a *tabula rasa* nor is it fully genetically determined. Our nature is both somewhat plastic and somewhat determined. Our moral identity is linked to culturally evolutionary processes that link our individuality to social groups.

Religious traditions educate the emotions.[38] They train us to see how we fit into history, literally from the beginning of time.[39] Once we see where and how we fit, we can understand what our role is within that history.

When the root metaphor of a mythic tradition is ingested, one apprehends that ultimate facts and values have the same source. In mythic insight, the ultimate facts and values have the same source. In mythic insight, the ultimate explanation is also the ultimate validation. The root metaphor renders the real sacred and the sacred real. The force of the naturalistic fallacy – the separation of facts and values – is dissolved by the metaphors that generate myth. Thus we see that the root metaphor of a religious tradition links cosmology to morality. In the Abrahamic traditions, for example, the root metaphor is God-as-person. God is both creator and judge, and the cosmic order and the moral order are unified under God's ultimate plan. The Greek tradition reality and value were unified by *logos*, the divine rationality inherent both in the cosmos and the human spirit. The root metaphor underlying much of Chinese myth is the Tao, the ultimate principle of balance and harmony that governs fulfillment.[40]

Religion, therefore, is multifaceted. It is intellectual, experiential, ritual, aesthetic, and institutional.[41] Moreover, religion allows us to have an identity beyond that of the small group. While "campsite morality was governed by gut reactions, reunion life was unnatural, counterintuitive. In the reunion context there were things you could not do, no matter how intensely you felt like doing them."[42] Belonging to a larger culture, which had survival benefits, requires one to extend trust beyond where one could see immediate consequences of actions. Interestingly, one needs to understand emotions such as compassion, empathy, and gratitude and these are nourished in these small groups, but then one needs to learn to extend these sentiments to larger associations. Culture and religion were ways to do this.

The bad news is, of course, that the way this can happen is by making non-believers into an evil enemy to be fought. As Scott Appleby has written in his brilliant book, *The Ambivalence of the Sacred*, religion and spirituality have good and bad sides. Like business, there is a side to religion that is associated with peace, justice, serenity, compassion, and good works. There is something to build upon here and because the spiritual, ecologizing sense is part of our nature, we cannot simply sublimate it. It won't stay quiet nor will it remain private. We might as well engage and try to figure out, like business, how to find ways to encourage its positive expression while minimizing its negative possibilities.

The literary sense

Henry Kissinger once wrote that "almost as a matter of natural law, in every century there seems to emerge a country with the power, the will, and the intellectual and moral impetus to shape the entire international system in accordance with its own values. In the seventeenth century, France ... the eighteenth century, Great Britain ... nineteenth century, Metternich's Austria reconstructed the Concert of Europe ... twentieth century ... United States ..."[43] In the twenty-first century, it is plausible that the shaper of the international system may be the market and its agents, corporations. Whether corporations really will have that kind of organizing influence or whether they simply have a significant influence, how might corporations optimally contribute to a system that is more likely to foster peace than violence? How might corporations be instruments of peace?

There is a story to tell here and I believe that the first task is to tell those stories. I mean that in a serious way, but also in a lighter way as well. As has been clear, I suspect, one of the more important influences in my professional career has been Bill Frederick. Frederick's creativity and courage in synthesizing ethics and the sciences has always resonated with me. Once Fredrick was giving a lecture at a prestigious conference, the Ruffin Series in Business Ethics. A member of the audience, a long-time friend of Frederick's asked him, "Bill, what are you doing? Seriously Bill, I don't know what you are doing? You're not doing philosophy. You're not doing science. You're telling a story and it's an interesting one, but I don't know what analysis to apply in understanding and evaluating what you are doing."

Frankly, I don't remember Bill's reply (nor does Bill), but it struck me that the same question could just as easily be asked of me. And I am quite content in telling a story. Stories have power. They allow us to see things. Legal rules, philosophical principles, and social science analysis are all helpful, but the most natural way to understand ethics is to tell stories. We learn from fireside tales, from films and novels, and from biographies. This book has been a story that tells the tale of how businesses might be instruments of peace and how they might do this via Total Integrity Management. I really couldn't care less if "Total Integrity Management" is exactly the right approach. The point of the book has been to tell a story intriguing enough to get people smarter than me engaged in the deeper analysis that will get things right.

Similarly, Ed Freeman gave his presidential address to the 1995 Annual Meeting of the Society for Business Ethics. The provocative title was "Business Sucks". Freeman's point was not that business was really bad, but that people speak as if that was the case. Since we assume that business is bad, a manger might think that it isn't worth the time to try to do good in business. If you did, you might be something of a naïve chump. Freeman argued, quite rightly I think, that we need stories about good business actions too so that our expectations become that of the positive possibilities businesses can make to society. This could include contributing to Peace Through Commerce. This book has attempted to provide a foundation for how this could happen and the next chapter will begin with some real stories of how businesses have made such contributions. To further lay out the thinking of how the literary/aesthetic could contribute to this effort, I would like to think a bit more about some tales of the good.

A narrative model

Professional responsibility

There is no one structure for corporations. Their ownership structure, legal attributes, and social responsibilities have developed over time and will continue to do so. In this light, corporate responsibility is a narrative; our current time and place is simply a chapter in that history.

The history of the firm, and how it has varied among aggregate, concession, and entity approaches is one solid way of undertaking such a narrative analysis. But there are other ways as well, particularly within the narrative tradition of legal analysis. In such analysis, one looks to literature to open up vistas of seeing that might otherwise be obscured by materialistic interpretations of history, politics, and economics. For instance, Thomas Shaffer and Robert Cochran have used various images from literature and film to characterize various roles a lawyer may play. Lawyer as Godfather, Lawyer as Hired Gun, Lawyer as Guru, and Lawyer as Friend.[44] Shaffer and Cochran demonstrate an important point: there is more than one role a lawyer can play. Depending on the time and place, a hired gun may step out of the "do what the client wants" role to offer some sage counsel as to what is truly in the client's best interests.[45]

This differentiation occurs even though lawyers' roles are fairly well defined and subject to a specific code of conduct. Lawyers are to zealously represent their clients' interests while maintaining an eye toward a position as being an officer of the court. Detailed professional responsibility codes mandate what this may mean in many situations. Within such Hard Trust, however, Shaffer and Cochran note that a client could be so deferential to a lawyer's advice, wisdom, or power so as to accept the lawyer's view of what would be in the client's best financial interest; in such cases, the lawyer acts as a godfather.[46] On the other hand, a lawyer could also eschew any pretense of advising a client as to what the client should do and simply carry out the client's interests, as defined by the client, so that the lawyer acts as a hired gun.[47] As a guru, the lawyer advises what is best not for the client's pecuniary interests, but what is morally the right thing to do.[48] Finally, lawyers and clients develop relationships in which there is genuine dialogue as to what is in the client's overarching best interests: dialogue that is advisory, not binding, but which also does not limit the lawyer's role to the interpretation of the law. In such cases, the lawyer acts as friend.[49]

It is possible that a particular lawyer or a particular law firm could adopt one of these approaches, or a blend of them, as the way the individual or firm practices law. The firm could be comprised of "hired guns", for instance, whether in the practice of litigation or corporate law, conceiving of professional duties with the "zealous representation" model as the paradigmatic value.[50] In such cases, the lawyer/firm is not far away from the economic, shareholder value model in which managers don't ask ultimate questions as to whether what they are doing is a good thing, but instead simply act as though their duty is to maximize the interests of their principal. In the legal case, that principal is the client; in corporations, the principal is the shareholder. On the other hand, a lawyer or firm could adopt an approach where the lawyer weighs in on what s/he considers to be the best interests of the client even when the client cannot seem to see their own best interests. In other words, the client may be so obsessed with the winning of a particular case that their judgment fails to consider that settling a case may be in their better long-term interests. A wise lawyer can provide that perspective and in so doing, follow a model more akin to the Jensen "enlightened stakeholder management" model.[51] That is, a lawyer who counsels a client to consider a longer-term perspective may enhance the client's overall financial interests better than simply doing what the client wants. In addition, a lawyer could simply approach a client with respect to a moral good that might be achieved by the client – say for instance, in philanthropic terms – that the client had not considered. In doing so, the lawyer may provide moral leadership to the client drawing from their relationship but going beyond a dyadic principal–agent model.

A lawyer/firm may not simply practice one of these models, but may practice some or all of them within the same day. For some clients, a hired gun model might be appropriate, for others, a friend, and for still others, the guru might be best. Each manifests a different role within an overarching understanding of what it means to be a lawyer.

The same holds true of other professionals as well. An accountant does follow client instructions as to what services are being contracted for, just as a patient sees a doctor for certain treatments. Yet, an accountant, such as Arthur Andersen the man, performs his role well when refusing to follow client orders to inadequately audit the corporation's books. The role to guard the public's confidence by conducting accurate audits takes precedence over satisfying the client. In addition, even prior to the escalation of consulting practices by accounting firms, accountants regularly provided business advice and counsel to their clients in addition to bookkeeping and auditing. As with lawyers, a given accountant or accounting firm may fulfill all of these roles in a single day, perhaps even with respect to one client. Doctors may well follow patient requests for conducting a particular examination or even a procedure, but not without providing professional assessment of the wisdom of doing so.

These models are fairly well suited for individuals just as the metaphor of Honest Brokers was suitable in Chapter 4. But institutions, not being sentient creatures, have a difficult time developing a sense of moral maturity that characterizes an Honest Broker or movement between Shaffer and Cochran's roles for lawyers. Such maturity or wisdom is necessary to know what role is appropriate at a given time and place.

Playing the role of the hired gun when a client not only needs, but wants counsel is to fail to be a good lawyer. A corporate executive may develop such wisdom, but such individual maturity can be an institutionalized trait only with significant attention to the culture and traditions of the company so that the default mechanisms within the company are those that consider the variety of roles inherent in corporate life.

Literary tales

J. R. R. Tolkien's *Lord of the Rings* can be a narrative source for thinking about moral development and applying the results of that thinking to corporate responsibility. Tolkien's magic ring, the ring to lead them all, possesses a powerful trait of making the person wearing it invisible. Tolkien follows Plato, who explores what a person might do if he found such a magic ring. Gyges, the shepherd who finds the ring in Plato's *Republic*, uses the ring for evil purposes, including killing the king, seducing the queen, and becoming ruler of the land, in large part, in the view of Glaucon, because he cannot be caught and held accountable for his indiscretions. Plato wants to refute this idea and instead argues that the evil life is an unhappy one, more so than a virtuous life, and living an evil life corrupts the soul, leading to unhappiness. Because the ring "corrupts the desires, interests, and beliefs of those who wield it", Tolkien is able to demonstrate Plato's argument and particularly so through Gollum.[52]

Gollum is a miserable creature who is "afraid of everything, friendless, homeless, constantly seeking his 'precious' ring".[53] Although both Gollum and Sam are hobbits, Gollum has lost all companionship and friendship. The only thing that Gollum thinks will make him happy is to possess the ring, although he was "altogether wretched" even when he did have it. Because he has nothing else – no friends or love for himself – he cannot resist the temptation of the ring so that it becomes a single-minded obsession.[54]

On the other hand, other characters face the temptation of the ring and their ability to resist the temptation is largely dependent upon how well they are able to distance themselves from it and link themselves with other values and loves. For instance, Frodo offers the ring to the elf-queen Galadriel as he does to Gandalf. Each, however, refuses the ring because they recognize the threat to their integrity and principles and know that, if they possess the ring, even if they might desire to do good, they would end up corrupted by its power.[55]

Tom Bombadil, a character absent from the film version, who is a merry "Master of wood, water, and hill" is wholly unaffected by the ring; it neither makes him disappear when he puts it on nor does it blind him to the invisibility of Frodo when he puts it on. Bombadil is, according to Gandalf, "his own master". Sam holds the ring for a short time when he believes Frodo is dead, but easily gives it back to him when Frodo is found alive because of his love of Frodo and "his own sense of self".[56]

Frodo and Boromir are more mixed. In his desire to use the power of the ring for the good of defeating Sauron, Boromir is seduced by the ring's power and tries to take it from Frodo. He is, as one commentary noted, Glaucon's honest man in Plato's Ring of Gyges who is unable to resist the power of the ring.[57] Frodo conducts a three-volume battle with the ring, resisting it and succumbing to it; ultimately he is "saved" by a combination of luck (Gollum's obtaining it by biting off Frodo's finger and then plunging to his death and the ring's extirpation) and his friends, the "fellowship" and, particularly, Sam.[58]

Although this sketch is very brief, one can still derive at least four lessons applicable to corporate life as well. First, it is interesting that in Tolkien's books, the "fellowship of the ring" is frequently referred to as the "company". In contemporary usage, company does connote corporate business, but company denotes friendship and fellowship as well. One has company over for dinner. Friends enjoy each other's company. When traveling together one accompanies another. There is, in the word company, a connotation of mutual support that, as we have seen, is critical for resisting the power of temptation. The fellowship keeps others in check. They consult in order to find the right route to take. Even when personal integrity prevents Gandalf, Galadriel, Sam, or Bombadil from taking the ring, it is fair to ask if each somehow intuits what it is they should do or whether they have been formed by other members of company – family, tutors, history, etc. – to form the sense of self that is able to resist the ring's temptation.

The quest to return the ring to its origin in order to destroy it cannot be borne by one person; it requires a company, a fellowship. This suggests a moral dimension to the engagement of people who form a corporate company. Whether one endorses an aggregate or entity, communitarian or contractarian approach, there are rules of behavior that become implicit, and sometimes explicit, in knowing how the work of the "company" should take place. Even an individualistic, contractarian view of the firm must have rules of behavior for the joint project to evolve and, as countless articles on contractarian approaches address, knowing how to check another party's shirking behavior – a behavior that succumbs to a temptation of not contributing to the good of the company – is vitally important to the company itself and to the individuals that comprise it.

The company can form the "self" of individuals who comprise it in two ways. One way, an aggregate way, is for the parties to a company to detail what behavior is acceptable and what is not. This itself is not that far afield from the plight of the fellowship, where a diverse group of four hobbits, two men, a wizard, an elf, and a dwarf, seek to overcome their biases in order to form a working company. This kind of self is one that recognizes that individual self-interest is dependent on sacrificing some measure of self-interest to the common good. It also recognizes checks implicit in a company that one has to recognize whether one likes the interests of others or not.

A second sense of self is as the company forms the individual moral framework of the people participating in it. A frequent charge against the teaching of ethics in professional schools is that students are far too old to have their behavior influenced. Yet if adults do absorb and internalize the actions of those around them at work and make such actions into their daily habits then the moral practices of the companies with which we associate may have a decided impact on the development of our moral intuitions and character. This is a more communitarian reason to note the connection of community and self and it requires additional attention to how such character is molded.

A second lesson from Tolkien is the danger of a single-minded pursuit of any object. Gollum, who along with Sauron, seeks the ring more than anyone, is utterly miserable. Frodo, increasingly through the tale as he deals with the burden of the ring, is miserable as well. Yet, it is also true that it is hard for any character not to desire it. It is power and freedom for the possessor or at least it seems to be. The teaching of Tolkien, however, is that it is in life's complex balancing of values and loves and interests that moral maturity and integrity develops so that the corrupting power of the ring does not control. The single-minded pursuit of the ring, as with anything else, may clarify what a person needs to do in order to obtain the "precious", but it also renders one vulnerable to the dark side of the ring's corrupting power. To the extent that corporations follow a single-minded pursuit of money and profitability and to the extent that individuals in firms pursue money and power, one should not be surprised that such a culture produces exactly the kind of corruption that makes headlines. Even if one posits that an enlightened form of shareholder value will include treating stakeholders reasonably well, the difficulty is that the quality of the motivation may ultimately fail. It is akin to Gollum agreeing to lead Frodo and Sam to the back gates of Mordor – although seemingly a decent thing to do, it nearly ultimately failed because Gollum didn't care about Sam and Frodo, but only the "precious".[59]

The third lesson, very much following from the above, is that ethical behavior arises not from a single-minded pursuit of an object, but in the realization of the complexity of goods and evils that exist and in developing the "company" and the "self" that is able to differentiate between what is helpful and what is corrupting. Gollum, to put it bluntly, acts like a two-year-old. He only wants his "precious" and he stops grasping for it only when (physically) prevented. His single-minded pursuit of a material object places him, rather obviously, rather low on Kohlberg's chart of moral development. One can make the same comment about public corporations, whose purpose, it is argued, is to single-mindedly pursue profits with attention to legal or moral norms only with respect to making sure that one does not get caught for an indiscretion.

As Aristotle long ago argued, ethical behavior results, not from a narrow pursuit of a single good, but in recognition of the complex balancing of goods that requires wisdom and judgment – phronesis – that is fostered by a "good company" in order to develop the self that is able to stand up to corrupting temptation.[60]

Fourth, the sense of moral goodness entails some notion of renunciation. This is not to say that ethics are simply those actions that cost one something, because there are moral actions that are rewarded because a community has had the wisdom to align its values so as to reward people for good behavior. Nevertheless, those characters who were able to resist the power of the ring had to renounce it. Gandalf and Galadriel renounced it because they intellectually knew that it would corrupt them, even if they wanted to try to use it for good. Bombadil and Sam renounced it because their values were so apart from any sense of their own self-aggrandizement that they simply didn't care about the ring.[61] Similarly, any corporate company that wishes to engage in ethical behavior will face, at some point, a choice of whether to pursue profits or renounce them. Because a central purpose of the firm is to produce economic value, firms will certainly choose profitability, but if it chooses that only, it will blind itself to the dangers that can undermine it. Today, what can undermine it is potential global violence. The good news is that companies are already addressing this issue and provide models for behavior.

Now I shudder to think what a cranky critic will do with analogizing *The Lord of the Rings* to serious issues of corporate governance and world peace. Nevertheless, *The Lord of the Rings* insightfully lays out the possibilities for a "company" and the dangers of the pursuit of desirable things. If companies pursue profit and profit only, they doom their own profitability and, perhaps, our survival.

There are two additional aspects of M^3. These dimensions help to foster the spiritual/aesthetic dimension of human nature while dampening some of its incendiary fire. They are organization dimensions and the bias adjustments necessary to hem in the potentially negative, passionate dimensions that will leave a larger connection between spiritual individuals and organizations as well as the "more mediation" aspect, which is about how to connect these notions directly to sustainable peace.

The organizational dimension: mediating institutions

As introduced in Chapter 1, recent research suggests that human beings are hard-wired to live and work in relatively small organizations. Anthropologists and psychologists have shown that this is because of the ratio of the neocortex of the brain to body mass. Human beings, and other primates too, simply short-circuit when put into too large a group. For instance, at a cocktail party, there will rarely be conversations in groups larger than 4 to 6. Even if the room is relatively quiet, it is very hard to have a conversation with a group bigger than that. The group automatically fissions. There are similar breaking points at the numbers 30 and 150 where it becomes almost impossible for individuals to understand the consequences of their actions on others. And if they cannot see the consequences of their actions, they don't care as much about them.[62] When that happens, they are less concerned with ethical behavior.

As noted in Chapter 1, we are most comfortable – and most aware of – the consequences of our actions in groups that are relatively small sizes of 4 to 6, 30, and 150. The importance of these numbers reaches to ethics as well. Within small groups, people must consider the consequences of their actions. That doesn't mean that they necessarily like each other; only that they have to get along with others so that their actions matter. This insight connects to a deep strain of philosophy, particularly rooted in the natural law tradition and, more specifically within some dimension of Catholic Social Thought.[63] The normative argument is that human beings have their moral character formed in relatively small "mediating institutions". Families, religious organizations, neighborhoods, and voluntary associations form moral character, at least in part, because individuals must deal with the consequences of actions; the groups are small enough and enduring enough so that one must seriously consider how one's behavior impacts communal relationships. These organizations also provide a "double-meaning" to its members. They provide an internal sense of moral identity within so that one has a sense of belonging. They also provide an external gateway to the larger world. The way in which they fulfill this role is complex and has been characterized as simply an enhancement of self-interest, as socialization groupings that teach individuals to reach beyond self-interest and consider their citizenship obligation to others, and as naturalistic reactions to an urban world in terms of dysfunctional, anti-social groups (inner city youth gangs and rural militas) that provide identity *against* the outside world. In this last respect, the organizations might be more aptly called quarantining institutions rather than mediating institutions, because they discourage a mediated, constructed response to the outside world in favor of an exclusivist, confrontational and/or withdrawing relationship to the world. Phrased descriptively, human beings do seem to naturally group themselves. Phrased normatively, for human beings to group themselves in a way that is socially engaged, the institutions must mediate the relationship between the individual and the outside world rather than quarantine the individual from a constructive relationship with it.[64] Like religion, the importance of mediating institutions is that they are a naturalistic reality that will extrude into our lives. Because our nature also has plasticity as well, the question is how we can best integrate various hardwired aspects of our nature. We are neither genetically determined nor are we free from certain hardwired limitations. Both religion and mediating institutions can inspire passionate commitment to ethical behavior. We might as well marshall them constructively. In doing so, we may well find corporate ways to lead to Peace Through Commerce.

One of the advantages of working with the concept of Business as Mediating Institution (BMI) is that it helps to bring together some of the stronger aspects of management theory related to ethics. Efficaciously speaking, if a central aim of developing culture is to explain to employees the reasoning behind rules, then structuring corporate groups so that employees are aware of the consequences of their actions would seem to be a smart strategy. Employees would then experience the reason behind corporate rules and, if truly a mediating institution, these rules would have to be developed, in part by the employees themselves. Doing this would merge both kinds of natural law I have described. Because voice, participation, subsidiarity, and communication were natural law attributes, a mediating structure fosters small group interaction, discussion, and application of rules within a framework of overarching legal checks (i.e. a group would not legally build internal solidarity by focusing on shared racial hatreds), and would coincide with a classic sense of natural law. Because this structure would promote ethics as a shared way of life, it would promote the Ellulian sense as well. In short, BMI allows for an efficacious integration of the research that shows what works and also with two important natural law formulations.

Moreover, this approach allows for the integration of normative business ethics too. Stakeholder theory suggests that a business should be managed for the benefit of all stakeholders.[65] That has justly been criticized as a too-broad approach. How can a manager manage for everyone? To that question, many attempts have tried to place weights on stakeholder interests, such as looking at the rights and the protection of the vulnerable. I would suggest that while it may be difficult to manage for everyone, a business can provide a chance for voice in the organization. Companies can and do solicit employee perspectives. There is no reason they cannot do so on issues of ethics too. They can ask employees what virtues they think are important. They can offer half-day retreats every two to three years to allow employees to simply share stories about what they find ethically inspiring. I have used both techniques in classes and in consulting and the impact is striking. Employees (and students) will all likely value the same things such as honesty, loyalty, accountability, creativity, and respect. In one form or another, I have asked participants in over one hundred audiences to "elect" the virtues they admire and these five virtues are always present in the list of seven or eight they "elect".

In classes and in consulting, I regularly ask participants to tell me stories they find to be ethically inspiring. Even when they disagree with each other about what they value, the discussion opens up ethics as something that draws them together. This best occurs when one is in a small enough group so that one really interacts with others as human beings, exactly the kinds of interaction Fabbro identified as characteristic of relatively non-violent societies. Moreover, in hearing these stories, one quickly finds that employees and students are concerned about more than themselves. That is what ethics is about. The employees and students are also concerned with others and that, by proxy, provides voice for those other stakeholders as well. Thus, although a mediating institution's approach would focus on employee voices (the two other key stakeholder groups of shareholders and customers already being heard through markets and the law), these voices have the potential to be an efficacious and practical way to consider stakeholder interests. And so, BMI draws on the best of stakeholder theory while minimizing the practical difficulties of administering it.

Similarly, the social contracts of Tom Donaldson and Tom Dunfee look at an overarching sense of justice through social contracting in the Rawlsian tradition.[66] Its two-tiered approach also looks at existing "contracts". These contracts, such as a nation-state's laws, express what a society believes is just. If that contract allows for voice and exit, then the contract passes a first test of justice: authenticity. It passes a second test if it also conforms to the overarching sense of justice: legitimacy. With respect to the issue of authenticity, Donaldson and Dunfee claim that these capture a communitarian sense. In a way, they are right because contemporary "communitarians" use states and nation-states as examples of communities. But these really aren't communities, they are societies. A community has more of a mediating institution feel. There is personal engagement with the collective that truly establishes voice. My "voice" in a society of 250 million people is quite low. My voice in a group of 30 is significant. The combination of voice in a mediating institution plus overarching tests applied on larger scales is a good way to test ethical actions. And so, BMI can agree with Integrative Social Contracts Theory (ISCT) on the need for a multi-tiered model of testing for moral norms. But by emphasizing the level of mediating institutions, one truly engages meaningful voice. That voice engages personally meaningful experiences.

Finally, communities have a strong role in inculcating moral values in individuals as an Aristotelian conception of morality. Those individuals, in turn, affect the moral character of organizations in conjunction with the reciprocal experience of being shaped by those institutions, which gives rise to a dialectical sense of moral development. Mediating institutions capture this dimension because families, neighborhoods, voluntary associations, and religious organizations all shape and are shaped by individual moral development. Communitarians, such as Amitai Etzioni, also emphasize the importance of connecting individuals to organizations, but typically they do so by making the relevant organizations mammoth megastructures such as the nation-state.[67] Yet, the anthropological data on the importance of small numbers suggest that there may be a particular kind of a community – a relatively small mediating institution – whereby moral development is optimally developed. In short, while it is clear that large organizations are with us to stay (and, on a positive note, they do allow human beings to achieve things that they would not be able to realize in small bands), a central dilemma for contemporary normative behavior is matching where people learn about ethics to where they are practiced.

Very few companies recognize this, in part because this view of moral development rarely extends to business. Those that have tried to characterize businesses as being mediating organizations tend to do so in a very vague sense; that is because they are neither government nor individuals, businesses "mediate" or stand between individuals and governments. Such a conception, however, is very different than one that actually forms moral character. Yet, there is evidence that a person's moral behavior is affected by the character of the business organization, a conclusion that should not be surprising given the amount of time people spend at work. Indeed, James Coleman claims that "The family has been replaced by the modern corporation as the central social unit in society; the social net within which first men, and now women, carry out their daily productive activities and find their psychological home."[68] If this is true, attention needs to be given to how businesses are developed as moral communities fostering moral individuals who, in turn, reinforce moral organizations. Two dimensions of this dialectical community-building are the articulation of clear rules (Hard Trust) and the development of the perception of

organizational justice (Real Trust). Yet, a third dimension is that of
Good Trust, where the actual motivational caring to be ethical results,
at least in part, from an institutional setting that matches anthropological realities of human nature with demonstrable characteristics of moral
development. Making businesses into mediating institutions is the central element of this effort.

Thus, the concept of mediating institutions is a way to integrate both
normative and descriptive managerial approaches to business ethics. It
can blend the best parts of the normative approaches and it can do so in
a particularly efficacious way. In order to prevent these small groups
within a large corporation from running amok, they do need to be
hemmed in by society's laws (Hard Trust) that prevent egregious,
dehumanizing behavior. And so, BMI is dependent on Hard Trust.
Good Trust is then about the aesthetic/spiritual quests for moral excellence. One way to do this is to place people into organizations most
conducive to their hardwired tendencies, to have voice, and to engage
in meaningful behaviors at work. The third part of Good Trust then
looks at a final element of issues that result when engaging the passions.

Psychological considerations, wisdom, and Peace Through Commerce

Bias adjustments

Arguing that businesses might tap into deep aspects of human nature in
order to generate a passionate commitment to certain moral duties
raises immediate concerns, however, because as already noted, some
small organizations are paragons of vice rather than virtue. This concern is amplified by the problem that human beings do not always see
moral situations clearly due to various kinds of psychological blinders.
Engendering passion may create admirable commitments to wanting to
do good, but that passion must also be routed in ways that limit
destructive bias.

David Messick and Max Bazerman provide a helpful framing of how
bias affects moral judgments.[69] Messick and Bazerman argue that
people make decisions based on their theories of the world, theories
of other people, and theories about ourselves. A problem, they argue, is
that we aren't necessarily very good at making moral judgments. We
deceive ourselves because of our biases. That is particularly true if we

already possess a very strong way of interpreting the world (through, for instance, religion) and if we have a strong identity in a group, which provides such a strong sense of purpose so as to limit outside perspectives (through, for instance, mediating institutions). Thus, while spiritual quests for excellence and belief may produce passionate identity, they do require checks to reduce bias.

Theories about the world, Messick and Bazerman argue, include predispositions toward ignoring low probability events, limiting the search for potentially affected parties, and ignoring the possibility that the public might find out. Another example of theories of the world include assessment of risk. This includes denying that decisions need to be made in the midst of genuine ambiguity, the fact that every decision requires an assessment of how to tradeoff risks, and that how one frame risk (either as a gain or as a loss) makes a difference as to how human beings are prone to perceive the magnitude of that risk. In other words, we think decisions are cleaner than they really are. Finally, how one perceives causation can vary. Human beings are prone to focus on people as causing problems rather than looking at the systems in which people act, to categorize otherwise similar events from which one can learn as differentiated occurrences, and to ignore sins of omission. In short, we don't tie things together, but view problems as personal errors.

The second kind of framing occurs through theories about other people. This largely rests on notions of ethnocentrism and stereotyping. People tend to divide the world into us versus them. As Messick and Bazerman explain, this tendency does not necessarily lead to one group actively discriminating against another group as much as it may mean simply favoring one's own perceived group. Even more interestingly is their claim that the reasons for the determination of who is an "us" and who is a "them" is very arbitrary. As they put it, persons living in various parts of the State of Illinois could, on one day, be "us" as fans of the Chicago Cubs and, on the next day, "them" as downstaters rather than Chicagoans debating political power.[70] The bad news in this is that we are prone to making others into an enemy. Given Ray Kelly's warning about how social substitutability is a key, dehumanizing move that opens the door for organized violence, this is a very worrisome aspect of human nature. The good news is that we define the "other" in ways that allow us to find new friends. Sometimes we may be in different groups; sometimes in the same one. Cross-cutting ties of identity serve as a potential check against simply grouping an "other" as enemy. This is very much Amartya Sen's point.[71] It is a mistake, he argues, to think of grouping on the basis of religion or ethnic identity alone. People belong to many associations. Well, perhaps. But here is where businesses can provide another sense of identity that cuts against ethics and religious identity.

The final theory concerns ourselves. Messick and Bazerman argue that we tend to have illusions of our own superiority. This includes a sense of favorability viewing ourselves vis-à-vis others (most people consider themselves as moral, but not others), an optimistic sense that things will turn out in our favor, and an illusion that we have more control over events than we, in fact, do.[72]

Attention to these biases and external accountabilities that force individuals to face up to impediments to making good judgments about these biases are necessary to improve the quality, breadth, and honesty of decisions. They also serve to make sure that individuals excited about integrating their work and their ethical identity do not become so confident in what they are doing that they fail to consider the impact of those outside of the immediate line of their vision or engage in destructive behavior.[73] The discussion of Hard Trust and Real Trust helps to provide these external accountabilities that check bias.

Rules, both from external (legal) sources and from internal (corporate policy) sources, are necessary to hem in misbehavior. Rules and laws provide landmarks including stop signs, and they punish violations. Hard Trust is coercive and therefore tough enough to require attention. It is also an essential aspect of trust. One can trust a product's efficacy more if the company will be fined for not making it so that it conforms to government standards. Managerial integration of behavior also promotes trust. The management literature shows that there are financial rewards possible for trust-building behavior. In order to garner Real Trust, one cannot exclude stakeholders and society. Engaging them builds social capital and the very process also checks excesses of Good Trust. So Good Trust depends on Hard Trust and Real Trust just as Hard Trust and Real Trust depend on the Good Trust motivation to care about ethics. This brings us to one past aspect of Good Trust, one that serves as its own correction against bias and which serves to provide motivation for Hard Trust and Real Trust: Peace Through Commerce.

Peace Through Commerce

If passion has been corrected by bias adjustments, there remains a final issue regarding what that passion for moral excellence should be directed toward. The ambivalent nature of spiritedness – that is that it can be used for great good and great evil[74] – means that a passionate quest for moral excellence needs to be handled with great care. This chapter has already suggested several ways to handle this passion. Adjusting for bias is an important dimension as is social rules (Hard Trust) and an objective set of standards comprising both subjective perceptions of justice as well as more formal, deep theories of moral behavior (Real Trust). These three aspects all subject passionate quests for excellence to accountabilities that protect against harmful effects. That is, they all constrain passion and for good reasons. However, in this discussion of Good Trust, I wish to also suggest a particular kind of passion that is itself corrective without falling to the problematic dimension that unchecked passions can produce and which marries a teleological, inspirational commitment to good to the other kinds of passionate work already described.

Theologian Stanley Hauerwas explains why a commitment to non-violence is such a critical one for religious individuals, in his case, for Christians.[75] Hauerwas believes that non-violence is not simply an important commitment, but one that is a hallmark of ethical (for him, Christian) life. He believes that ethics are not universal, but instead highly contingent. That is, there is no set of universal natural law ethics (or if there is, they operate at such a high level of generality so as to make little difference in solving particular problems). Our ethics are, instead, very dependent upon traditions, religions, and history. This does not take Hauerwas into situational ethics at all. Instead, he argues that the moral life is lived with a set of communal commitments and that one's duty is to be loyal and obedient to those commitments. Of course, dutiful obedience to communal commitments can lead to violence performed on behalf of the community. That violence is counter to the ethic Hauerwas wishes to live up to, so an important additional aspiration that operates as an identity-defining check on communal citizenship is that of non-violence.

Seeing that ethical business behavior can make a contribution to peace strikes me as a potentially powerful motivation. Reducing violence helps business and it helps the world. Particular actions – as developed in Part One and as elaborated in Part Two are the behaviors businesses can implement to foster sustainable peace. But that objective elevates a value of non-violence itself and that value is one that, just as Hauerwas argued, corrects against the exact negatives associated with spiritual quests for excellence and with mediating institutions. Peace Through Commerce becomes its own bias adjustment.

Thus, Good Trust provides the emotional foundation for Hard Trust and Real Trust and results in three important upshots. First, the things corporations can do to contribute to sustainable peace correlate with a good deal of what we have already seen in Hard Trust and Real Trust. Supporting the rule of law, avoiding corruption, fair treatment of internal and external constituents, and economic development all relate to an enlightened notion of shareholder responsibility that incorporates specific attention to contemporary recommendations for business ethics practices. Second, aiming at a quest for sustainable peace provides perhaps the most compelling existential teleology one can aim for and hooks passionate quests for this particular kind of moral excellence to the practices viewed to be good business ethics. Further, it does so in a way that, by its own principles, prevents some of the problematic excesses of spirited quests for excellence by stressing principles of non-violence. Third, there is now research that shows that while corporations will not create world peace – the causes of violence are too vast for any one person, group, or even sector to remedy – there are important contributions that businesses can make to it.

In short, Total Integrity Management may be an effective synthesis of contemporary approaches to business ethics. Total Integrity Management integrates the legal, the managerial, and the spiritual. This holistic combination is likely to be the approach that makes business organizations into cultures that foster ethics and compliance, the test for the Federal Sentencing Guidelines, as amended in 2004. What really brings Total Integrity Management to life is Good Trust. And what Good Trust suggests is that there are personal and social excellences available by integrating Hard Trust, Real Trust, and Good Trust. Those excellences go to the heart of spiritual identity. They suggest the kinds of mediating structures necessary to optimally foster that identity *and* lead to social common goods. These goods, if aligned with consensus-based business ethics practices of economic development, rule of law political structures, and sensitivity to internal corporate community, as well as to external community relations, have an unexpected consequence: Peace Through Commerce. In a recursive fashion, Total Integrity Management's outcome itself serves as a strong reason for why business should focus on ethical business behavior. Doing so may pay off in greater stability in which business itself would better thrive. It also is a profound good within the reach of business. It is a powerful enough good to get individuals to drop their cost-benefit guard for a time to consider how their actions might prevent a kid from getting his head blown off.

Notes

1. CHRIS HEDGES, WAR IS A FORCE THAT GIVES US MEANING (2002).
2. LOYAL RUE, RELIGION IS NOT ABOUT GOD (2005).
3. Tom Peters, *Business Leaders Should be Spirited, Not Spiritual*, CHI. TRIB. (June 5, 1993).
4. JAMES A. AUTRY, LOVE AND PROFIT: THE ART OF CARING LEADERSHIP 14–15 (1991).
5. JOSEPH M. JURAN, MANAGERIAL BREAKTHROUGH: A NEW CONCEPT OF THE MANAGER'S JOB 49 (1964), citing Exodus 18:20–2.
6. *Id.* at 15.
7. MARY WALTON, THE DEMING MANAGEMENT METHOD 58 (1986).
8. LAURA NASH, BELIEVERS IN BUSINESS (1994).
9. See SAM HARRIS, BEYOND BELIEF, THE END OF FAITH: RELIGION, TERROR, AND THE FUTURE OF REASON (2004) for a passionate argument along these lines.
10. THIERRY C. PAUCHANT, ETHICS AND SPIRITUALITY AT WORK 7 (2002).
11. *Id.* at 14.
12. *Id.* at 2.
13. RUE, *supra* note 2, at 9.
14. RUE, *supra* note 2, at 10.
15. RUE, *supra* note 2, at 28.
16. RUE, *supra* note 2, at 29.
17. RUE, *supra* note 2.
18. RUE, *supra* note 2, at 30.
19. RUE, *supra* note 2, at 37.
20. RUE, *supra* note 2, at 38.
21. RUE, *supra* note 2, at 38–9.
22. RUE, *supra* note 2, at 40.
23. RUE, *supra* note 2, at 42.
24. RUE, *supra* note 2, at 42.
25. RUE, *supra* note 2, at 43.

26. RUE, *supra* note 2, at 44.
27. RUE, *supra* note 2, at 44.
28. RUE, *supra* note 2, at 45.
29. RUE, *supra* note 2.
30. RUE, *supra* note 2, at 63–4.
31. RUE, *supra* note 2, at 64.
32. RUE, *supra* note 2, at 66.
33. RUE, *supra* note 2, at 67.
34. RUE, *supra* note 2, at 70.
35. RUE, *supra* note 2, at 70.
36. RUE, *supra* note 2, at 73.
37. RUE, *supra* note 2, at 75.
38. RUE, *supra* note 2, at 79.
39. RUE, *supra* note 2, at 86.
40. RUE, *supra* note 2, at 127.
41. RUE, *supra* note 2, at 143–4.
42. RUE, *supra* note 2, at 156–7.
43. HENRY KISSINGER, DIPLOMACY 17 (1994).
44. THOMAS L. SHAFFER AND ROBERT E. COCHRAN, JR., LAWYERS, CLIENTS, AND MORAL RESPONSIBILITY (1994).
45. *Id.*
46. *Id.* at 8.
47. *Id.* at 15.
48. *Id.* at 31.
49. *Id.* at 44.
50. See generally William E. Nelson, *Moral Ethics, Adversary Justice, and Political Theory: Three Foundations for the Law of Professional Responsibility*, 64 NOTRE DAME L. REV. 911 (1989); E. Wayne Thode, *The Ethical Standards for the Advocate*, 39 TEX. L. REV. 575, 583 (1961); cf. MODEL RULES, *supra* note 100, R. 3.1, cmt.
51. Michael D. Jensen, *Value Maximization, Stakeholder Theory, and the Corporate Objective Function,* 12 BUSINESS ETHICS QUARTERLY 235 (2002).
52. See Eric Katz, *The Rings of Tolkien and Plato: Lessons in Power, Choice, and Morality,* in THE LORD OF THE RIGHTS AND PHILOSOPHY: ONE BOOK TO RULE THEM ALL (Gregory Bassham and Eric Bronson, eds., 2003).
53. *Id.* at 9.
54. Jorge J. E. Gracia, *The Quests of Sam and Gollum for the Happy Life, in* THE LORD OF THE RIGHTS AND PHILOSOPHY: ONE BOOK TO RULE THEM ALL (Gregory Bassham and Eric Bronson, eds., 68–71, 2003).
55. Katz, *supra* note 52, at 7, 13.

56. Katz, *supra* note 52, at 17–18.

57. Katz, *supra* note 52, at 11.

58. Katz, *supra* note 52, at 15–19.

59. Katz, *supra* note 52, at 9–10.

60. ARISTOTLE, NICOMACHEAN ETHICS (David Ross, trans., 1984, III3., 11112b11).

61. J. R. R. TOLKIEN, THE LORD OF THE RINGS (1954, 2004).

62. TIMOTHY L. FORT, ETHICS AND GOVERNANCE: BUSINESS AS A MEDIATING INSTITUTION 51 (2001).

63. PETER BERGER AND JOHN NEUHAUS, TO EMPOWER PEOPLE: THE ROLE OF MEDIATING STRUCTURES IN PUBLIC POLICY (1977).

64. FORT, *supra* note 62.

65. See R. EDWARD FREEMAN, STRATEGIC MANAGEMENT: A STAKEHOLDER APPROACH (1984).

66. See THOMAS DONALDSON AND THOMAS W. DUNFEE, TIES THAT BIND: A SOCIAL CONTRACTS APPROACH TO BUSINESS ETHICS (1999).

67. AMITAI ETZIONI, THE NEW GOLDEN RULE 127 (1996). For a critique of Etzioni, see Timothy L. Fort, *On Golden Rules, Balancing Acts and Finding the Right Size*, 8 BUSINESS ETHICS QUARTERLY 347.

68. JAMES COLEMAN, FOUNDATIONS OF SOCIAL THEORY 397 (1990).

69. David Messick and Max Bazerman, *Ethical Leadership and the Psychology of Ethical Decision Making*, 37 SLOAN MGMT. REV. 9 (1996).

70. *Id.* See also David Messick, *Social Categories and Business Ethics*, BUSINESS ETHICS QUARTERLY. *Special Issue: Ruffin Series 1*, at 149 (1998); cf. Edwin M. Hartman, *Altruism, Ingroups and Fairness: Comments on Messick*, BUSINESS ETHICS QUARTERLY. *Special Issue: Ruffin Series 1*, at 179 (1998); and Donna J. Wood, *Ingroups and Outgroups: What Psychology Doesn't Say*, BUSINESS ETHICS QUARTERLY. *Special Issue: Ruffin Series 1*, at 176 (1998).

71. AMARTYA SEN, IDENTITY AND VIOLENCE: THE ILLUSION OF DESTINY (2006).

72. Messick and Bazerman, *supra* note 69.

73. NGOs are a good example of this. Convinced of the moral virtue of their mission, they are also among the least transparent of organizations, raising questions as to the methods and interests masked by not being fully accountable to the public while demanding such accountability from corporations and governments.

74. See SCOTT APPLEBY, THE AMBIVALENCE OF THE SACRED (2000), arguing that religion is used for great good and great evil.

75. See STANLEY HAUERWAS, THE PEACEABLE KINGDOM (1983).

8 | *Instruments of peace*

Lord, make me an instrument of thy peace.
Where there is hatred, let me bring love;
where there is injury, pardon. Where there is
doubt, faith, where there is despair, hope.
Where there is darkness, light; where there is
sadness, joy, and all for thy mercy's sake. O
divine master, grant that I may not so much
seek to be consoled as to console; to be
understood as to understand; to be loved as
to love. For it is in giving that we receive; it is
in pardoning that we are pardoned, and it is
in dying that we are born to eternal life.

(Prayer of St. Francis of Assisi)

In 1999, under the leadership of Madeleine Albright, the State Department established the Award for Corporate Excellence. The award continued under Colin Powell and Condoleezza Rice, proving a bi-partisan dimension. The award is given for the actions of US companies in their work overseas that attends to a variety of economic development, human rights, labor rights, and environmental issues. Such actions, the State Department believes, tend to improve diplomatic relations between the host country and the United States.[1]

One of the 2003 Awards went to Chevron/Texaco for its work in a variety of places and, in particular, Nigeria. This included educational, health, and humanitarian assistance related to equipping riverboats as traveling healthcare clinics. The company also provided airlifts for villagers caught in ethnic and political conflict; the company is also active in Nigeria's HIV/AIDS program. US Steel, another 2003 winner, was recognized for its work in Slovakia, where after purchasing a local ironworks, they raised salaries, improved incentive programs, and improved healthcare and benefit packages. Philanthropically, the company also built an oncology wing at a hospital, donated funds to orphanages, assisted in adoption placements, and sponsored a youth hockey league.[2]

In 2002, the Secretary of State recognized Chindex and Coca-Cola. Chindex partnered with the Chinese Academy of Medical Sciences to establish medical facilities in Beijing with part of the services donated to the care of orphans. Chindex also sponsored educational programs for healthcare professionals on US trends in healthcare and has facilitated dialogue between the Food and Drug Administration and its counterpart in China. Coca-Cola supported educational programs in Egypt, assisted in funding for wastewater and air treatment plants, raised funds for children's cancer programs, and funded housing initiatives for the poor.[3]

Other winners have been SELCO Vietnam for its work in providing wireless household electricity, employment of local citizens, providing good salaries and benefits, and focusing special hiring attention on women. The company has a reputation for attention to safety, and adherence to the Foreign Corrupt Practices Act. Because of its focus on solar energy, it pays attention to environmental issues of battery recycling and, of course, its very work is an ecologically advantageous alternative to carbon-based fuels.[4] Like a 2000 winner, Motorola Malaysia, Selco provides valuable technological transfer to the host country as well as managerial training that has spillover effects throughout the country. Motorola also shares a characteristic with another 2000 winner, Rayonier (for its work in New Zealand) because of the support of employee educational advancement. Both companies share high standards of employment practices; Rayonier is also noted for providing supplies for local farmers, radios for school buses, scholarships for students, recreational use of land, and money for civic projects.[5] Frigorifico Canelones has converted a bankrupt meat-packing plant into the country's largest beef exporting unit while earning a reputation for a strong safety record, providing donations for homeless shelters, counseling for abused children, and recreational activities for youth.[6] F. C. Schaffer's work in Ethiopia was recognized in 1999 not only for its environmental and employment practices, but also because the company not only built a successful sugar-refining factory, but also shared its expertise with competitors when floods destroyed some of their plants.[7]

This growing interest *from businesses* to promote peace is hardly an exclusively US phenomena. It is worldwide. As I have already noted,

International Alert's report, *Local Business, Local Peace* presents dozens of examples as well as case studies showing businesses from many countries engaging in peacemaking. This validates the way in which peace can be an identity-forming embodiment of an entity theory of the firm that is not dependent on nationalism and extends beyond an aggregate approach on shareholders. These actions are the hope of Peace Through Commerce. They include a telecommunications company in Somalia partnering with UNICEF and a local NGO to promote training for former child soldiers to the South Caucasas, where women entrepreneurs engage in microfinance, to interethnic dialogue fostered by companies in Nigeria and in Northern Ireland as well as in Sri Lanka.

Are these anecdotal examples exceptions only? Don't we need hard, statistical evidence, at least correlative and preferably causative, to really link peace and business? Well, yes, they may be exceptions (perhaps they are new leaders) and yes, better statistical validation is always nice. But the fact that these examples exist suggest that there *are* models of the firm that can contribute to Peace Through Commerce. If that is true, then the possibility of such firms' success means that there is a *choice* companies can make between being instruments of domination and instruments of peace.

These examples provide evidence of good actions that companies can take. It is not that companies forego economic profitability in doing so, but that the companies integrate a variety of approaches that, probably for a variety of motives, are more sophisticated than a narrow view of short-term money-making. The risk in all of this is, though, that companies can simply make this into a cynical public relationship blow (that because it is dishonest is contrary to ethical business behavior). Or, what happens when *good* companies do *bad* things?

Few companies in American business history, for instance, have had as high a profile as the Ford Motor Company. With that history comes controversy. It also has had ongoing battles as to its interaction with society. This reaches back to Henry Ford's attempt to deny the payment of an extraordinary dividend to the shareholders of the company, including the Dodge brothers, in favor of increasing compensation to employees.[8] In the landmark case, *Dodge vs. Ford*, the Court held that Henry Ford's purported desire to provide societal benefits to employees and customers were outweighed by his responsibility to his corporate shareholders.[9] Given the emphasis on fair treatment of employees and customers by various social responsibility initiatives, including the Secretary of State, one might expect that, today, Henry Ford's decision would be a front-page, "good corporation" story.[10] In a similar vein, William Clay Ford, Jr. maintained a high-profile commitment to creating an ecologically friendly company and automobile during his tenure as CEO.[11] And, the Secretary of State gave Ford Motor Company one of its 2001 Awards for Corporate Excellence for its leadership in providing HIV/AIDS training to the employees of its South African subsidiary. This program provides education and testing of its employees, partners with local programs as well as global programs such as the Center for Disease Control, and has reached more than 12,000 people in South Africa.[12] At the same time, Ford is regularly bashed for opposition to increased mileage standards for its vehicles, finds itself frequently in the midst of union struggles, and became a lightning rod for controversy in the Firestone tire controversy.[13]

Similarly, in the 1980s, Shell was the poster child for bad company behavior with charges against it from human rights and environmental activists. Environmentally, the company was castigated for its sinking of the Brent Spar oil rig in the North Sea. Its decision to simply sink an oil rig seemed incomprehensible and was protested vehemently by groups such as Greenpeace. Later evidence demonstrated that the company may have had a legitimate point that the least environmentally damaging alternative was, in fact, to sink the rig, but such evidence did little to protect the company from the protests. Even more caustic were the protests against Shell's alleged complicity in the oppression of the Ogoni people in Nigeria in order to protect Shell's oil supplies: complicity that even grew to allegations of active participation in the assassination of the leader of the Ogoni people, Ken Saro-Wiwa. The company denied any such complicity or participation, but heading into the 1990s, it was hard to find many defenders of Shell among scholars and advocates of corporate responsibility.[14]

In the 1990s, however, Shell became one of the stars of the corporate responsibility movement. It virtually recreated its company image, not only philanthropically sponsoring "best practices" kinds of programs and studies, but implementing them. The company became much more transparent in answering questions about its activities, adopted a variety of environmental programs and initiatives, and became an advocate for human rights. Along with BP Amoco, Shell became one of the oil leaders of the corporate responsibility movement. Yet in 2004, the company was mired in admissions that it had significantly overstated its expected oil resources, prompting serious corporate governance charges, stock price plunges, and threatening the very economic sustainability of the company.[15]

Companies, like the human beings who populate them, are complex things. They do good things and bad things and the motives driving each can be bewilderingly diverse as well. It isn't particularly helpful to characterize one company as good and another as bad. It is worthwhile to recognize the positive and negative actions they take and to see how those actions relate to larger public goods. The fact of the matter is that companies have already engaged in Peace Through Commerce. The story of this book is simply that the twenty-first century is a time and season in which a more mindful pursuit of Peace Through Commerce as an aim could be particularly beneficial and that an integrated strategy of Total Integrity Management is an efficacious way of approaching this because it links deeply rooted aspects of our human nature to documented contributions to peaceful societies.

Next steps

Peace Through Commerce is obviously a huge, complex subject. Figuring out exactly how it could be achieved is beyond my capabilities. Yet my hope is that the ideas are intriguing enough to foster additional research. That research and action might concentrate on more empirically grounded connections between attributes of non-violence and corporate behavior. What Real Trust behaviors are most efficacious? What are the optimal ways for corporations to be agents of social change? What procedures and programs best match rewards and rhetoric so that any engagement is efficacious? Because Hard Trust is essential, what is the proper interaction between government and business in fostering Peace Through Commerce? For instance, property rights may advocate for more rational property rights, but ultimately government protects them. What is the best way for that to occur? If Good Trust is critical – which I obviously believe is the case – then exactly how does business act to foster religious harmony rather than fanning the flames of intolerance, a trait that can be incendiary?

These are the tip of the iceberg. In Chapter 1, I analogized the work done to that of a lawyer making a *prima facie* case as one that has enough merit to be heard in full by a court. There is evidence to consider; it is not merely a wisp of an argument. At the same time, a *prima facie* case is not conclusive. A *prima facie* case does not mean that the party bringing the case has proved the case by either a reasonable doubt or by a preponderance of the evidence. Similarly, I think this book, together with the other literature cited, presents a *prima facie* case that corporations could become instruments of peace.

The argument is, though, only a *prima facie* case. I have not, nor has anyone else to my knowledge, established the case beyond reasonable doubt nor with a preponderance of the evidence that businesses do significantly improve the chances for peace. Unlike a court case, however, I do not view my role as the person responsible for getting to that level of evidence. I am happy to do my part, but this is an issue that will require many minds. So the court I hope to engage is the court of scholars, policy-makers, business leaders, NGO activists, and others to figure out how we can make for a more peaceful, just world. I do not want to suggest that the mountain we must climb isn't steep. Historically, the systematic evidence suggests that businesses may be prone to foster violence rather than peace.

Why would this be the case? Why would the supposedly sophisticated, global society, at least compared to hunter-gatherer times, be so much more violent? Let me draw on anthropology one last time. Jonathan Haas and Cynthia Mahmood explain why and the studies of David Fabbro and Raymond Kelly shed light on what might be done. Combining those notions provides a sense of not just what the world as a collective body might do, but what businesses might do.

Haas represents a school of thought that suggests that the very economic structure of contemporary society poses a tendency toward violence.[16] This theory contends that organized warfare cannot be maintained by the small bands of hunter-gatherer societies. Bands and clans may periodically raid, but this is a relatively minor affair compared to the organized violence of the twentieth century.[17] Organized warfare is possible only when there is enough surplus labor and materiel to build specialized armaments and train soldiers. This becomes possible when the economic structure turns from hunting and gathering to agriculture. Sedentary economic life not only proved capable of providing surplus so that rather than looking for food each day, societies had the time and wherewithal to create armies. They also had the need to protect more geographically specific areas of land – those used for the growing of crops – rather than the more disperse geographic areas utilized in a foraging range. Moreover, rather than tents or other easily movable shelters, homes became permanent lodgings necessitating their protection as well.[18]

In addition, social structure tended to evolve from that of relatively egalitarian governance structures found in hunter-gatherer societies to more hierarchical forms found in agricultural societies.[19] Kings, chiefs, or Big Men proved their strength by fighting, by redistributing food from farming, and by being perceived as being blessed by the gods through good harvests and successful battles.[20] The tendency toward centralization of authority in early agricultural societies was further strengthened by industrialization. In short, a sedentary economic structure led to a more hierarchical social system, which was reinforced through organized warfare.[21]

This economic transformation also produced inequality. While pre-civilized societies emphasized the importance of sharing, sedentary economic life began to shift toward an ethic of consumption. Haas notes that violence typically results when a society becomes desperate because of its economic plight and witnesses the suffering of its children.[22] Mahmood extends this analysis to contemporary situations, where the economically disadvantaged may resort to violence. Her argument is that it is not simply that the poor resort to terrorism, but that the inequalities of the world is sufficiently perceived to be problematic so that enough individuals with wealth and power are drawn to use this plight (perhaps sincerely and perhaps manipulatively) to strike out against those in power.[23] Echoing the research of anthropologists Peter Richerson and Robert Boyd, who argue that our Pleistocene brain simply is not constructed to deal well with significant inequality,[24] R. T. Naylor argues that an approach to prevent terrorism is to address issues such as inequality so that there is not as fertile a breeding ground for violent sentiments.[25]

We have already seen the theories of David Fabbro and Raymond Kelly further provide a sense of how contemporary society, including business organizations, might build upon attributes of peaceful societies. If James Coleman's assertion that the modern corporation has now replaced the family as the organization point of human identity, then to the extent business organizations are able to counteract this contemporary trend toward Kelly's social substitutability and replicate Fabbro's peaceful societies, then it would seem that corporations at least have the opportunity to contribute an important good to society by structuring their organizations along the lines of mediating institutions. More specifically, by integrating Hard Trust, Real Trust, and Good Trust, they have the best chance of promoting Peace Through Commerce.

Getting rocks to the right spot

The state, as Phillip Bobbitt puts it, "exists to master violence".[26] Yet, the technological advances that allowed parliamentary democracy to defeat fascism and communism also make it very difficult for any nation-state to control its own borders and even to master the deadly violence that terrorist groups can wreak disruptively on a market society that needs stability to thrive.[27] While "bandits, robbers, guerrillas, gangs" have been around for a long time, they are more deadly now than they ever have been in the past.[28] Such groups, according to Samuel Huntington, do not possess the time or money to create a "first-class conventional military" so that they concentrate instead on the shortcut of attempting to acquire weapons of mass destruction.[29] Thus corporations, as well as the rest of us, face potential terrorist challenges of a magnitude not previously encountered. Moreover, the 1990s have seen "the emergence of religious fundamentalist and new religious groups espousing the rhetoric of mass-destruction terrorism ... such as Aum Shinrikyo, Hizballah, and al-Qaeda.[30]

Making matters even worse is that the economic success of business people can make them a ready target for retribution.[31] That may not be because of a kind of jealousy that may exist toward those who are successful, but because a good deal of economic success that occurs within a country frequently is in the hands of what Amy Chua calls a market-dominant minority.[32]

Market-dominant minorities are the Achilles' heel of free market democracy ... Markets concentrate wealth, often spectacular wealth, in the hands of the market-dominant minority, while democracy increases the political power of the impoverished majority. In these circumstances the pursuit of free market democracy becomes an engine of potentially catastrophic ethnonationalism, pitting a frustrated 'indigenous' majority, easily aroused by opportunistic vote-seeking politicians, against a resented, wealthy ethnic minority. This confrontation is playing out in country after country today, from Indonesia to Sierra Leone, from Zimbabwe to Venezuela, from Russia to the Middle East. Since September 11, 2001, this confrontation has also been playing out in the United States ... Americans today are everywhere perceived as the world's market-dominant minority, wielding outrageously disproportionate economic power relative to our size and numbers. As a result, we have become the object of mass, popular resentment and hatred of the same kind that is directed at so many other market-dominant minorities around the world.[33]

As Chua notes, democracy in these contexts all too frequently consists simply of majority rule based on universal suffrage without constitutional protection or a variety of minority rights.[34] But it is into this context that corporations operate and where their success can make them perceived as agents of the problems in the society itself, particularly when local cultural changes are linked with religious belief.

Sociologist Fatema Mernissi writes that when visiting a Muslim country, the noticeable attitude is one of bitterness at all levels of society over "blocked ambition and ... frustrated desires for consumption".[35] Mernissi relates a story of a carpet weaver, who had been fired after a workplace accident without any offer of medical coverage or compensation.[36] When urged to take her case to a labor inspector, the injured worker exploded:

Listen, Fatima, just because you are educated and I am illiterate, you have no right to treat me like an idiot. You tell me to go see the labor inspector as if I had not thought of it; you tell me to go to the labor union as if I had not thought of it! I tell you that Allah is my defender; he is my union and my inspector![37]

As Mernissi concludes, "Islam gives someone like Mina a framework within which to express her pain and to change it into anger and a program for vengeance."[38]

Corporations find themselves engaged in this milieu because they may be viewed as institutions that deprive workers of their rights, because of resentment (sometimes tinted with religious objections to the sundering of a local culture, because the technology developed by companies can be turned against them by terrorists, because the nation-state has difficulty in policing such problems so that private security firms frequently attempt to fill the void left by the state in responding to such challenges, and because there is a market for "corporations to sell sensitive military technology to potentially dangerous foreign states".[39]

Thus, corporations find themselves in the crosshairs of anger and resentment because they can be perceived as instruments of oppression and poverty. They also find themselves in the crosshairs of public accountability because they have a tendency toward scandal. We already know that corporations are prone to misbehavior. The corporate scandals of the turn of the century simply are the latest chapter. Even before the glut of scandals featuring Enron, Arthur Andersen, Worldcom, Global Crossing and others, there were cigarette companies; before them, junk bonds and savings and loans; and before them, asbestos manufacturers and defense industry kickbacks. Such a list provides the barest tip of the iceberg of other tales of woe of corporate misbehavior. And one could go much further back to catalogue abuses of the building of railroads, or landlord confiscation of real estate. Sometimes, these tales are directed to domestic controversy, but at other times, in a global marketplace, they claim geopolitical attention as witnessed in controversies over abuses associated with diamond mining in Africa or oil extraction in Indonesia. It may be that one way to establish more trustworthiness is for corporations to practice behaviors that attend to multiple dimensions of trust, such as Hard Trust, Real Trust, and Good Trust.

In a previous book, *The Role of Business in Fostering Peaceful Societies*, Cindy Schipani and I offered a hopeful vision of how businesses might contribute to Peace Through Commerce. I conclude this book with a similar kind of (perhaps tempered) optimism. If ever there was a time and place for corporations to consider why they should behave ethically, it may be now. That's not just because the district attorneys of the world have them in prosecutorial crosshairs. It is also not just because the media, the Internet, and the NGO community have honed modern telecommunications to make corporate reputation increasingly noted and important. Both of those are important, but in addition, the world is a more dangerous place now than ever before because disaffected individuals and countries can get their hands on materials that could have devastating consequences if used. Certainly governmental action to prevent such things from happening is critical. But corporations are global actors and if sustainable peace has anything to do with how people perceive the justness of their plight, then to the extent corporations can develop the moral maturity to be Honest Brokers, to be good citizens, they may just do more than what they thought possible. Issues such as this are of the nature of those confronted by Honest Brokers such as Everett Dirksen, Howard Baker, and Paul Simon. They are moral goods that transcend partisanship, ideology, and self-interest.

It would be great, of course, if the collective action of corporations along with government and civil society could act to push the cause of sustainable peace to the top of a hill where it could be a city shining to inspire all around. But even if the cause of sustainable peace is not a city, but simply a rock, and not a rock that stays on top of the hill, but one that tends to slip down the side in Sisyphean fashion, it's important to make sure the rock doesn't roll all the way back to the bottom. There is an opportunity and indeed need for twenty-first century businesses to push the rock. Indeed, there is an intermediate goal of ethical business behavior that *could* be achieved by Total Integrity Management. That goal is within reach, but if an additional motivation is desired for promoting ethical business behavior, it is that in doing so, there may be an unexpected payoff: it may lessen the likelihood that a child will have her head blown off.

Or maybe, the prophet Mohammed is someone to consider in this task. He knew something about getting rocks into places of peace. When the sacred Kaaba stone in Mecca, placed there by Abraham himself, was in need of repair, leaders of various religious groups wanted to have the honor of returning it to its central place. To avoid feuding, Mohammed, a businessman as well as a prophet, proposed that four leaders take each corner of a rug, place the Kaaba stone in the middle, and together, peacefully, carry it back to its place. Mohammed saw that sharing the carrying of the rock this way fostered peace rather than feuding. It was an action of someone who avoided scandal, who demonstrated respect for the other religious leaders, and who saw a common good of peace that transcended their immediate self-interests. It was another action of Honest Brokering, a practice whose time has come for business.

Notes

1. www.state.gov/e/eb/cba/bs/ace/, accessed November 25, 2005.
2. www.state.gov/e/eb/cba/bs/ace/2003, accessed November 25, 2005.
3. www.state.gov/e/eb/cba/bs/ace/2002, accessed November 25, 2005.
4. www.state.gov/e/eb/cba/bs/ace/2001, accessed November 25, 2005.
5. www.state.gov/www/about_state/business/cba_award_corp.html, accessed November 25, 2005.
6. www.state.gov/www/about_state/business/cba_award00_corp.html, accessed November 25, 2005.

7. www.state.gov/www/about_state/business/cba_award99_corp.html, accessed November 25, 2005.

8. See Dodge vs. Ford Motor Co., 170 N.W. 668 (Mich. 1919).

9. Dodge vs. Ford, at 684.

10. One recent example of a "good corporation" story is that of Malden Mills, a textile producer in Lawrence, Massachusetts. A 1995 fire destroyed Malden Mill's textile production facility. However, the CEO Aaron Feuerstein immediately committed to rebuild the company and continued to pay workers and provide health benefits during the period it took to make the plant operational. Matthew W. Seeger and Robert R. Ulmer, *Virtuous Responses to Organizational Crisis: Aaron Feuerstein and Milt Cole*, 31 JOURNAL OF BUSINESS ETHICS 369 (2001).

11. Chairman William Clay Ford, Jr. plans to incorporate environmental technologies such as hydrogen combustion engines in future automotive designs, stating: "It's a fraction of the cost, it's a fraction of the complexity, and yet it gets you 99% of the environmental benefit of a fuel cell." J. Muller and J. Fahey, *Hydrogen Man*, FORBES 46 (December 27, 2004). However, the article notes that environmentalists may not welcome such technology with open arms due to the smog-causing nitrogen oxide such engines emit.

12. See www.state.gov/e/eb/cba/bs/ace/2001/7291.htm, accessed November 27, 2005.

13. Note to Firestone and those who argue that Ford took the more responsible approach. R. Noggle and D. Palmer, *Radials, Rollovers and Responsibility: An Examination of the Ford-Firestone Case*, 56 JOURNAL OF BUSINESS ETHICS 185 (2005).

14. Stelios C. Zyglidopoulos, *The Social and Environmental Responsibilities of Multinationals: Evidence from the Brent Spar Case*, 36 JOURNAL OF BUSINESS ETHICS 141 (2005).

15. Nicholas Beale, *Oil and Troubled Waters*, 83 HARVARD BUSINESS REVIEW 24 (2005).

16. Jonathan Haas, presentation at 2003 William Davidson Institute Conference on Corporate Governance and Sustainable Peace, held at Ann Arbor, Michigan, October 4, 2003 (paper on file with author).

17. LAWRENCE KEELEY, WAR BEFORE CIVILIZATION (1995). See Chapter 2 for a more complete discussion of this topic.

18. Haas, *supra* note 16.

19. See Kent vs. Flannery, *Prehistoric Social Evolution*, in RESEARCH FRONTIERS IN ANTHROPOLOGY 3 (Carol R. Ember and Melvin Ember, eds., 1995).

20. See e.g. VALERI VALERIO, KINGSHIP AND SACRIFICE: RITUAL AND SOCIETY IN ANCIENT HAWAII (Paula Wissing, trans., 1985). See also MARSHALL SAHLINS, ISLANDS OF HISTORY (1985).
21. Haas, *supra* note 16.
22. Haas, *supra* note 16.
23. Cynthia Mahmood, presentation at 2003 William Davidson Institute Conference on Corporate Governance and Sustainable Peace, held at Ann Arbor, Michigan, October 4, 2003 (paper on file with author).
24. Peter J. Richerson and Robert Boyd, *Complex Societies: The Evolutionary Origins of a Crude Superorganism*, 10 HUMAN NATURE 253 (1999).
25. R. T. NAYLOR, WAGES OF CRIME 131–2 (2002).
26. PHILLIP BOBBITT, THE SHIELD OF ACHILLES: WAR, PEACE AND THE COURSE OF HISTORY 216 (2002).
27. See *id.* at 215–16.
28. *Id.* at 219.
29. HUNTINGTON, THE CLASH OF CIVILIZATIONS AND THE REMAKING OF WORLD ORDER 186 (1996).
30. REX A. HUDSON, WHO BECOMES A TERRORIST AND WHY: THE 1999 GOVERNMENT REPORT ON PROFILING TERRORISTS 6 (1999).
31. See generally AMY CHUA, WORLD ON FIRE: HOW EXPORTING FREE MARKET DEMOCRACY BREEDS ETHNIC HATRED AND GLOBAL INSTABILITY (2003).
32. *Id.*
33. *Id.* at 6–7.
34. *Id.* at 14.
35. FATEMA MERNISSI, ISLAM AND DEMOCRACY: FEAR OF THE MODERN WORLD 56 (Mary Jo Lakeland, trans., 2002).
36. *Id.* at 57.
37. *Id.*
38. *Id.* at 58.
39. Bobbitt, *supra* note 26, at 237.

Index

war
  debt financing, British model 65
  driving forces 36
  expense of technology 64–5
  representative taxation to finance
    war 65
  state's need to raise money
    64–5
  to secure economic advantage
    39–41
  see also anthropological rootedness
    of war and peace
war-making capability
  and popular support 66–7
  dangers of the military-industrial
    complex 37–8
  effects of ethical business 68–71

weapons of mass destruction
    (WMDs) 69
  acquisition by terrorists 95
  proliferation, effects of corporate
    cultures 107–8
  sale of components 13–15
  technology sales and export controls
    101–5
weapons technology, market
    opportunities 13–15
weapons trade *see* arms sales and
    exports
Weaver, Gary 175–6, 184–5
Werhane, Patricia 178–9
Wolfowitz, Paul 102–4
World Bank 4–5, 106
Worldcom 11, 136–7

Made in the USA
Lexington, KY
10 August 2012